Exploring the Philosophical Roots that Influence Financial Fruit: A Christian Perspective

Robert E. Brooks

Front Cover: Photo by Baesil on Unsplash accessed on July 30, 2024.

Copyright © 2025 Financial Risk Management, LLC

Published by: Financial Risk Management, LLC
                13157 Martin Road Spur
                Northport, AL 35473
                U.S.A.

Email: frmhelpforyou@gmail.com
Website: www.frmhelp.com

December 2024

ALL RIGHTS RESERVED. No part of this work covered by the copyright herein may be reproduced, stored in a retrieval system or transmitted in any form or by any means, electronic, graphic, mechanical, digitizing, photocopying, recording, scanning, web distribution, information networks, or otherwise, except as permitted under Sections 107 and 108 of the 1976 United States Copyright Act, without the prior written permission of Robert Brooks.

Limit of Liability/Disclaimer of Warranty. The author and publisher of this work have used their best efforts in preparing this work, they make no representations or warranties regarding the accuracy or the comprehensiveness of this work and specifically disclaim any implied warranties of merchantability or fitness for a particular purpose. No warranty may be created or extended by sales representatives or written in sales documents. The advice and strategies, explicit or implicit, may not be suitable for your situation. You need to consult with professionals where appropriate. Neither the publisher nor the author shall be liable for any loss of profit or any other commercial damages.

Unless otherwise indicated, all Scripture quotations are from The ESV® Bible (The Holy Bible, English Standard Version®), © 2001 by Crossway, a publishing ministry of Good News Publishers. Scripture quotations taken from https://www.biblegateway.com/. Used by permission. All rights reserved.

Library of Congress Cataloging-in-Publication Data
Brooks, Robert, 1960-
      Exploring the Philosophical Roots that Influence Financial Fruit: A Christian Perspective/Robert E. Brooks.
          p.   cm.
      ISBN-13: 979-8301783135
      1. Christian Apologetics. 2. Finance. 3. Theology. 4. Philosophy.

Dedication

To my wife Ann,
as well as my children,
and ever-growing number of grandchildren

Exploring the Philosophical Roots that Influence Financial Fruit: A Christian Perspective

Table of Contents

DEDICATION I
TABLE OF CONTENTS II
OPENING QUOTE I

PREFACE **1**

ACKNOWLEDGEMENTS **4**

PART 1. PHILOSOPHICAL ROOTS **7**

CHAPTER 1. FOUNDATIONS **9**

LEARNING OBJECTIVES 9
OPENING QUOTE 9
OVERVIEW 9
CASE STUDY 1.1: HOME PURCHASE 10
CHRISTIAN APOLOGETICS DEFINED 12
   Three Tests for Truth *12*
   Four Questions to Be Answered *12*
   Five Subjects to Be Understood *13*
PURPOSE OF APOLOGETICS 15
ORIGINS OF APOLOGETICS 15
APPROACHES TO APOLOGETICS 17
   Defense (Negative Apologetics) *17*
   Offense (Positive Apologetics) *18*
SOURCES FOR FINANCIAL WISDOM 18
   Harnessing Wisdom and Understanding *20*
FINANCIAL MANAGEMENT 23
CASE STUDY 1.2: EXPERIENCE WITH CHRISTIANITY AND FINANCE 24
CHRISTIAN FINANCIAL MANAGEMENT 25
TARGET AUDIENCE 26
WHERE DO WE GO FROM HERE? 28
SUMMARY 29
CASE STUDY 1: YOUNG BANKER'S TRANSPORTATION DECISION 30
CASE STUDY 2: THOMAS, THE RESURRECTION, AND PERSONAL FINANCE 31
CASE STUDY 3: AMERICA'S MOST EXPENSIVE HOME 32
CASE STUDY 4: HOME PURCHASE DECISION 32
CASE STUDY 5: IS FAITH A BLIND LEAP? 32

CASE STUDY 6: CHRISTIANITY AND FINANCE 33
REFERENCES 33
    Books *33*
    Useful Websites *33*

CHAPTER 2. PHILOSOPHY: LOGIC AND EPISTEMOLOGY 34

LEARNING OBJECTIVES 34
OPENING QUOTES 34
OVERVIEW 35
PHILOSOPHY DEFINED 36
    Philosophical Worldview *37*
    Decision-Making Process *38*
    Coherence *39*
    Correspondence *40*
    Ontic Referent Error *41*
CASE STUDY 2.1: ONTIC REFERENT ERROR AND FINANCE 41
LOGIC 43
    Law of Non-Contradiction *43*
CASE STUDY 2.2: JESUS USED LAWS OF LOGIC TO REFUTE OPPONENTS 44
    Logic and Budgeting *46*
EPISTEMOLOGY 48
    Correspondence Theory of Truth *49*
    Epistemology and Budgeting *51*
SUMMARY 54
CASE STUDY 1: DECISION-MAKING PROCESS 54
CASE STUDY 2: BIBLICAL LOGIC 55
CASE STUDY 3: GRATIFICATION, CREDIT CARD, AND THREE TRUTH TESTS ... 55
CASE STUDY 4: LOGIC OF CHRISTIANITY 56
CASE STUDY 5: NON-WORLDVIEW WORLDVIEW 56
CASE STUDY 6: FAITH AND BUDGETING 56
REFERENCES 56

CHAPTER 3. PHILOSOPHY: METAPHYSICS AND ETHICS 58

LEARNING OBJECTIVES 58
OPENING QUOTES 58
OVERVIEW 59
LOGIC AND EPISTEMOLOGY REVIEW 59
METAPHYSICS 60
    Selected Definitions Useful in Metaphysics *61*
CASE STUDY 3.1: METAPHYSICS AND BUDGETING 62
    Quotes Connecting Metaphysics with Finance *64*
ETHICS 65
    Alternative views of right *66*
    A Christian View of Right *67*
CASE STUDY 3.2: CFA INSTITUTE'S CODE OF ETHICS 68
    Ethics and Budgeting *70*

- SUMMARY 71
- CASE STUDY 1: MONTE HALL PROBLEM 72
- CASE STUDY 2: PRICE DISCRIMINATION – INFORMED VERSUS UNINFORMED 72
- CASE STUDY 3: BOND PRICE, 102% OF PAR, AND CHILD TEMPERATURE 73
- REFERENCES 73

CHAPTER 4. NATURE OF INFORMATION 74

- LEARNING OBJECTIVES 74
- OPENING QUOTE 74
- OVERVIEW 74
- EXAMPLES OF INFORMATION 75
  - *Nature* 75
  - *Cultivated Nature* 76
  - *Clear Communication* 76
- CASE STUDY 4.1: DIFFERENT LANGUAGE AND COMMUNICATION 77
  - *Human Emotive Communication* 78
  - *Financial Information* 79
- DATA ANALYSIS 80
  - *Categories of Explanations* 80
  - *Syntactic Information* 82
  - *Semantic Information* 82
- CASE STUDY 4.7: DATA ANALYSIS AND BEAR STEARNS STOCK PRICE 84
- BIBLICAL PERSPECTIVE ON THE NATURE OF INFORMATION 85
  - *Role of Information in Questions of Origins* 86
  - *Role of Information in Defending a Proposition* 88
  - *Biblical Ideas on the Nature of Financial Information* 89
  - *Selected Quotes Regarding Information* 91
- SUMMARY 91
- CASE STUDY 1: EXECUTIVE COMMUNICATION, EARNING CALL, AND POTENTIAL TAKEOVER 92
- CASE STUDY 2: MECHANISM, AGENCY, AND LAUNCHING A STARTUP BUSINESS 92
- CASE STUDY 3: IMAGO DEI AND POLITICAL SYSTEMS 93
- REFERENCES 93

PART 2. THEOLOGICAL SOILS 95

CHAPTER 5. EXISTENCE OF GOD 97

- LEARNING OBJECTIVES 97
- OPENING QUOTE 97
- OVERVIEW 97
- NATURE OF THE THEISM DEBATE 98
  - *Burden of Proof* 98
  - *Rebuttal and Refutation* 99
  - *God's Existence Is Properly Basic Belief* 100
- CASE STUDY 5.1: CHALLENGING THE INTERNAL LOGIC OF THE ATHEIST 101
- ATHEISM'S THEOLOGICAL PROBLEMS 101
  - *There Are No Moral Laws* 101

- Life Lacks Meaning 103
- Humans Have No Hope 104
- WILLARD'S THREE-STAGE APPROACH TO GOD'S EXISTENCE 104
  - Stage 1: No Physical Quantity Completely Explains Its Own Existence 105
  - Stage 2: Argument From and To Design 105
  - Stage 3: Human Events 112
- CHRISTIANITY'S THEOLOGICAL BEAUTY 113
  - Immutable Moral Law 113
  - Deeply Meaningful Life 114
  - A Satisfying Hope 114
- CASE STUDY 5.2: GOD'S EXISTENCE AND PERSONAL FINANCE 115
- SUMMARY 117
- CASE STUDY 1: GOD, FINANCE, AND FIDUCIARIES 118
- CASE STUDY 2: CHRISTIAN WORLDVIEW, FINANCE, AND MEANING 118
- CASE STUDY 3: DNA-DANCING, DANCING BEFORE GOD, AND FINANCE 119
- REFERENCES 120

CHAPTER 6. COMPETING WORLDVIEWS 122

- LEARNING OBJECTIVES 122
- OPENING QUOTE 122
- OVERVIEW 122
- WORLDVIEW EXPLAINED 123
- SKEPTICISM, METHODISM, AND PARTICULARISM 125
  - Problem of the Criterion 125
  - Skepticism 127
  - Methodism 127
  - Particularism 127
  - Biblical Particularism 128
- ERROR ANALYSIS RELATED TO WORLDVIEWS 131
  - Tight (Intolerant, Dogmatism) 131
  - Loose (Overly Tolerant, Relativism) 131
- CASE STUDY 6.1: ERROR TYPES AND ETERNITY 132
- BRIEF REVIEW OF SELECTED WORLDVIEWS 133
  - Scientism 133
  - Positivism 134
  - Verificationism 134
  - Post-Modernism 134
  - Critical Realism 135
- NATURE OF BELIEFS 135
- WORLDVIEW AND PERSONAL FINANCE 137
- CASE STUDY 6.2: VIEWS ON PERSONAL DEBT 139
- SUMMARY 140
- CASE STUDY 1: PAUL'S PARTICULARIST CLAIM 140
- CASE STUDY 2: ATHEISM, AI, AND ECONOMIC FORECASTING 140
- CASE STUDY 3: CHRISTIANITY, AI, AND ECONOMIC FORECASTING 141
- REFERENCES 142

CHAPTER 7. NATURALISM, CHRISTIANITY, AND SCIENCE 143

- LEARNING OBJECTIVES 143
- OPENING QUOTE 143
- OVERVIEW 143
- NATURALISM 144
- NATURALISM AND PERSONAL FINANCE 146
- CHRISTIANITY 147
- CASE STUDY 7.1: CHRISTIAN WORLDVIEW AND SUICIDE 149
- CHRISTIANITY AND PERSONAL FINANCE 151
- SCIENCE 151
- SCIENCE AND PERSONAL FINANCE 154
- NATURALISM, CHRISTIANITY, AND SCIENCE 155
- CASE STUDY 7.2: FOUNDATIONS OF PERSONAL FINANCE 158
- SUMMARY 159
- CASE STUDY 1: SENSATE VERSUS IDEATION: BUDGETING 160
- CASE STUDY 2: CAR PAYMENTS AND THE CHRISTIAN WORLDVIEW 160
- CASE STUDY 3: CHARITY: NATURALISM VERSUS CHRISTIANITY 161
- REFERENCES 161

CHAPTER 8. PROBLEM OF EVIL 162

- LEARNING OBJECTIVES 162
- OPENING QUOTES 162
- OVERVIEW 163
- PAIN, SUFFERING, AND EVIL 163
- ATHEISM AND THE PROBLEM OF EVIL 164
- THEISM AND THE PROBLEM OF EVIL 165
- BIBLICAL INSIGHTS ON THE PROBLEM OF EVIL 166
- CHRISTIAN EXPERIENCE 168
  - *Fate of the Apostles* *169*
- CASE STUDY 8.1: HORATIO G. SPAFFORD 170
- ENDURING FINANCIAL LOSS 173
- CASE STUDY 8.2: THE ARTIST, HIS FAITHFUL FATHER, AND THE DRUNK 174
- SUMMARY 174
- CASE STUDY 1: SERVING THOSE WHO STEAL FROM YOU 175
- CASE STUDY 2: JESUS'S APPROACH TO EVIL 175
- CASE STUDY 3: AN UNJUST DEATH 176
- REFERENCES 176

PART 3. FERTILIZING FINANCIAL FRUIT 177

CHAPTER 9. THE BIBLE AS HEARSAY OR HERESY 179

- LEARNING OBJECTIVES 179
- OPENING QUOTE 179
- OVERVIEW 179
- HEARSAY, HERESY, OR HISTORY 180

IS THE BIBLE JUST HEARSAY?	181
CASE STUDY 9.1: BIBLE AS HEARSAY AND PERSONAL FINANCE	183
IS THE BIBLE PROMOTING A HERESY?	184
Direct Manuscript Evidence	*185*
Indirect Manuscript Evidence from Early Church Leaders	*186*
CASE STUDY 9.2: BIBLE AS HERESY AND PERSONAL FINANCE	188
SUMMARY	188
CASE STUDY 1: PROBLEM OF CURRENTLY UNKNOWN EXPLANATION	188
CASE STUDY 2: BIBLICAL INTEGRITY AND PERSONAL DEBT	189
CASE STUDY 3: BIBLICAL INTEGRITY, BORROWING, AND GENEROSITY	189
REFERENCES	190

CHAPTER 10. THE BIBLE AS HISTORY 191

LEARNING OBJECTIVES	191
OPENING QUOTE	191
OVERVIEW	191
THE BIBLE IS SIMPLY THE BEST BOOK	191
THE BIBLE IS INFALLIBLE, INERRANT, AND INSPIRED	193
CASE STUDY 10.1: LOGIC APPLIED TO INSPIRATION	193
THE BIBLE IS BELIEVABLE	197
THE BIBLE IS VERY LOGICAL	198
THE BIBLE IS ETERNAL	200
Bible as History and Personal Finance	*200*
CASE STUDY 10.2: "THE BIBLE STANDS"	203
SUMMARY	203
CASE STUDY 1: FOUNDING DOCUMENTS	204
CASE STUDY 2: JEFFERSON COUNTY, ALABAMA SEWAGE PROBLEM	205
CASE STUDY 3: BORROWING UNDER THE OLD TESTAMENT LAW	206
REFERENCES	206

CHAPTER 11. MIRACLES 207

LEARNING OBJECTIVES	207
OPENING QUOTE	207
OVERVIEW	207
MIRACLES DEFINED	208
Atheist Claim	*208*
Weak Theist Claim	*208*
Strong Theist Claim	*208*
MIRACLES RECORDED IN THE GOSPEL ACCORDING TO JOHN	210
PROPHECY	213
CASE STUDY 11.1: PROPHESY FULFILLMENT AS RANDOM CHANCE	214
What Day Would the Messiah Be Executed?	*215*
LIST OF PROPHESIES	218
CASE STUDY 11.2: MIRACLES AND PERSONAL FINANCE	220
SUMMARY	220
CASE STUDY 1: BIBLE AS A BEST SELLER	221

CASE STUDY 2: WHEN TO TAKE SOCIAL SECURITY 221
CASE STUDY 3: DEBT AND PERSONAL FINANCIAL DECISION-MAKING 222
REFERENCES 223

CHAPTER 12. RESURRECTION OF JESUS CHRIST 224

LEARNING OBJECTIVES 224
OPENING QUOTE 224
OVERVIEW 224
JESUS'S CLAIM 225
EVIDENCE FOR JESUS'S BODILY RESURRECTION 228
    1. Eyewitness Accounts and Experiences 228
    2. Early, Preserved Accounts of the Gospel 228
    3. Transformed from Fear to Martyrdom 229
    4. Empty Tomb 229
    5. Resurrection Was Declared in Jerusalem 229
    6. No Contrary Evidence 229
    7. Some Jews Changed the Day of Worship 229
    8. Conversion of Saul of Tarsus 230
    9. Key Initial Evidence Given to Women 230
    10. Physical Resurrection—the Cornerstone 230
    11. Fulfilled Prophesy 230
    12. Clarity of Biblical Teaching Related to Finance 231
BAYES'S THEOREM AND THE RESURRECTION 231
    Technical Details of Bayes's Theorem 233
    Bayes's Theorem 234
    Bayes's Theorem and the Resurrection of Jesus Christ 235
CASE STUDY 1: BAYES'S THEOREM AND THE TWELVE APOSTLES 236
PASCAL'S WAGER 237
CASE STUDY 2: FINANCE AND JESUS'S RESURRECTION 239
SUMMARY 241
CASE STUDY 1: COKE CONSOLIDATED 241
CASE STUDY 2: BAYES'S THEOREM REDONE 242
CASE STUDY 3: BAYES'S THEOREM WITH PASCAL'S WAGER 243
REFERENCES 243

CHAPTER 13. LOVING YOUR NEIGHBOR 244

LEARNING OBJECTIVES 244
OPENING QUOTE 244
OVERVIEW 244
LOVE AS THE COMPELLING ARGUMENT 245
CASE STUDY 1: FOUNDATIONS FOR FARMING (FFF) 248
HOSPITALITY AS THE GATEWAY TO THE WORLD 249
CASE STUDY 2: TUSCALOOSA INTERNATIONAL FRIENDS 252
THE SERVANT LEADER 253
BIBLE-BASED FINANCIAL MANAGEMENT 254
SUMMARY 255

CASE STUDY 1: THE GOLDEN RULE	256
CASE STUDY 2: ETERNAL LIFE AND THE MARKETPLACE	256
CASE STUDY 3: CONTINENTAL REALTY GROUP	257
REFERENCES	257

CHAPTER 14. THE NATURE OF THE HARVEST ... 259

LEARNING OBJECTIVES	259
OPENING QUOTE	259
OVERVIEW	260
FROM JESUS TO WALL STREET	260
Naturalism, Christianity, and Finance	*265*
Two Economic Frameworks	*268*
Products or people	*270*
THE HARVEST	273
CASE STUDY 14.1: PRECEDENCE: EXISTENCE OR ESSENCE	275
CASE STUDY 14.2: NAPOLEON'S QUESTION	277
ENCAPSULATING QUOTES	278
SUMMARY	279
CASE STUDY 1: HOME PURCHASE DECISION REVISITED	280
CASE STUDY 2: PHILOSOPHICAL ROOTS	280
REFERENCES	280

BIBLIOGRAPHY ... 283

MAJOR BIBLE REFERENCES ... 288

Opening Quote

"If God had perceived that our greatest need was economic, he would have sent an economist. If he had perceived that our greatest need was entertainment, he would have sent us a comedian or an artist. If God had perceived that our greatest need was political stability, he would have sent us a politician. If he had perceived that our greatest need was health, he would have sent us a doctor. But he perceived that our greatest need involved our sin, our alienation from him, our profound rebellion, our death; and he sent us a Savior." D. A. Carson, A Call to Spiritual Reformation: Priorities from Paul and His Prayers

Preface

Thank you for joining this exploration of personal finance foundations. My academic interest for over 40 years has been finance. Based on extensive research and industry consulting, I have concluded that one key to human flourishing is improved financial decision-making. At its core, decision-making rests on philosophical presuppositions or one's worldview. Although covered in detail later in this material, a worldview is simply a conceptual arrangement by which one fits everything they believe and through which they interpret and judge reality. It is analogous to eyeglasses.

    The goal here is an attempt to express reasons for the truthfulness of the Christian worldview. If the Christian worldview is true — and I believe it is — then those who embrace it will make significantly different financial decisions. Thus, I seek to establish the link between worldview and finance. You will find here various arguments for the truthfulness of the Christian worldview. An apologist is simply a person who seeks to defend a particular worldview.

    I am an apologist though not professionally trained. It is important to disclose the lack of formal theological or philosophical training. Rather for well over 40 years, my wife and I have been engaged in various apologetic encounters primarily with international students and visiting scholars.

    Thus, my hope is to follow C. S. Lewis who observed the following:

> *It often happens that two schoolboys can solve difficulties in their work for one another better than the master can. When*

> *you took the problem to a master, as we all remember, he was very likely to explain what you understood already, to add a great deal of information which you didn't want, and say nothing at all about the thing that was puzzling you. ... The fellow-pupil can help more than the master because he knows less. The difficulty we want him to explain is one he has recently met. The expert met it so long ago that he has forgotten. He sees the whole subject, by now, in such a different light that he cannot conceive what is really troubling the pupil; he sees a dozen other difficulties which ought to be troubling him but aren't.*[1]

The material presented here is drawn from many sources and is built upon the hard work of numerous other authors. Thus, one way to view this material is my effort to organize apologetic materials in a form that is useful, particularly in the context of personal finance. As this material developed over decades and without any thought of eventually publishing it, every effort has been made to appropriately attribute quotes, but many have been lost. My hope is that you will benefit from how this material is organized and gain your own insights related to the foundations of finance.

Although not written initially for this purpose, one could see this book as a response to works from other authors who are grappling with philosophical foundations of personal finance but from a non-Christian perspective. Examples of these books include the following:

- Brian Portnoy, *The Geometry of Wealth: How to Shape a Life of Money and Meaning*, Harriman House, 2018.
- David Dubofsky and Lyle Sussman, *Your Total Wealth: The Heart and Soul of Financial Literacy*, HSF Publishing, LLC, 2021.
- Mark Spitznagel, *The Dao of Capital Austrian Investing in a Distorted World*, Wiley, 2013.
- Pulak Prasad, *What I Learned About Investing From Darwin*, Columbia University Press, 2023.

---

[1] The idea for this approach is taken liberally from C. S. Lewis, *Reflections on the Psalms* (Orlando, FL: Harcourt, Inc., 1958), 1–2.

Any book of this length and of this nature will contain errors. I would be deeply grateful if you could help me locate them. Please email your feedback to frmhelpforyou@gmail.com. Once known, an errata sheet will be available at www.robertebrooks.org. Further, you will find several other supporting materials at this website.[2]

Robert Brooks

Tuscaloosa, Alabama
December 2024

---

[2]For more information about the author, see www.robertebrooks.org. Further, you can read his story at https://meettheprof.com/view/professors/entry/robert-brooks/.

Acknowledgements

This work is based on more than forty years of working with financial concepts as well as interacting with students and scholars at universities, primarily internationals that had an interest in appraising the legitimacy of Jesus Christ's claims. Many people have provided insights that have helped improve communicating Christian perspectives on various topics, especially finance. To paraphrase an ancient proverb, a short conversation over tea with a wise person is better than reading many books. I am deeply indebted to the many people who engaged me in conversation relating to the claims of Jesus Christ as well as various academic finance-related claims.

I am particularly grateful to one of my finance professors in graduate school who believed I should not be in a graduate finance program because I was a Christian. In his mind, being a finance professor was incompatible with being a follower of Jesus Christ. It was the first significant challenge to my worldview.

Further, I am grateful to a student, who over thirty years ago, asked permission to convert me to atheism. He had taken several of my classes and concluded that I was a rational person given his experiences in my finance classes. As before, in his mind, being a finance professor was incompatible with being a follower of Jesus Christ. He was a brilliant student, and his arguments were systematic, clear, but simply not compelling against the sheer weight of evidence favoring the Christian worldview.

The many hours we spent evaluating the arguments and considering the evidence was deeply beneficial to me. The effect was opposite from his intentions—it resulted in me having a much deeper understanding of the solid foundation upon which the Christian worldview rests.

I am also the beneficiary of numerous conversations with international scholars, many of whom were from countries openly hostile to followers of Jesus Christ. Many of them while in America desire to explore various worldviews, including the Christian worldview. It is a unique experience to share various Bible passages with thinkers who have no background in anything involving God.

I recall being with about eight scholars as the account of Lazarus' death and resurrection was being covered.[3] Most of these scholars did not know what was recorded in verse 44 when in verse 43 it was recorded that Jesus spoke at Lazarus's tomb, "Lazarus, come out." In verse 44, it is recorded, "The man who had died came out …." One of the scholars turned and looked at me and said, "This verse changes everything." He was right. It does change everything. C. S. Lewis said, "I believe in Christianity as I believe that the Sun has risen, not only because I see it, but because by it I see everything else."[4] To me, everything else particularly includes finance.

Many people have invested time to improve this material. I am deeply indebted to Ann, my wife, for long hours of editing early drafts. I also am deeply grateful for the excellent copyediting services provided by Michael Brooks who can be reached at michaelbrookseditor@gmail.com. Further, this book was significantly improved with the insights and wisdom provided by Professor Klaus Issler.

Further, corrections and insights were provided by participants in several organizations, including members of various organizations at the University of Alabama such as the Christian Faculty Fellowship, Navigators International, and Living International Fellowship. Several individuals provided editorial insights, including Professor Don M. Chance, Scott

---

[3]See the Gospel According to John, Chapter 11.
[4]C. S. Lewis, *Is Theology Poetry?* (Samizdat University Press). Originally presented in 1944 at the Socratic Club, an Oxford debating society. Later published in the collection of essays entitled *They Asked for a Paper* (1962).

Green, Andrew Southwell, and many others. This material has been taught in various forms at my home church, Emmanuel Baptist Church in Tuscaloosa, Alabama.

My hope is you will give this material serious consideration.

Part 1. Philosophical Roots

The core premise for this book is that financial fruit grows on philosophical roots. As you might surmise, farming is in my background, and currently, I am a gentleman farmer, primarily for the sheer enjoyment and physical exercise.

Part 1 covers Chapters 1-4 focused on digging around the philosophical roots. Part 2 covers Chapters 5-9 focused on different theological soils. Finally, Part 3 covers Chapters 10-14 focused on fertilizing financial fruit and the resultant harvest. A detailed overview is provided at the end of Chapter 1.

In Chapter 1, foundational issues are introduced and their connection to personal finance demonstrated. Apologetics, making a rational defense for a particular worldview, is introduced and its connection to finance. Chapter 1 provides a couple of case studies within the chapter as well as a few additional case studies at the end. This pattern of case studies will continue throughout the book.

Chapter 2 formally introduces philosophy. Philosophy informally is simply thinking hard about something. I provide more formal definitions as well as briefly cover two pillars of philosophy: logic and epistemology. In one case study, Jesus' use of logic to refute opponents is illustrated.

Chapter 3 provides the remaining two pillars of philosophy, metaphysics, and ethics. In this chapter, the case is made that much of finance is metaphysical in nature. Ideas always precede financial actions. The CFA Institute's Code of Ethics is highlighted as a robust illustration of the link between ethics and finance.

Chapter 4 addresses the nature of information. Finance is

information-heavy. The challenge is sorting through the vast quantity of available information. But what exactly is information? If someone mentions fried chicken, exactly what is happening in your mind? Understanding the fundamental nature of information is critical to laying a solid philosophical foundation.

Chapter 1. Foundations

Learning Objectives

- Define and explain the foundational approach.
- See personal finance outcomes as unavoidably based on the philosophical foundation.
- Provide roadmap for the remaining materials.

Opening Quote

"The real trouble with this world of ours is not that it is an unreasonable world, nor even that it is a reasonable one. The commonest kind of trouble is that it is nearly reasonable, but not quite. Life is not an illogicality; yet it is a trap for logicians. It looks just a little more mathematical and regular than it is; its exactitude is obvious, but its inexactitude is hidden; its wildness lies in wait."[5]

Overview

The goal of the material presented here is to provide an

---

[5] G. K. Chesterton, "The Paradoxes of Christianity," *Orthodoxy*. See https://www.biblestudytools.com/classics/chesterton-orthodoxy/the-paradoxes-of-christianity.html.

alternative way to explore personal finance. Personal finance rests on philosophical foundations; hence, various candidate foundations are explored, and the case is made for the truthfulness of the Christian perspective.

In this chapter, Christian apologetics is introduced and a roadmap is provided. The goal is to help remove the fog in our thinking to be able to think appropriately about God. If successful, do not be surprised if you find yourself desiring heavenly treasure far more than earthly material possessions.

First, Christian apologetics is carefully defined and its purpose and origins explored. Second, both negative and positive approaches to Christian apologetics are introduced. Finally, the target audience is identified and an overview is provided.

Overarching all this material is the notion that your financial fruit depends on your philosophical roots. If you are rooted in a false worldview, then do not be surprised if the financial fruit is distasteful for a host of reasons. For example, no amount of budgeting will benefit if you lack the willpower to change your financial habits. It is true, however, that if our financial habits are aligned with the solid truthfulness of the correct worldview, then the resultant financial fruit will be sweet, even if not monetarily large in value.

We turn now to illustrate one financial application that makes the connection between our philosophical roots and one of life's many choices. With this illustration, case studies are introduced. The goal for these case studies is to assist in making the connection between ideas presented and day-to-day financial practice.

Case Study 1.1: Home Purchase

One of the most long-lasting financial decisions made relates to our homes. Although renting for a lifetime is increasingly popular due to mobility advantages, most U.S. families eventually seek to live in a place they can call their home.

Is the home purchase decision simply an analytical and

rational choice, or is there more that typically goes into it? Figure 1.1 illustrates four home choices — consider them carefully. What issues or objections come to mind if you and your family (assume young couple with two children) had to choose only one?

Figure 1.1 Illustration of four houses[6]

There are several issues involved, including functional utility, maintenance cost, structural soundness, and overall safety. The often unspoken but profound driving factor in home purchase decisions relates to how we will be perceived among peers. This is not a tangible, physical, or utilitarian issue, rather an issue of human pride.

Regardless of the home selected, one of the core tenets explored here is whether we are owners or simply God's managers. If we were designed by God to be his managers, then taking on the role of owner will not be fruitful. Biblically, a God-designed earth suggests economic abundance, not dwindling scarcity as is often portrayed. Finally, if the biblically-based worldview is true, then we are deeply loved by God, able to

---

[6] 1) Photo by Redd F on Unsplash, 2) Photo by Phil Hearing on Unsplash, 3) Photo by todd kent on Unsplash, 4) Photo by Daniel Barnes on Unsplash. Accessed on October 23, 2024.

unconditionally love other, and enjoy deep contentment in this life.

As the above case study illustrates, the question is whether the home choice is primarily physical or metaphysical in nature? Is it driven by human desire or rational analytics? Is it primarily a mental exercise, or is it more driven by our will? Do we even have this choice because we are just dancing to our DNA? One objective for exploring this material is to think more deeply about the financial choices we make daily. The goal is to then make choices that are more in line with our worldview. Improving the alignment with the correct worldview will naturally lead to human flourishing. As will be shown later, worldviews are mutually exclusive. If one worldview is true, then other worldviews are false. It is therefore imperative to find the correct worldview requiring careful analysis and assessment of various types of evidence. This evidence will be explored within the context of finance.

We now turn to carefully to define Christian apologetics.

Christian Apologetics Defined

Apologetics refers, in part, to making a rational defense for a particular worldview. Every worldview must pass three tests for truth, answer four questions, and address five subjects. The word "claim" here to simply a statement, idea, or declarative proposition, such as, "Jesus Christ rose bodily from the dead."

Three Tests for Truth
1) Is the claim logically consistent?
2) Is the claim empirically adequate?
3) Is the claim experientially relevant?

Four Questions to Be Answered
1) Origins: Where did we come from?

2) Meaning: Is life meaningful?
3) Morality: Are there immutable moral laws?
4) Destiny: Where am I going?

Five Subjects to Be Understood

1) God – theology
2) Reality – metaphysics
3) Knowledge – epistemology
4) Morality – ethics
5) Humankind – anthropology

It is important to emphasize that every worldview, such as Christianity or naturalism, must stand these three tests for truth, must answer these four ultimate questions, and integrate these five subjects. No worldview is exempt.

One's worldview makes a difference in how we feel, think, and act. There is an existential aspect to our worldview even if it is not central. That is, it impacts how we live and thus how we make financial decisions. There is an entailment or an inevitable consequence of our worldview to personal financial decisions. If we change our worldview from one that is wrong to the correct one, it is not surprising that our financial decision-making improves. Further, we may find ourselves no longer measuring life's choices in their transitory financial currency implications. There is wealth that is much more enduring.

Christian apologetics simply seeks to produce reasons for believing and addresses challenges to one's belief. More formally, Paul Coulter defines Christian apologetics in the following way:

The task of developing and sharing arguments for the truth and rationality of Christianity and the falsehood and irrationality of alternatives with the aim of strengthening the faith of believers and provoking non-believers to consider Christ.[7]

---

[7]Paul Coulter, "An Introduction to Christian Apologetics," Be Thinking, https://www.bethinking.org/apologetics/an-introduction-to-christian-apologetics.

Voddie Baucham Jr. defines apologetics simply as

> ... *knowing what we believe and why we believe it, and being able to communicate that to others effectively.*[8]

Cornelius Van Til's definition is simply,

> *Apologetics is the vindication of the Christian philosophy of life against the various forms of the non-Christian philosophy of life.*[9]

The language of the New Testament is Koine (common) Greek. The Greek word apologia (ἀπολογία) from which our word apologetics derives carries the meaning of making a legal defense or a carefully reasoned defense of one's beliefs or actions.[10] It is important to note that Christians were expected to be able to provide a carefully reasoned explanation for following Jesus Christ. The apostle Peter puts it this way.[11]

1 Peter 3:15
> [15]*But in your hearts honor Christ the Lord as holy, always being prepared to make a defense (ἀπολογίαν) to anyone who asks you for a reason (λόγον) for the hope that is in you; yet do it with gentleness and respect...*

Thus, Christians need to be ready to give a defense of the Christian faith through well-reasoned or rational means (λόγον – words, reason). Thus, Christians need to provide evidence or arguments that provide rational justification for their Christian belief.

---

[8]Voddie Baucham, Jr., *Expository Apologetics: Answering Objections with the Power of the Word* (Wheaton, IL: Crossway, 2015), 20.
[9]Ibid., 21.
[10]Quoted in Coulter.
[11]All scripture is taken from the *English Standard Version* unless otherwise noted.

Purpose of Apologetics

There are two main objectives for apologetics: to draw seekers to faith in Jesus Christ and strengthen the faith of Jesus Christ's followers. These two objectives at times rely on different approaches. Whereas followers of Christ can be strengthened using in-family arguments, such as biblically-based perspectives, seekers can be drawn using out-of-family arguments, such as empirical evidence and rational persuasion.

For many issues, the arguments are independent of whether a person is a Christ-follower or not. There are times, however, where an in-family perspective will not be relevant to a seeker.

Origins of Apologetics[12]

Christian apologetics has a very long history. As Christianity emerged in the second century AD, Justin Martyr (c. AD 100–165) appeared to have the biggest impact as he was well versed in numerous philosophies prior to following Jesus. From its origins, apologists have been criticized. For example, Tertullian (c. AD 155–240), who was also an early apologist himself, argued that various philosophies and Christianity are incompatible, famously asking, "What has Athens to do with Jerusalem?"

The New Testament writer, Luke, documented several apologetic arguments made by Paul in Acts. Paul used rational arguments to support Christianity as fulfilling the Old Testament as well as demonstrate that Christianity was better than pagan philosophical ideas. Note in Acts 17:17, provided below, Luke describes Paul as using reason in both the Jewish synagogue as well as within the Athenian business marketplace.

---

[12]See Coulter.

Acts 17:17–21

> [17]So he reasoned in the synagogue with the Jews and the devout persons, and in the marketplace every day with those who happened to be there. [18]Some of the Epicurean and Stoic philosophers also conversed with him. And some said, "What does this babbler wish to say?" Others said, "He seems to be a preacher of foreign divinities" — because he was preaching Jesus and the resurrection. [19]And they took him and brought him to the Areopagus, saying, "May we know what this new teaching is that you are presenting? [20]For you bring some strange things to our ears. We wish to know therefore what these things mean." [21]Now all the Athenians and the foreigners who lived there would spend their time in nothing except telling or hearing something new.

Paul was able to defend the Christian perspective based on the context of the Old Testament as well as from a strictly philosophical perspective within the marketplace. In Acts 26, Paul is making a rational defense of the truthfulness of the Christian perspective and requesting the king to be patient. Paul also speaks from his own personal experience. Following this approach, the material presented here seeks to make a rational defense while illustrating finance implications from one perspective as a finance professor. In the opening three versus of Acts 26, Paul is seeking patience from King Agrippa as Paul lays out his deep-seated rational explanation for preaching the gospel of Jesus Christ.[13]

Acts 26:1–3

> [1]So Agrippa said to Paul, "You have permission to speak for yourself." Then Paul stretched out his hand and made his defense: [2]"I consider myself fortunate that it is before you, King Agrippa, I am going to make my defense today against all the accusations of the Jews, [3]especially because you are familiar with

---

[13]The entire passage is provided in the online supplement available at www.robertebrooks.org.

all the customs and controversies of the Jews. Therefore I beg you to listen to me patiently."

Later in Paul's ministry, he continues repeatedly to serve as an apologist making a defense of the gospel. One illustration is in Philippians.

Philippians 1:7, 16
> *⁷It is right for me to feel this way about you all, because I hold you in my heart, for you are all partakers with me of grace, both in my imprisonment and in the defense and confirmation of the gospel. … ¹⁶The latter do it out of love, knowing that I am put here for the defense of the gospel.*

Approaches to Apologetics

There are two core approaches to apologetics: defense and offense. Within these approaches, the key task of a Christian apologist is to serve as an ambassador for Jesus Christ. Remember too that ambassadors do not seek to represent themselves. Rather they represent the King whom they serve.

Defense (Negative Apologetics)

The goal of negative apologetics is to address challenges to the Christian faith. The apologist seeks to defend Christianity in a winsome way. An apologist seeks to remove boulders from the path that hinder seekers from finding the truthfulness of Christianity. For example, the role of defense would seek to address the rationality of creation over naturalistic evolution. The apologist might ask the opposition the source of his belief. For example, how does nothing create something?

Further, there are numerous misconceptions about 1) what it means to be a follower of Jesus Christ, 2) proper interpretation of the Bible, 3) interpreting various scientific claims, 4) refuting historical and archeological assertions, and 5) rightly interpreting the Bible with respect to personal finance.

With defensive strategies, the apologist seeks to defend Christianity against various charges in a logical way without being too offensive. Thus, the goal is to provide a rational defense for the personal finance implications of the Christian worldview.

Offense (Positive Apologetics)

The goal of positive apologetics is to produce reasons to believe the Christian faith. An apologist seeks to demonstrate the rationality of Christianity. The role of offense is to seek evidence for the existence of God and the bodily resurrection of Jesus Christ. For example, the apologist could address differing explanations for what happened to Peter after Jesus's crucifixion. With offense strategies, the apologist seeks to exalt Christianity in a logical way without being too offensive.

With our focus, the goal is to exalt the Christian worldview, particularly how it applies to personal finance. If one concludes that the Bible is in fact God's divine communication, then it would not be surprising at all that the Bible provides a truthful perspective of all things related to wealth.

Sources for Financial Wisdom

When navigating life's challenging terrain, wisdom and understanding are essential. But where can high wisdom and genuine understanding be found? How can it be acquired to make prudent financial decisions? Ultimately, there are only two possible ways: God's way and not God's way.

For many, wisdom and understanding are found in academies, secular books, podcasts, and the like. There is much knowledge and practical insights to be gained from these resources. Unfortunately, poor financial decisions are often still made. The goal here of apologetics focused on finance is to aid in developing wise and understanding financial decision-makers. Job 28 puts an interesting perspective on this pursuit and provides warrant for the essential need to examine one's foundational beliefs.

Job 28:1–28

> ¹"Surely there is a mine for silver, and a place for gold that they refine. Iron is taken out of the earth, and copper is smelted from the ore. ³Man puts an end to darkness and searches out to the farthest limit the ore in gloom and deep darkness. He opens shafts in a valley away from where anyone lives; they are forgotten by travelers; they hang in the air, far away from mankind; they swing to and fro. ⁵As for the earth, out of it comes bread, but underneath it is turned up as by fire. ⁶Its stones are the place of sapphires, and it has dust of gold. ⁷"That path no bird of prey knows, and the falcon's eye has not seen it. ⁸The proud beasts have not trodden it; the lion has not passed over it. ⁹"Man puts his hand to the flinty rock and overturns mountains by the roots. ¹⁰He cuts out channels in the rocks, and his eye sees every precious thing. ¹¹He dams up the streams so that they do not trickle, and the thing that is hidden he brings out to light.
>
> ¹²"But where shall wisdom be found? And where is the place of understanding? ¹³Man does not know its worth, and it is not found in the land of the living. ¹⁴The deep says, 'It is not in me,' and the sea says, 'It is not with me.' ¹⁵It cannot be bought for gold, and silver cannot be weighed as its price. ¹⁶It cannot be valued in the gold of Ophir, in precious onyx or sapphire. ¹⁷Gold and glass cannot equal it, nor can it be exchanged for jewels of fine gold. ¹⁸No mention shall be made of coral or of crystal; the price of wisdom is above pearls. ¹⁹The topaz of Ethiopia cannot equal it, nor can it be valued in pure gold.
>
> ²⁰"From where, then, does wisdom come? And where is the place of understanding? ²¹It is hidden from the eyes of all living and concealed from the birds of the air. ²²Abaddon and Death say, 'We have heard a rumor of it with our ears.' ²³"God understands the way to it, and he knows its place. ²⁴For he looks to the ends of the earth and sees everything under the heavens. ²⁵When he gave to the wind its weight and apportioned the waters by measure, ²⁶when he made a decree for the rain and a

way for the lightning of the thunder, ²⁷then he saw it and declared it; he established it, and searched it out. ²⁸And he said to man, 'Behold, the fear of the Lord, that is wisdom, and to turn away from evil is understanding.'"

Job 28:1-11 highlights human cleverness when in pursuit of material wealth, such as gold and silver. Mountains are literally moved, deep tunnels dug, and entire rivers stopped. Even in Job's day, human ingenuity was on display especially in pursue of precious metals and gems. Generally, it is within our human nature to pursue material wealth. But navigating this life, especially related to personal finance, requires way more than material wealth.

In Job 28:12, two critical questions are posed: Where is wisdom found? Where is the place of understanding? Ellicott summarizes, "But where shall wisdom be found?--With magnificent effect comes in this question, after the gigantic achievements of man just recounted; notwithstanding his industry, science, and skill, he is altogether ignorant of true wisdom. Neither his knowledge nor his wealth can make him master of that; nor can he find it where he discovers so many other secret and precious things."[14]

From Job 28:13-19, humans do not appreciate wisdom's worth, cannot locate it by searching efforts, and cannot buy it with materially valuable means. Perhaps for emphasis, these two critical questions are asked again in Job 20:20.

From Job 28:21-27, wisdom and understanding are in fact hidden from everyone except the God who created all things. Job 28:28 is key for our pursuits. Wisdom is found in the fear of the Lord and understanding is gained from turning away from evil. In this book, a careful examination is made of the God of the Bible and focus on His definition of evil, which should be abandoned.

Harnessing Wisdom and Understanding

There is a recuring theme in the Bible related to wisdom and

---

[14]See Ellicott's Commentary for English Readers, https://biblehub.com/job/28-12.htm#commentary.

understanding, particularly wisdom that comes from above. In Romans 11:33, Paul exalts God's wisdom and recognizes that it is not acquired by sheer human effort or searching.

Romans 11:33

> [33]Oh, the depth of the riches and wisdom and knowledge of God! How unsearchable are his judgments and how inscrutable his ways!

God's wisdom, however, is accessible to humans. James 1:5 holds the key: Ask! This appears to be simplistic at best. It is important to interpret biblical instructions within context. Within Christian circles there is a common saying, "A text without a context is a pretext for a proof text."[15] It is common in biblical discussions to pull a passage out of context to prove a point, commonly referred to as proof-texting. James 1:5 has that risk; thus, the context is provided.

James 1:1–5

> [1]James, a servant of God and of the Lord Jesus Christ, To the twelve tribes in the Dispersion: Greetings. [2]Count it all joy, my brothers, when you meet trials of various kinds, [3]for you know that the testing of your faith produces steadfastness. [4]And let steadfastness have its full effect, that you may be perfect and complete, lacking in nothing. [5]If any of you lacks wisdom, let him ask God, who gives generously to all without reproach, and it will be given him.

The first thing to notice is James's use of "servant." The Greek word, δοῦλος (doo'-los), indicates "a slave." Thus, James self-identifies as a slave of his master (Lord: κύριος (koo'-ree-os)). Thus, the author is a slave, and the master is Jesus Christ—very odd indeed in modern context. The second thing to notice is the audience is "brothers." The Greek word, ἀδελφός (ad-el-fos'), defined by Strong's concordance as "a brother, member of the same religious community, especially a fellow-

---

[15]See, for example, https://deeperchristian.com/prooftexting/.

Christian." James's expectation is not that followers of Jesus Christ will be prosperous. Rather trials are more likely. So strong was the fellowship bonds of early believers that the ancient Romans accused Christians of incest because they married their brothers and sisters in Christ.[16]

Jesus's invitation to be "yoked" to him is explained in Matthew 11:28–30. As with many biblical paradoxes, entrusting one's life to Jesus Christ, often termed being a slave, results in deep and abiding rest as well as peace.

Matthew 11:28–30

[28]Come to me, all who labor and are heavy laden, and I will give you rest. [29]Take my yoke upon you, and learn from me, for I am gentle and lowly in heart, and you will find rest for your souls. [30]For my yoke is easy, and my burden is light."

King Solomon comes to the same conclusion as recorded in Job.

Ecclesiastes 12:11–14

[11]The words of the wise are like goads, and like nails firmly fixed are the collected sayings; they are given by one Shepherd. [12]My son, beware of anything beyond these. Of making many books there is no end, and much study is a weariness of the flesh. [13]The end of the matter; all has been heard. Fear God and keep his commandments, for this is the whole duty of man. [14]For God will bring every deed into judgment, with every secret thing, whether good or evil.

So how does this high wisdom and understanding translate into financial management? Financial management is first explored in general and then a specific focus on Christian-based financial management is illustrated.

---

[16]For an excellent treatise on the early Christian church, see Nijay K. Gupta, *Strange Religion*, (Grand Rapids, MI, Brazos Press, 2024).

Financial Management

Financial management is categorized as a subfield of microeconomics within the broad field of economics. Economics is a subfield of the social sciences, and the social sciences are a subfield of science itself. Often Christian apologists find themselves interacting with formal sciences like logic or mathematics categories or the natural sciences like the physical or biological categories.

The unique approach taken here is to intentionally intersect Christian apologetics with finance, mainly personal finance. When Christianity and finance are raised in the same sentence, many immediately think of the word of faith movement that is also known as the health-and-wealth gospel, the prosperity gospel, or the name-it-and-claim-it gospel. This movement in various forms asserts that it is always God's will for his followers to be healthy and wealthy. Based on clear biblical teaching as well as casual empirical observation, it is simply false.

The existence of counterfeits is often an indication of something valuable. Thieves counterfeit $100 bills because the true $100 bill is valuable. Thus, the true gospel of Jesus Christ has had numerous counterfeits over the centuries.

By intersecting Christian apologetics and finance, the goal is to demonstrate the truthfulness of the Christian worldview. The goal is not to give you ten tips on how to die rich. Remember, you will eventually die one day—rich or not. Rather, based on a review of the Bible and experience, the decision to follow Jesus Christ will result in suffering. You may wake up one day and find yourself making disciples in a place that is rather hostile to Christianity. Many followers of Jesus Christ have discovered that as stewards of God's resources money is a great servant but a horrible master. Simply put, the Christian worldview has a completely different perspective on wealth management. This Christian perspective is either true or false. So let us investigate.

Case Study 1.2: Experience with Christianity and Finance

Early in my PhD coursework, I began to make the connection between Christianity and personal finance. One early connection occurred after acquiring an old copy of an English translation of Max Weber's *The Protestant Ethic and the Spirit of Capitalism* first published in 1904. He made a compelling argument for the link between free markets and the Christian worldview.

The first major challenge to this connection arrived in a PhD-level class. A world famous professor asked the class of four PhD students the following: Suppose you were offered the following game. The professor would flip a coin and if it lands heads, we receive $100, and if it lands tails, we receive $0. The objective was to estimate the maximum amount we would be willing to pay to play the game only once. As the discussion surrounded investor risk aversion, the expected answer was some number less than $50, but each student's answer would vary. For example, married students with children might say $40 as they would be highly risk averse, whereas rich single students may say $49.5 as they are less risk averse.

As students gave their respective answers, I found myself saying that I would not play as I do not gamble. The goal was not to be self-righteous, rather I was wrestling with the notion that as a follower of Jesus Christ, I was a manager of God's resources, and this game did not seem to serve a redemptive purpose. At the time, it seemed clear that the actual existence of God changes our relationship with money. Needless to say, my response sparked an intense somewhat hostile discussion.

From my perspective, money serves a useful purpose in fulfilling God's purposes. Alternatively, money is a horrible task master when enlisted for the purpose of fulfilling our own narcissistic desires. As many have witnessed, the materialism addiction is deadly.

Around this same time in the early 1980s, I came across Larry Burkett's Christian Financial Concepts ministry and books. Nearing the end of my PhD training, I began an intense study of what the Bible communicated related to finance. Over the past several decades, I have taught a wide variety of Bible-based personal finance classes. My wife and I have seen firsthand how Bible-based finance concepts effectively transforms lives. College-aged people are enlightened to realize it is easily possible to never make a car payment in their lifetime through financial saving discipline. Young couples drowning in debt are radically delivered from materialism to go on to be courageous followers of Jesus Christ. Older adults' transition from an owner-perspective to God's manager-perspective and are liberated from crushing finance-related stress.

Over the past forty years or so, numerous organizations have emerged within the Christian personal finance advisory space. From Crown Ministries (current organization from the legacy of Larry Burkett) that has served over fifty million people to Dave Ramsey's Financial Peace University, these and many other related organizations provide helpful materials in aiding people of the journey seeking Bible-based financial principles.[17]

Christian Financial Management

Our objective here is not to recreate the fine work of numerous Christian-based finance organizations. Rather, our objective is to provide the philosophical foundation for the merits of Bible-based financial decision making.

According to Faith Driven Investor, Christians manage over $150 trillion, comprising over half of the world's wealth.[18] Faith Driven Investor makes a compelling argument for the necessity to use this wealth to influence the world for good. The idea that where we invest our wealth is somehow separate from

---

[17]See https://www.crown.org and https://www.daveramsey.com. For a more related organizations, see https://www.sharefaith.com/blog/2015/07/top-10-christian-based-financial-organizations/. For a listing of related books, see https://www.lifeway.com/en/shop/books/christian-living/life-issues/personal-finance.
[18]See https://www.youtube.com/watch?v=610v60gbKYc.

how we seek to influence culture is robustly rejected.

Ideas have consequences. The idea that the Bible addresses personal finance has a direct consequence to those of us who are biblically responsive. Can we really trust the biblical perspective, or should we turn to naturalism and modern sages?

As we will see, not only do ideas have consequences, but ideas also have antecedents. Why should we entrust the weight of our lives to the biblical perspective for the purpose of taking us across life's harrowing bridge? Will the bridge fail us just when our children head off to college and depend on our help? Thus, our focus is primarily foundational. For example, although budgeting is addressed in the next few chapters, it is left to other quality sources for the practical issues related to establishing a budget and the challenges of living within it.

Foundational issues are the focus as they get at the heart of why budgeting often fails to achieve the desired objective. If the foundation is firmly established on the biblical rock, then the unique strategies adopted will withstand the withering pressures of the day. One's grasp on a particular biblically-based strategy may weaken if it is not firmly gripped with a robust understanding of its deep truthfulness. The Christian-based finance perspective is radically different from alternative approaches, particularly those taught in academic institutions. Thus, a robust philosophical foundation to the Christian-based finance approach is provided.

Target Audience

The target audience for this material is not the evangelical atheist and others deeply committed to the expulsion of Christianity from the marketplace of ideas.[19] Rather, the target audience includes two categories, maturing believers and genuine seekers.

Apologetics serves a useful role in helping young

---

[19]Often on college campuses, not only is atheism a popular worldview, students and faculty often seek to convert theist, particularly Christians, to their atheistic or at least agnostic worldview.

believers as they seek to grow in their newfound Christian faith. Clearly, the greater the confidence we have in the truthfulness of Jesus Christ, the more fully we embrace his lordship. Interestingly, the more fully we embrace his lordship, the easier it is to return from our natural tendency to wander away. As we realize that he was in fact who he claimed to be, then we better understand his unique position in world history. I personally found great benefit from being introduced to and studying numerous apologetic materials as a young Christian while in the PhD program at the University of Florida.

Apologetics is also beneficial for genuine seekers considering the truthfulness of Christianity. As a former finance faculty member serving in that capacity for thirty-seven years, it is amply evident that there has been a concerted effort to remove Christianity from the academic marketplace of ideas. Thus, genuine seekers find it difficult to locate unbiased materials when considering various perspectives. It is interesting to watch intellectuals, particularly PhD students from countries deeply hostile to Christianity, begin to explore the truth claims of Christianity. They are typically deeply surprised at Christianity's logical foundation, its deep empirical and rational support for various claims, ability to address life's main questions, and the resultant ethic's ability to navigate life's difficult challenges.

One goal here, regardless of which category you are in, is to find common ground. The goal is to identify foundational beliefs that most people share. For example, most people are deeply interested in and desire to know the truth. Further, it is generally recognized that we believe many things unproven as will be demonstrated later. All human knowledge rests on many things that we accept by faith. That is, we presuppose. For example, rational humans believe the law of non-contradiction. In general, the law of non-contradiction states that two mutually exclusive propositions cannot both be true at the same time in the same sense.[20] Thus, Christianity and any one of numerous other perspectives cannot both be true. It is deeply

---

[20]For a more complete discussion, see Logic section of Session 2.

disingenuous to make assertions such as truth depending on whether you believe it or not. Truth is objective in nature.

Finally, quality Christian apologetic approaches assert various truth claims with as much rational support as possible, but it is not appropriate for the Christian apologist to be antagonistic. Jesus's approach was genuine and gentle.

Where Do We Go From Here?

One objective is to demonstrate conclusively that our philosophical foundation is the driving force for financial decision-making. Further, the Christian foundation is the most logically coherent and it provides the best correspondence with financial realities. The following table provides a sketch of the thirteen chapters covered within this material.

Chapter	Topic
1	Foundations
2	Philosophy: Logic and Epistemology
3	Philosophy: Metaphysics and Ethics
4	Nature of Information
5	Existence of God
6	Competing Worldviews
7	Naturalism, Christianity, and Science
8	Problem of Evil
9	The Bible as Hearsay or Heresy
10	The Bible as History
11	Miracles
12	Resurrection of Jesus Christ
13	Loving Your Neighbor
14	The Nature of the Harvest

One's philosophical foundation matters greatly. With an eye toward the following thirteen chapters, in the next table a contrast is made between the Christian worldview and atheistic naturalism (existence exists and that is all that exists).[21]

Chapter	Christianity	Naturalism
1	Manager of God's resources	Owner of my resources
2	Intricate design and order	Chaos
3	Immutable ethics	Mutable and tentative social arrangements
4	Objective reality	Subjective perceptions, never sure real
5	Beauty	Preference
6	Particularism–know particular claims	Skepticism–somehow sure no absolutes
7	Economic abundance	Dwindling scarcity
8	Meaningful life	Meaninglessness of all of life
9	Transcendent reality pervades everything	Existence is all that exists and that is it
10	Truth is known with certainty	Truth is not knowable
11	Divine declared communication	Divine silence
12	Deep and abiding hope in life	Hopelessness
13	Loved deeply by God and others	At best tolerated by others
14	Contentment and generosity	Wanting and forsaken

Summary

Again, the goal of this material is to spark discussion. Being a good discussant is a lost art in today's culture.

---

[21] We will go into much more detail on the concept of worldview. Chapter 7 is particularly focused on Christianity and naturalism.

Personal finance rests on philosophical foundations, and in future chapters several different philosophical foundations are explored. In this Chapter, the Christian foundation was introduced and the concept of apologetics as well as provide a roadmap on where we will be going over the next several chapters.

Christian apologetics was defined, and its purpose and origins explored. Second, both negative and positive approaches to Christian apologetics was introduced. Finally, the target audience was identified for using this material, and an overview of the thirteen chapters provided. Various financial issues will be integrated as part of appraising different worldviews.

As you begin to work your way through this material, what questions would you like to have answered or what issues would you like to have addressed? Your feedback will help with future projects. Please email your comments or questions to the email address given in the preface.

Case Study 1: Young Banker's Transportation Decision

Sam was graduating from a major university with a master's degree in finance and was recently married. He drove a twenty-year-old car he had inherited from his grandmother. His grandmother had backed into a few poles and her solution was to use duct tape to keep the back bumper from falling off. As you might expect, the car was not aesthetically pleasing to the eye. When he accepted a banking job, what would the U.S. culture expect him to do? Buy a brand new car on payments primarily to be seen as being financially well off. Sam actually drove that car another five years or so for the purpose of getting his family's financial foundation strong and saving enough to pay cash for his next car. He will likely never make a car payment in the remainder of his life. Reflecting on your own circumstances, are there specific actions you could take to improve your family's financial foundation?

Case Study 2: Thomas, the Resurrection, and Personal Finance

In the passage below, one of the few recorded actions of a man called Thomas is given. Most know him as "doubting Thomas" because he did not believe Jesus had rose bodily from the grave.

John 20:24–29

> ^{24}Now Thomas, one of the twelve, called the Twin, was not with them when Jesus came. ^{25}So the other disciples told him, "We have seen the Lord." But he said to them, "Unless I see in his hands the mark of the nails, and place my finger into the mark of the nails, and place my hand into his side, I will never believe." ^{26}Eight days later, his disciples were inside again, and Thomas was with them. Although the doors were locked, Jesus came and stood among them and said, "Peace be with you." ^{27}Then he said to Thomas, "Put your finger here, and see my hands; and put out your hand, and place it in my side. Do not disbelieve, but believe." ^{28}Thomas answered him, "My Lord and my God!" ^{29}Jesus said to him, "Have you believed because you have seen me? Blessed are those who have not seen and yet have believed."

Based on Thomas' interaction with the risen Jesus, he no longer doubted. One key insight is that since Jesus rose bodily from the grave, just as he said, then he validates all the other things he said. For example, Jesus asserted that he had the power to forgive sin.

Matthew 9:1–2

> ^{1}And getting into a boat he crossed over and came to his own city. ^{2}And behold, some people brought to him a paralytic, lying on a bed. And when Jesus saw their faith, he said to the paralytic, "Take heart, my son; your sins are forgiven."

As expected, the scribes did not believe Jesus had this sin-forgiving power. Assuming Jesus rose bodily from the grave, what does that suggest regarding his authority to forgive sin?

Case Study 3: America's Most Expensive Home[22]

The Donohue family owns a 60-acre estate in Florida. They decided to sell the "crown jewel of the estate — a roughly 9-acre compound in Naples' Port Royal neighborhood with three houses and a private yacht basin — for a potentially record-setting $295 million." Is super affluence somehow anti-Christian? Does knowing the creators of a 60-acre estate had 13 children and 84 grandchildren change your perspective?

Case Study 4: Home Purchase Decision

John and Melinda, a young married couple, recently decided to take the plunge and buy a house. They were excited to learn that the friendly banker would make them a sizeable mortgage with no money down. They seek your advice. How would you advise them based solely from an economic perspective? If you have a biblically-based worldview, how does your advice change?

Case Study 5: Is Faith a Blind Leap?

Your non-Christian friend claims that the Christian faith is a

---

[22] E. B. Solomont, "America's Most Expensive Home for Sale Hits the Market for $295 Million," *Wall Street Journal*, February 7, 2024, https://www.wsj.com/real-estate/luxury-homes/americas-most-expensive-home-for-sale-naples-florida-81535a6b.

blind leap and perhaps useful for those who are afraid. By contrast, he claims science is based on rationality and thus a leisurely justifiable walk and deeply useful for those willing to brave the chaos of life. How does one respond from a biblical perspective?

Case Study 6: Christianity and Finance

Appraise the following statement: "Christianity may be beneficial by providing an ethical framework for living, but it does not aid in managing your money."

References

Books

Craig, William Lane, *Reasonable Faith: Christian Truth and Apologetics*, 3rd edition (Crossway, 2008).
Keller, Tim, *The Reason for God: Belief in an Age of Skepticism* (Dutton, 2008).
Lennox, John C., *God's Undertaker: Has Science Buried God?* (Lion, 2009).
Lewis, C. S., *Mere Christianity* (Harper Collins, 1952).
Lewis, C. S., *Miracles* (Harper Collins, 1947).
Lewis, C. S., *The Problem of Pain* (Harper Collins, 1940).
McDowell, Josh, *A Ready Defense* (Thomas Nelson, 1990).
Strobel, Lee, *The Case for a Creator* (Zondervan, 2004).
Strobel, Lee, *The Case for Faith* (Zondervan, 2000).
Strobel, Lee, *The Case for Christ* (Zondervan, 1998).

Useful Websites

https://www.bethinking.org/apologetics: Managed by the Universities and Colleges Christian Fellowship (UCCF) whose goal is to "make disciples of Jesus Christ in the student world."
https://carm.org: Christian Apologetics and Research Ministry — contains a wide array of useful materials.

Chapter 2. Philosophy: Logic and Epistemology

Learning Objectives

- Briefly introduce philosophy.
- Illustrate basic concepts in logic and how it is used in apologetics.
- Define epistemology and demonstrate its importance in apologetics.
- Explore important connections between logic and epistemology with financial budgeting.

Opening Quotes

"(T)o be ignorant and simple now — not to be able to meet the enemy on their own ground — would be to throw down our weapons, and to betray our uneducated brethren who have, under God, no defense but us against the intellectual attacks of the heathen. Good philosophy must exist, if for no other reason, because bad philosophy needs to be answered."[23]

---

[23] C. S. Lewis, *The Weight of Glory*, (San Francisco: Harper, 2001), 58.

Exploring the Philosophical Roots that Influence Financial Fruit

"Our economic future is not now and never has been tied to the physical assets we now see, but to the vast untapped potential of creative thinking — the metaphysical process which can show us entirely new reserves and new and easier ways of doing things, extending value and increasing wealth without depleting our planet."[24]

Overview

In this Chapter, a quick tour through the field of philosophy is given. These philosophical concepts are applied to the often not-so-popular topic of budgeting. After exploring definitions of philosophy and philosophical worldview, a quickly journey through philosophy's four pillars: logic, epistemology, metaphysics, and ethics, is provided. In this chapter a brief introduction to the first two pillars, logic and epistemology, is given. In the next chapter, a brief review with the final two pillars of metaphysics and ethics is provided.

The material in these two chapters is rather dense. It will be challenging and likely frustrating at times. To provide encouragement, consider the following quote, "The primary and essential character of wealth is metaphysical, not physical, and is the direct result of the creativity of mind, not the availability of raw materials — the sum product of individual efforts, not the manipulated static resources of collective nations or governments or lands."[25] What is Warren T. Brookes asserting here?

Most of us have been educated to believe that the primary and essential character of wealth is physical. It is our nice house and car, and if things go well, then houses and cars. One objective here is to seek more deeply to understand the dominant role the non-physical plays in each of our lives. With this new understanding, we are better able to make financial decisions that lead to human flourishing.

---

[24]Warren T. Brookes, *The Economy in Mind* (New York: Universe Books, 1982), 36.
[25]Ibid., 12.

Philosophy Defined

Philosophy is derived from two Greek words (phileos or φίλος "to love" and sophia or σοφία "wisdom") meaning loving wisdom.[26] "Philosophy is ... the critical analysis of fundamental concepts of human inquiry, and the normative discussion of how human thought and action ought to function, as well as the description of the nature of reality."[27] "Philosophy is just thinking hard about something."[28]

We inherently know that there is something amiss between say normative behavior and positive behavior. Normative is defined as what ought to be. Positive is defined as what actually is. We easily observe in other people's lives and even within our own lives a significant disconnect between what ought to be (normative) and what actually is (positive). In today's intellectual culture, there is a heavy focus on the positive informing the normative. For our purpose, with an emphasis on finance, we can see this contrast played out in that the mantra for finance in today's culture is "data rules." From a Christian perspective, perhaps the mantra should be "data fools" as history repeatedly demonstrates that those things that have never happened in history do happen. The closer one's worldview is to the truth; your financial management decisions will improve. For example, a deep understanding of what it really means to be human will solve numerous problems when entering financial contracts.

When budgeting, we clearly need to keep our earning above our yearning (normative). Unfortunately, we will struggle when our yearning results in actual spending exceeding our earning (positive).

---

[26]Norman L. Geisler and Paul D Feinberg, *Introduction to Philosophy A Christian Perspective* (Grand Rapids, MI: Baker Academic, 1980), 13.
[27]Ibid., 17.
[28]Alvin Plantinga quoted in J. P. Moreland and William Lane Craig, *Philosophical Foundations for a Christian Worldview* (Downers Grove, IL: InterVarsity Press, 2003), 28.

Philosophical Worldview

A worldview is an ordered set of propositions that one believes, especially propositions about life's most important questions.[29] In the context here, a philosophical worldview means a perspective based on an ordered set of propositions that govern all aspects of life. Worldview is derived from a German word, Weltanschauung that means wide world perspective. Specifically, from welt (world) and anschauung (perspective).

      These propositions tend to be presuppositions and core assumptions as opposed to the decision-making process taken for a particular task. Presuppositions are implicit assumptions about the world for it to make sense. It is often core to any argument to posit a philosophical worldview. One's worldview is like a pair of glasses used to see the world as illustrated in Figure 2.1.

Figure 2.1. One's Worldview Illustrated with Eyeglasses[30]

---

[29]Moreland and Craig, *Philosophical Foundations*, 13.
[30]Photo by Alan King on Unsplash.com. Accessed on July 23, 2024.

Once a person has established their philosophical worldview — knowingly or not — then one has the capacity to make decisions that are coherent as an outcome stemming from his or her worldview. Various worldviews are examined in more detail in Chapters 6 and 7. Once one has adopted a particular philosophical worldview, then the analytical process of making decisions are better grounded by reason.

If our identity is linked to our material possessions, then the budgeting process will be a lifelong challenge. If our identity is not linked to our material possessions, then the budgeting process will simply be a part of the decision-making process involved to achieve our purpose.

Decision-Making Process

In the context here, the decision-making process means any method of assessing the "correctness" of a particular "idea" within a particular worldview. Ideas, or more precisely, propositions, are essentially truth claims. For example, one proposition is "Jesus Christ rose bodily from the dead." Whether or not this proposition is deemed "valid" will depend on both the particular   deployed as well as the philosophical worldview.

The philosophical worldview always precedes the decision-making process. Note the biggest influence on how decisions are made is often not the decision-making process, rather the philosophical worldview. Figure 2.2 illustrates how "ideas" are evaluated first through the philosophical worldview and then through a decision-making process. When understanding how we make financial decisions, it is crucial to understand our worldview as it will explain these decisions better than a particular decision-making process.

Figure 2.2. Processing "ideas"

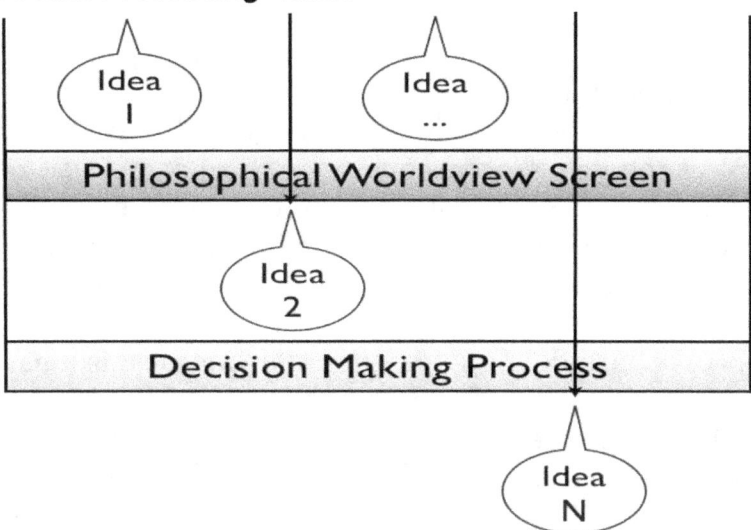

When our decisions fail to correspond to reality—that is, when we consistently make poor financial decisions—often the culprit is a faulty worldview. Hence, our own decisions are an important piece of evidence regarding the truthfulness of our worldview. Note when "ideas" are evaluated, there are two key considerations, coherence and correspondence.

Budgeting is a key component for performance analysis. Budgeting is not a process of checks and balances—the checks wiping out the balances! The budgeting process is deeply helpful when first seeking to understand the flow of finance throughout any organization, including a family.

Coherence

Is an "idea" coherent within a particular philosophical worldview? Coherence is focused on the internal consistency of the "idea" with one's philosophical worldview. The focus is not on whether the "idea" is true, but rather whether there are any inconsistencies between the "idea" and the philosophical worldview. These inconsistencies are often known as defeaters. Absent any defeaters, then the "idea" is likely to be coherent.

Selected examples:

"I am absolutely certain that there are no absolutes." (Incoherent)

"In the beginning, God created the heavens and the earth." (Coherent within a theist's worldview)

Coherence is normative, what ought to be, in flavor. For example, suppose you were considering the lunar cycle stock investing strategy. Specifically, the strategy involves buying stocks during the fifteen days surrounding the new moon dates and shorting stocks (a process where one sells stocks they do not own) during the fifteen days surrounding a full moon. For most people, including investment professionals, this lunar cycle investing strategy does not fit their philosophical worldview. Thus, the empirical evidence or any other decision-making process is never considered.

Correspondence

Does an "idea" correspond to reality? Correspondence is focused on how well an "idea" aligns with observations within the space-time universe. Here the focus is on whether an "idea" is more likely to be true considering empirical observations when compared with a contrary "idea."

Selected examples:

"All swans are white." (Lacks correspondence)

"All swans are not white." (Correspondence)

Correspondence is positive in flavor. For example, Yuan, Zheng, and Zhu[31] find significantly positive returns to the lunar cycle investing strategy identified above across forty-eight countries. These positive returns cannot be explained by standard approaches. Thus, an empiricist may adopt this strategy only if it initially passed through their philosophical worldview screen.

Similarly, budgeting aids in identifying lack of correspondence. The amazing features of that new car, even though $40,000 over budget, spark the idea of acquisition. The

---

[31]Kathy Yuan, Lu Zheng, and Qiaoqiao Zhu, "Are Investors Moonstruck? Lunar Phases and Stock Returns," *Journal of Empirical Finance* 13, no. 1, (January 2006): 1–23.

lack of correspondence to the budget-driven plan hopefully negates an impulsive purchase.

One particularly nasty yet common mistake is to confuse an "idea" with the evidence related to it.

Ontic Referent Error

The ontic referent error relates to confusing an "idea" with the underlying reality either supporting or refuting the "idea." Ontic is defined as "relating to entities and the facts about them; relating to real as opposed to phenomenal existence."[32] Phenomenal is defined as "perceptible by the senses or through immediate experience."[33] A referent is "the thing that a word or phrase denotes or stands for."[34] Thus, the ontic referent is the actual approach one uses as the basis to evaluate an "idea."

For example, consider the "idea" that the "grass outside my front door, on the date of writing this sentence, is green." Thus, the ontic referent would be evaluating whether the grass exhibits a dominant color wavelength around 495–570 nanometers. Ergo, does it look green?

Case Study 2.1: Ontic Referent Error and Finance

Emmanuel Derman, a famous finance practitioner and professor, makes the ontic referent error in his book *Models. Behaving. Badly.* He states,

> A theory is not a fetish; when it is successful ... it describes the object of its focus so accurately that **the theory becomes virtually indistinguishable from the object itself.** Maxwell's equations are electricity and magnetism; the Dirac equation is the electron; the Weinberg-Salam model of weak and

---

[32]Dictionary on Mac computer (New Oxford American Dictionary).
[33]Dictionary on Mac computer (New Oxford American Dictionary).
[34]Dictionary on Mac computer (New Oxford American Dictionary).

electromagnetic interactions matches the electrons and quarks in almost every detail, as closely as one can measure. You can layer metaphors on top of the equation, but the equation is the essence. (Bold above is italics in original.)[35]

If the Dirac equation is the electron, then do we say that Dirac created the electron? I think not! In this book, a strong distinction is made between an "idea" and its corresponding reality. For our purposes, an "idea" is not the corresponding object itself. An "idea" is normative, but the corresponding object is positive. Is there any equation that is the phenomenon the equation seeks to describe?

As the case study above illustrates, the process of budgeting aids in avoiding the ontic referent error. The idea that we will grow our income in the future to pay off current debts is attractive. Unfortunately, often due to unanticipated events, though rationally expected, result in lack of correspondence to future income.

As we move through philosophy, we heed the warning of the Apostle Paul:

Colossians 2:6–10

6Therefore, as you received Christ Jesus the Lord, so walk in him, 7rooted and built up in him and established in the faith, just as you were taught, abounding in thanksgiving. 8See to it that no one takes you captive by philosophy and empty deceit, according to human tradition, according to the elemental spirits of the world, and not according to Christ. 9For in him the whole fullness of deity dwells bodily, 10and you have been filled in him, who is the head of all rule and authority.

Philosophy rests on four main pillars, logic, epistemology, metaphysics, and ethics. This Chapter concludes with a brief journey through logic and epistemology.

---

[35] Emmanuel Derman, *Models. Behaving. Badly* (New York: Free Press, 2012), 61.

Logic[36]

Logic lies at the core of all intellectual activity. Logically absurd "ideas" such as a married bachelor, a square circle, and the smell of red, should be avoided. Other ideas must be studied more carefully to arrive at whether the "idea" is true or false. Logic is deeply objective; feelings are not involved in the reasoned result. At the core, budgeting is inherently logical. If the expenses exceed the revenue for sustained periods of time, then financial trouble is in the offing most of the time. It is simply logical. The law of non-contradiction is now introduced.

Law of Non-Contradiction

"In some ways the most fundamental area of philosophy is logic, since philosophy is a rational inquiry and since logic systematically sets forth the laws of thought and argument."[37] Logic is the study of the rules of reasoning.[38] The goal of logic is to reach a conclusion, specifically to improve one's ability to form good arguments as well as critically evaluate others' arguments. Expressing oneself logically requires the hard work of carefully crafting every statement. It should not be surprising then that the presentation of logical concepts is typically done with great care and precision. Consider the following example.

Example:
P – There is no resurrection from the dead.
Q – Christ has not been raised from the dead.
Premise #1: If P, then Q (denoted symbolically as $P \rightarrow Q$) (Read: If there is no resurrection from the dead, then Christ has not been raised from the dead. See 1 Corinthians 15:13.)
Premise #2: P (There is no resurrection from the dead.)
Conclusion #3: Q (Christ has not been raised from the dead.)

---

[36]Please see the supplement for this book available online at http://robertebrooks.org/project/christian-apologetics-and-finance/. Technical details beyond are scope here are provided for those who wish to delve deeper.
[37]Geisler and Feinberg, *Introduction to Philosophy*, 27.
[38]Moreland and Craig, *Philosophical Foundations*, 29.

Contradictory: not P (denoted $\neg P$), there is a resurrection from the dead.

Paul often used strict logical arguments when presenting the truthfulness of Christianity. Thus, logic is a critical component when appraising competing worldviews.

Case Study 2.2: Jesus Used Laws of Logic to Refute Opponents

Jesus was a master logician. Consider the following passage in Matthew.

Matthew 22:23–33

> [23]*The same day Sadducees came to him, who say that there is no resurrection, and they asked him a question,* [24]*saying, "Teacher, Moses said, 'If a man dies having no children, his brother must marry the widow and raise up offspring for his brother.'* [25]*Now there were seven brothers among us. The first married and died, and having no offspring left his wife to his brother.* [26]*So too the second and third, down to the seventh.* [27]*After them all, the woman died.* [28]*In the resurrection, therefore, of the seven, whose wife will she be? For they all had her."* [29]*But Jesus answered them, "You are wrong, because you know neither the Scriptures nor the power of God.* [30]*For in the resurrection they neither marry nor are given in marriage, but are like angels in heaven.* [31]*And as for the resurrection of the dead, have you not read what was said to you by God:* [32]*'I am the God of Abraham, and the God of Isaac, and the God of Jacob'? He is not God of the dead, but of the living."* [33]*And when the crowd heard it, they were astonished at his teaching.*

Note that Jesus does not chide the Sadducees for their hypothetical-based inquiry. Rather Jesus answers the question factually based on a biblical foundation that he presupposes is true. What are the implications for us when seeking to address various hypothetical questions?

The Law of Non-Contradiction (LNC) can be expressed as follows: P cannot be both Q and not-Q at the same time and in the same sense. Interestingly, philosophers argue that you cannot prove the LNC. Any argument whatsoever must rely on the LNC. Further, you need argument to prove the LNC.

Aristotle noted indirect proofs. He shows you have nonsense if the LNC is repudiated. The LNC is therefore necessary, presupposed, and used for any significant thinking. You cannot think properly if you deny the LNC. For example, you cannot use language until you presuppose the LNC, assuming predicate, noun, adjective means what it means and not something else.

New Age religion repudiates the LNC. Eastern religions often allow contradictory beliefs. Both contradictory beliefs, however, cannot both be true as it requires the sacrifice of reason and the LNC. If you believe arguments are possible, then at least implicitly you are affirming the LNC.

LNC is basic. It is presuppositional. As Christians, we should accept the responsibility to adhere to the LNC. Based on the following passage, once again Paul is using formal logic.[39]

1 Corinthians 15:12–19

> [12]Now if Christ is proclaimed as raised from the dead, how can some of you say that there is no resurrection of the dead? [13]But if there is no resurrection of the dead, then not even Christ has been raised. [14]And if Christ has not been raised, then our preaching is in vain and your faith is in vain. [15]We are even found to be misrepresenting God, because we testified about God that he raised Christ, whom he did not raise if it is true that the dead are not raised. [16]For if the dead are not raised, not even Christ has been raised. [17]And if Christ has not been raised, your faith is futile and you are still in your sins. [18]Then those also

---

[39]Moreland and Craig, *Philosophical Foundations*, 115–120.

who have fallen asleep in Christ have perished. ¹⁹*If in Christ we have hope in this life only, we are of all people most to be pitied.*

We now apply logic to the traditional budgeting process.

Logic and Budgeting

One key area of finance is related to the discipline of budgeting. Budgeting is the process of estimating income and expenses over a period such as a month or year. Some have jokingly observed that budgeting involves checks and balances: the checks wipe out the balances. Given the calendar seasonality often observed in family income and expenses, most budgets include calendar months as well as the overall year.

There are numerous resources available from expensive apps to freely available forms. One free resource is provided by Crown Ministries.[40] In my experience, there is a tactile benefit to working with pencil and paper or a simple spreadsheet. When later temptations arrive to stray from then agreed budget, the labor of documenting the numbers proves beneficial. Further, there is no risk of misappropriation by the app vendor of your personal information.

The practice of budgeting is extremely logical, especially when documenting historical financial activities. If your expenses exceed your revenues in a particular month, then additional resources must be found to fill the gap. There is simply no way to avoid it.

Table 2.1 illustrates just such a case. Note in Panel A that this couple with two children have an expected income of $100,000. This income places them in the top third of the U. S. households. Unfortunately, between taxes, insurance, retirement savings, and debt this couple only has $10,000 per year for household items. As Panel B illustrates, household consumption puts them into a deficit. The logical implications are clear. Either generate more income or eliminate expenses as this family simply cannot continue deficit spending over the

---

[40]For example, numerous downloadable documents are freely available at https://www.crown.org/resources/fillable-forms-worksheets/.

long term. Gaining the knowledge and understanding of our family's income and expenses is something significantly different from having the wisdom to make the appropriate financial alterations.

Table 2.1. Sample Income Statement for Couple with Two Children

Panel A. Income and Major Expenses

Income	Expected Annual	TI Percentage	Jan	Feb	Mar	Apr	May	Jun	Jul	Aug	Sep	Oct	Nov	Dec
Source 1	$84,000	84%	$7,000	$7,000	$7,000	$7,000	$7,000	$7,000	$7,000	$7,000	$7,000	$7,000	$7,000	$7,000
Source 2	$15,000	15%	$1,250	$1,250	$1,250	$1,250	$1,250	$1,250	$1,250	$1,250	$1,250	$1,250	$1,250	$1,250
Source 3	$1,000	1%	$83	$83	$83	$83	$83	$83	$83	$83	$83	$83	$83	$83
Source 4	$0	0%	$0	$0	$0	$0	$0	$0	$0	$0	$0	$0	$0	$0
Source 5	$0	0%	$0	$0	$0	$0	$0	$0	$0	$0	$0	$0	$0	$0
Total Income	$100,000	100%	$8,333	$8,333	$8,333	$8,333	$8,333	$8,333	$8,333	$8,333	$8,333	$8,333	$8,333	$8,333
Tax and Deductions														
Tithe/Giving	$5,000	5.0%	$417	$417	$417	$417	$417	$417	$417	$417	$417	$417	$417	$417
Fed Tax 1	$7,000	7.0%	$583	$583	$583	$583	$583	$583	$583	$583	$583	$583	$583	$583
Fed Tax 2	$3,000	3.0%	$250	$250	$250	$250	$250	$250	$250	$250	$250	$250	$250	$250
Fed Tax 3	$20,000	20.0%	$1,667	$1,667	$1,667	$1,667	$1,667	$1,667	$1,667	$1,667	$1,667	$1,667	$1,667	$1,667
State Tax	$5,000	5.0%	$417	$417	$417	$417	$417	$417	$417	$417	$417	$417	$417	$417
Insurance 1 (Health)	$6,000	6.0%	$500	$500	$500	$500	$500	$500	$500	$500	$500	$500	$500	$500
Insurance 2 (Dental)	$1,200	1.2%	$100	$100	$100	$100	$100	$100	$100	$100	$100	$100	$100	$100
Insurance 3 (Vision)	$600	0.6%	$50	$50	$50	$50	$50	$50	$50	$50	$50	$50	$50	$50
Retirement 1 (Matching)	$5,000	5.0%	$417	$417	$417	$417	$417	$417	$417	$417	$417	$417	$417	$417
Retirement 2 (Supplemental)	$0	0.0%	$0	$0	$0	$0	$0	$0	$0	$0	$0	$0	$0	$0
Takehome Pay	$47,200	47%	$3,933	$3,933	$3,933	$3,933	$3,933	$3,933	$3,933	$3,933	$3,933	$3,933	$3,933	$3,933
Major Items														
Mortgage/Rent	$24,000	24.0%	$2,000	$2,000	$2,000	$2,000	$2,000	$2,000	$2,000	$2,000	$2,000	$2,000	$2,000	$2,000
Insurance 1 (Life)	$2,000	2.0%	$167	$167	$167	$167	$167	$167	$167	$167	$167	$167	$167	$167
Insurance 2 (Auto)	$700	0.7%	$58	$58	$58	$58	$58	$58	$58	$58	$58	$58	$58	$58
Insurance 3 (Disability)	$100	0.1%	$8	$8	$8	$8	$8	$8	$8	$8	$8	$8	$8	$8
Debt 1 (Auto)	$4,800	4.8%	$400	$400	$400	$400	$400	$400	$400	$400	$400	$400	$400	$400
Debt 2 (Student Loans)	$3,600	3.6%	$300	$300	$300	$300	$300	$300	$300	$300	$300	$300	$300	$300
Debt 3 (Other)	$1,900	1.9%	$158	$158	$158	$158	$158	$158	$158	$158	$158	$158	$158	$158
Other	$100	0.1%	$8	$8	$8	$8	$8	$8	$8	$8	$8	$8	$8	$8
Net Before Household	$10,000	10%	$833	$833	$833	$833	$833	$833	$833	$833	$833	$833	$833	$833

Panel B. Household Expenses

Household	Year	TI Percentage	Jan	Feb	Mar	Apr	May	Jun	Jul	Aug	Sep	Oct	Nov	Dec
Spiritual (Books, Retreats)	$300	0.3%	$25	$25	$25	$25	$25	$25	$25	$25	$25	$25	$25	$25
Auto 1 (Repair/Replacement)	$600	0.6%	$50	$50	$50	$50	$50	$50	$50	$50	$50	$50	$50	$50
Auto 2 (Gas and Oil)	$600	0.6%	$50	$50	$50	$50	$50	$50	$50	$50	$50	$50	$50	$50
Auto 3 (Other-License/Taxes)	$100	0.1%	$8	$8	$8	$8	$8	$8	$8	$8	$8	$8	$8	$8
Dining Out/Entertainment	$400	0.4%	$33	$33	$33	$33	$33	$33	$33	$33	$33	$33	$33	$33
Vacation	$1,200	1.2%	$100	$100	$100	$100	$100	$100	$100	$100	$100	$100	$100	$100
Pets	$300	0.3%	$25	$25	$25	$25	$25	$25	$25	$25	$25	$25	$25	$25
Cleaning (Laundry)	$600	0.6%	$50	$50	$50	$50	$50	$50	$50	$50	$50	$50	$50	$50
Clothing	$670	0.7%	$56	$56	$56	$56	$56	$56	$56	$56	$56	$56	$56	$56
Healthcare (Copays, OTC Drugs)	$240	0.2%	$20	$20	$20	$20	$20	$20	$20	$20	$20	$20	$20	$20
Electric	$3,000	3.0%	$250	$250	$250	$250	$250	$250	$250	$250	$250	$250	$250	$250
Garbage	$300	0.3%	$25	$25	$25	$25	$25	$25	$25	$25	$25	$25	$25	$25
Gifts	$300	0.3%	$25	$25	$25	$25	$25	$25	$25	$25	$25	$25	$25	$25
Groceries	$6,000	6.0%	$500	$500	$500	$500	$500	$500	$500	$500	$500	$500	$500	$500
Education (Lessons, Sports)	$300	0.3%	$25	$25	$25	$25	$25	$25	$25	$25	$25	$25	$25	$25
Mart Items	$1,200	1.2%	$100	$100	$100	$100	$100	$100	$100	$100	$100	$100	$100	$100
Communication (Phone, Internet)	$1,200	1.2%	$100	$100	$100	$100	$100	$100	$100	$100	$100	$100	$100	$100
Cable	$500	0.5%	$42	$42	$42	$42	$42	$42	$42	$42	$42	$42	$42	$42
Subscriptions (Apps, Clubs)	$300	0.3%	$25	$25	$25	$25	$25	$25	$25	$25	$25	$25	$25	$25
Other Personal	$150	0.2%	$13	$13	$13	$13	$13	$13	$13	$13	$13	$13	$13	$13
Allowances	$120	0.1%	$10	$10	$10	$10	$10	$10	$10	$10	$10	$10	$10	$10
Postage	$120	0.1%	$10	$10	$10	$10	$10	$10	$10	$10	$10	$10	$10	$10
Beauty/Hair	$300	0.3%	$25	$25	$25	$25	$25	$25	$25	$25	$25	$25	$25	$25
Home Maintenance	$600	0.6%	$50	$50	$50	$50	$50	$50	$50	$50	$50	$50	$50	$50
Miscellaneous	$300	0.3%	$25	$25	$25	$25	$25	$25	$25	$25	$25	$25	$25	$25
Other Household	$300	0.3%	$25	$25	$25	$25	$25	$25	$25	$25	$25	$25	$25	$25
Total Household	$20,000	20%	$1,667	$1,667	$1,667	$1,667	$1,667	$1,667	$1,667	$1,667	$1,667	$1,667	$1,667	$1,667
Surplus/Deficit	($10,000)	-10%	($833)	($833)	($833)	($833)	($833)	($833)	($833)	($833)	($833)	($833)	($833)	($833)

Note: TI Percentage denotes the yearly line item as a percentage of total income.

Remember, if your outflow exceeds your inflow, then your upkeep will be your downfall. There is a lot of analysis available regarding family financial structure, such as size of a home mortgage. Unfortunately, every family is unique, and averages often fail to provide appropriate guidance. Through careful analysis and honest reflection, this family needs more than deductive or inductive logic. Through abduction, we can seek the set of premises that best explain this difficult financial situation. One possible false premise is the belief that the family's income will grow to match its expenses. As we know, one's unrestrained yearning will consume whatever income is available. Economics generally includes the notion of scarce resources seeking to satisfy unlimited desires. It is assumed that humans will always want more.

There is always the challenge of gleaning a reasonable view of historical financial decision-making patterns. A set of premises consistent with the Christian worldview often provide the best explanation as well as a straightforward path to financial health. For example, in the case presented above, adequate preparation needs to be vigorously pursued in preparation for the situation where the family's income takes a significant drop. It is not unreasonable to experience significant revenue declines over one's lifetime. Companies fail, jobs are lost, health is not assured, and pandemics happen just to name a few.

Clearly, there is a lot more going on than simple logic when it comes to navigating personal finance. Also, there is a lot more to the field of logic, but we will now leave it. With this foundation in logic, knowledge is explored through the field of epistemology.

Epistemology

Geisler and Feinberg define epistemology as the "branch of philosophy that tries to make sense out of knowledge, rationality and justified or unjustified beliefs."[41] Epistemology refers to the philosophical positions on the nature of knowledge or a branch of philosophy that studies knowledge.

Reformed epistemology "… is the idea that belief in God is a 'properly basic belief': it doesn't need to be inferred from other truths to be reasonable." Based on John Calvin's doctrine

---

[41] Geisler and Feinberg, *Introduction to Philosophy*, 20.

of "sensus divinitatis" or an innate sense of God.

Central to epistemology is the correspondence theory of truth: "(T)ruth obtains when a truth-bearer stands in an appropriate correspondence relation to a truth-maker."[42] The truth-bearer is the content of declarative sentences/statements and thoughts/beliefs that is true or false (where content is often called a proposition). The truth-maker is the actual state of affairs or facts.

Correspondence Theory of Truth

Aristotle states, "Truth occurs when thought and reality coincide."[43] He also asserts, "We must believe something before we can know anything."[44] Recall that the truth-bearer (TB) is a declarative proposition. For example, consider the TB, "All swans are white." For a long period of time, empiricists believed this TB to be true based on innumerable observations from the western world as illustrated in Figure 2.3.

Figure 2.3. Illustration of Truth-Bearer, "All Swans Are White."[45]

---

[42]Ibid., 135.
[43]Aristotle (384–322 B.C.) Quoted in *Oxford Users' Guide to Mathematics* (1996), 895.
[44]Ibid.
[45]Photo by Simon Hurry on Unsplash. Accessed on October 24, 2024.

Recall the truth-maker (TM) is found in the space-time universe. For example, the TM observation of a black swan. Truth is said to obtain when TM corresponds to TB. Figure 2.4 illustrates the correspondence between the TB = "All swans are not white" and the TM = "Black swan observation."

Figure 2.4. Illustration of Truth-Maker, "All Swans Are Not White."[46]

Thus, the correspondence theory of truth asserts that "truth obtains when reality is the way a proposition represents it to be."[47] Alternatively, "truth obtains when a truth-bearer stands in an appropriate correspondence relation to a truth-maker."[48] Thus, we see that propositions have intentionality, that is, they are often directed toward an object. Correspondence is a two-placed relation between a proposition (TB) and the state of affairs (TM) that is its intentional object.[49] Note that while evidence is truth-conducive, it is actually the case that evidence is not the same thing as truth itself; therefore, "(t)ruth has always been a hard thing to countenance within the confines of an empiricist epistemology or a naturalist

---

[46]Photo by Teresa Pinho on Unsplash. Accessed on October 24, 2024.
[47]Moreland and Craig, *Philosophical Foundations*, 130.
[48]Ibid., 135.
[49]Ibid., 139.

worldview."⁵⁰ Figure 2.5 illustrate the correspondence theory of truth.

Figure 2.5. Illustration of Correspondence Theory of Truth

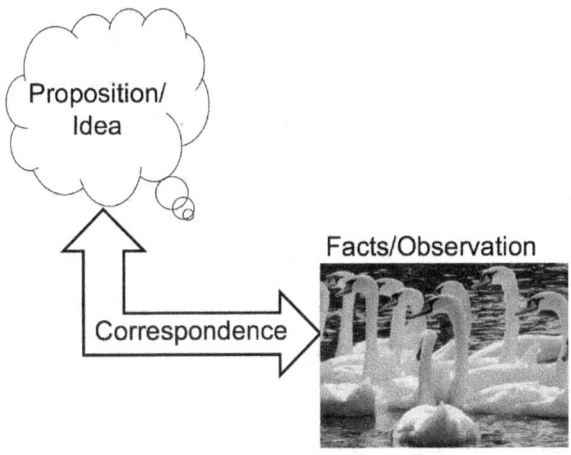

Epistemology and Budgeting

Finance is inherently linked to the task of valuation. Arthur Stone Dewing suggests that underlying all practical problems in connection with the financial aspects of the corporation, there is the problem of value.⁵¹ In finance, an instrument denotes anything that can be assigned a monetary value or used to assign monetary value to something else. Instrument examples include financial instruments, such as stocks, bonds, and mortgage contracts. Other instruments form the basis for financial instruments, such as temperature measurements, snow fall, and even number of votes. There are numerous ways to estimate a particular instrument's current value.

    Epistemology lies at the very foundation of all financial valuation exercises. Valuation involves the current monetary worth of perceived future benefits. For example, some people buy mutual funds, stocks, or even land because they believe in the future it will provide dividends, higher future sales prices,

---

⁵⁰Ibid., 141–142.
⁵¹Arthur Stone Dewing, *The Financial Policy of Corporations Book II Valuation and Promotion*, 4th ed. (New York: The Ronald Press Company, 1941), 173.

or other benefits. Perceptions of the future involve epistemic uncertainty. That is, we simply do not know the future. If anything, we are taught over our lifetime that the future brings events that simply are not anticipated.

History is littered with financial failures where beliefs related to valuations lie at the core. Numerous families have suffered bankruptcy because of the belief that certain asset values, such as a home, would always rise.

For example, consider a family of four living in a $700,000 home with a mortgage of $200,000 and they ran a small motorcycle shop that makes around $250,000 per year. They essentially had no other debts but also no other assets. What could go wrong, right? When the 2008 financial crisis was wreaking havoc on communities, the shop failed and was closed. Unfortunately, many people in their neighborhood were also in financial distress and selling their homes. The $700,000 home was auctioned for $180,000 and the family filed for bankruptcy.

Establishing budget-related practices involves planning and preparing for rare events. According to Forbes, 37% of U. S. homes are owned without a mortgage.[52] What is driving this decision, given the tax benefits of having a mortgage combined with "historically" low interest rates? You cannot go bankrupt unless you have liabilities that go unpaid. Clearly, the degree of leverage is a family choice. Upon what foundation do we make this choice? Do we base this choice on the latest financial advice sold by folks with multiple PhDs, in-depth data analysis, or even artificial intelligence? Or do we dust off the ancient documents and seek to understand the biblical basis for financial management? Understanding the level of epistemic uncertainty involved in finance is essential for improving financial decision-making.

Table 2.2 presents a sample balance sheet for the couple mentioned above. Most financial statements of this nature do not include implicit assets and implicit liabilities. An implicit asset is one that lacks tangibility such as one's human capital

---

[52]See https://www.forbes.com/sites/brendarichardson/2019/07/26/nearly-40-of-homes-in-the-us-are-free-and-clear-of-a-mortgage/?sh=3e1ae82447c2.

based on acquired skill. An implicit liability is similar such as parents' commitment to fund their children's college education. From Table 2.2 and the discussion above, there is significant epistemic uncertainty with many of these value estimates. For example, what is a reasonable estimate for one's human capital or future college costs? Further, what is the future range of possible outcomes for these valuation estimates? Clearly, financial valuation presently as well as estimating some potential future valuations poses epistemological challenges. History is filled with personal bankruptcies due to shocks in valuations coupled with unexpected loss of income or increase in expenses.

Table 2.2. Sample Balance Sheet for Couple with Two Children

Assets	Value	TA Percentage
Cash (Checking, Savings)	$5,000	1%
Vehicles	$10,000	1%
Household Items	$15,000	2%
Taxable Investments	$5,000	1%
Retirement Accounts	$25,000	3%
Primary Resiidence	$250,000	28%
Other Assets (Land, Business)	$75,000	8%
Other Assets (Human Capital)	$500,000	56%
Total Assets	**$885,000**	**100%**
Liabilities		
Payables (Rent, Utilities)	$5,000	0.6%
Credit Cards	$15,000	1.7%
Automobile Loans	$50,000	5.6%
Student Loans	$120,000	13.6%
Mortgage	$225,000	25.4%
Other Debts (Relatives)	$50,000	5.6%
Other Debts (Business)	$60,000	6.8%
Other Debts (Past Due Bills)	$5,000	0.6%
Implicit Debts (Children College)	$300,000	33.9%
Total Liabilities	**$830,000**	**94%**
Surplus	**$55,000**	**6%**

Facing our daunting personal financial challenges requires that we be able to think logically and understand the actual level of epistemic uncertainty encountered. There is a critical need for us to have correspondence between personal finance ideas and the factual realities of our financial situation.

Summary

In this chapter, various definitions of philosophy were explored and the notion of a philosophical worldview examined. Then a quick tour was taken through the first two pillars within the field of philosophy, logic and epistemology. This chapter concludes with an emphasis on the correspondence theory of truth and its relationship with personal financial budgets.

Case Study 1: Decision-Making Process[53]

Suppose you pull through a fast food restaurant and observe the following three screens (allegedly actually seen):

Screen 1: 4 chicken nuggets, $1.00, 170 calories.
Screen 2: Beef sandwich, $2.99, 450 calories.
Screen 3: 6 chicken nuggets, $2.99, 250 calories.

This case illustrates the importance of basic logic when making a financial decision. What should you purchase if interested in consuming six chicken nuggets? How many calories are consumed with these six chicken nuggets?

Calorie Count Per Nugget:
    4 Piece: 170 Calories/4 Nuggets = 42.5 C/N
    6 Piece: 250 Calories/6 Nuggets = 41 2/3 C/N

Thus, eating six nuggets from purchasing two of the four piece nuggets ($2) will save you $0.99, but will cost you an additional five calories (42.5 C/N x 6 N = 255 C).

---

[53]Source lost.

Case study 2: Biblical Logic

The Apostle Paul demonstrated robust logic when communicating the gospel. For example, in 1 Corinthians 15:12-19, he displays systematic and clear logical arguments.

1 Corinthians 15:12–19

[12]Now if Christ is proclaimed as raised from the dead, how can some of you say that there is no resurrection of the dead? [13]But if there is no resurrection of the dead, then not even Christ has been raised. [14]And if Christ has not been raised, then our preaching is in vain and your faith is in vain. [15]We are even found to be misrepresenting God, because we testified about God that he raised Christ, whom he did not raise if it is true that the dead are not raised. [16]For if the dead are not raised, not even Christ has been raised. [17]And if Christ has not been raised, your faith is futile and you are still in your sins. [18]Then those also who have fallen asleep in Christ have perished. [19]If in Christ we have hope in this life only, we are of all people most to be pitied.

Based on Paul's logic, if Jesus Christ did not rise bodily from the grave, where does that leave those who are his followers?

Case Study 3: Gratification, Credit card, and Three Truth Tests

Personal finance is related to gratification. Gratification is associated with pleasure, especially when a personal desire has been satisfied. The credit card industry seeks to have its customers not pay off the balances at the end of the pay period and thus accrue interest payments at extremely high rates. Logically, it does not make sense to satisfy a desire if that satisfaction results in paying over 25% interest on card balances. Thus, how does one explain there being over $1 trillion in credit card balances in the face of such high interest rates? Is there financial power in having the capacity to delay gratification?

Case Study 4: Logic of Christianity

Joe, an agnostic, asserts that Christianity is very illogical. In fact, Jesus and Paul writing were very mystical, lacking any appeal to human understanding. Appraise this.

Case Study 5: Non-Worldview Worldview

Some have asserted that one's worldview—an ordered set of propositions that one believes, especially propositions about life's most important questions—is like a pair of glasses. Appraise the following claim: "I am glad that as a rational person that I have chosen not to wear glasses."

Case Study 6: Faith and Budgeting

"Budgeting is not for spirit-filled Christians since we are merely God's managers. God will make sure the financial numbers work as we seek to fulfill His Kingdom mission." Is this a biblically-based assertion?

References

Geisler, Norman L. and Paul D Feinberg, *Introduction to Philosophy A Christian Perspective* (Grand Rapids, MI: Baker Academic, 1980).

Moreland, J. P. and William Lane Craig, *Philosophical Foundations for a Christian Worldview* (Downers Grove, IL: InterVarsity Press, 2003).

Moreland, J. P., *Love Your God With All Your Mind The Role of Reason in the Life of the Soul* (Colorado Springs, CO: NavPress, 1997).

Chapter 3. Philosophy: Metaphysics and Ethics

Learning Objectives

- Introduce briefly metaphysics and how it is used in apologetics.
- Explore ethics and demonstrate its importance in apologetics.

Opening Quotes

"We are dealing, no less, with the basic conflict between two entirely different concepts of man and his universe, concepts that affect every aspect of our social and economic lives, one determinedly physical and finite and the other profoundly metaphysical and infinite; the one (collective socialism) rooted in fearful concern about visible resources, the other (market capitalism) springing from faith in spiritual reality."[54]

"Since philosophy is foundational to every discipline of the university, philosophy is the most strategic discipline to be influenced for Christ."[55]

---

[54] Brookes, *Economy in Mind*, 23–24.
[55] Moreland and Craig, *Philosophical Foundations*, 2.

Overview

In this Chapter, the quick tour through the field of philosophy continues. In the last Chapter, the first two pillars of logic and epistemology were examined. In this Chapter, the brief tour of the remaining two pillars of metaphysics and ethics is given. But first, a brief review of logic and epistemology is provided.

Logic and Epistemology Review

Recall Plantinga defines philosophy as simply just thinking hard about something. Philosophy plays out in one's worldview. One's worldview is like a pair of glasses used to see the world. One key to quality thinking is the law of non-contradiction; an "idea" cannot be both true and false in the same sense at the same time.

    Logic is simply the study of the rules of reasoning. The goal of logic is to reach a conclusion, specifically to improve one's ability to form a good offense as well as critically evaluate and defend against others' unsubstantiated beliefs.

    According to Moreland and Craig, epistemology is a "branch of philosophy that tries to make sense out of knowledge, rationality and justified or unjustified beliefs."[56] Central to epistemology is the correspondence theory of truth. A truth-bearer is the content of declarative sentences/statements and thoughts/beliefs that are true or false (content is called a proposition). The truth-maker is the state of affairs (facts), any actual existing whole that is ordered by the relation of predication or exemplification (e.g. the apple being red).

---

[56] Moreland Craig, *Philosophical Foundations*, 71.

Metaphysics

Metaphysics is the study of "what we know about reality"[57] or the "... philosophical study of the nature of being or reality and the ultimate categories or kinds of things that are real."[58] Metaphysics involves the investigating such things that exist.

What counts as knowledge in finance is more tentative due to its social science nature. Let us consider knowledge with the following related definitions:

- "Facts, information, and skills acquired by a person through experience or education; the theoretical or practical understanding of a subject"[59]
- "A clear and certain perception of that which exists, or of truth and fact; the perception of the connection and agreement, or disagreement and repugnancy of our ideas."[60]
- "Justified true belief" attributed to Plato.[61]
- "Confident understanding of a subject with the ability to use it for a specific purpose"[62]

Within personal finance, confidence in financial facts, information, and skills is always tentative. We observe well-known patterns in financial data, such as stocks outperform bonds in the long run. Wisdom, however, requires one to realize that the future may not produce the same results as the past. For example, countries rise, and countries fall.

There are various forms of knowledge:
- Know that: Physics of balancing a moving bicycle
- Know how: Riding a bike
- Know how: Wisdom (actual choice, tacit)
- Know what: Facts (autonomous, unrelated)
- Know why: Understanding (science)

---

[57] Geisler and Feinberg, *Introduction to Philosophy*, 20.
[58] Moreland and Craig, *Philosophical Foundations*, 173.
[59] New Oxford American Dictionary available on MacBook Pro accessed on July 24, 2024.
[60] 1829 Webster's Dictionary.
[61] Moreland and Craig, *Philosophical Foundations*, 73.
[62] A widely used definition of knowledge.

- Know when: Tactical (not routine, but common)
- Know where: Strategic (not routine, rare, and major)
- Know who: Networks

Like riding a bike, knowledge of the underlying physics is not the same as knowing how to ride it. Thus, the list of various forms of knowledge above helps understand the differences. Within personal finance, understanding why various financial instruments are valued as they are is significantly different from managing a portfolio of financial instruments well.

Propositional knowledge can be understood in the following way. Consider the entire set of propositions, both true and false. This set is known as the feasible set. Only a subset of these propositions is true. Thus, the feasible set is split into two categories, those propositions that are true and those propositions that are false. Now the feasible set is divided into those propositions that we believe are true from those propositions that we believe are false. Knowledge is the set of propositions at the intersection of propositions that are true and propositions that are believed, where there is warrant or justification for such belief. For more effective personal finance decisions, we need to constantly increase our justified true beliefs and constantly decrease false beliefs that have snuck into our minds.

Selected Definitions Useful in Metaphysics

Notions of existence and being are often used in metaphysical analysis. *Existence* "is either the belonging of some property or the being belonged to by a property or, more simply, the entering into the nexus of exemplification."[63] For example, let z denote any number of entities, including substances (e.g., atoms, mountains, planes, stock certificate, mortgage document, plastic credit card), properties (e.g., color, goodness), relations (e.g., greater than, father of, sets (e.g., {1, 2, 3, 4, 5})), numbers (e.g., 1, 2, 3), and propositions (e.g., grass is green).

Being is defined as the existence of "that which is" or a

---

[63]Moreland and Craig, *Philosophical Foundations*, 191.

"something."[64] "Beings are similar (analogous), but not identical to one another. Yet there is a unity of being, since God is the one being; everything else *has* being because He gives it being (John 1:2, Revelation 4:11). 'In him we live, and move, and have our being.' (Acts 17:28). God is an infinite being; and all creatures are finite beings. ... All beings exist. The term *existence* is always defined in the same way, namely, 'that which is,' or 'that which is actual.'"[65]

John 1:2
²He was in the beginning with God.

Revelation 4:11
¹¹"Worthy are you, our Lord and God, to receive glory and honor and power, for you created all things, and by your will they existed and were created."

Acts 17:28
²⁸for "'In him we live and move and have our being'; as even some of your own poets have said, "'For we are indeed his offspring.'

Note: Paul is likely quoting Epimenides of Crete and Aratus's poem "Phainomena" (ESV notes). So what does this have to do with personal finance? Let us consider the often avoided topic of budgeting in the following case study.

Case Study 3.1: Metaphysics and Budgeting

Recall budgeting usually starts with the logical documentation of historical events, typically events related to receiving and spending money. Along with this historical documentation of our income statement, we also seek to estimate the balance

---

[64]Geisler and Feinberg, *Introduction to Philosophy*, 168.
[65]Ibid., 176.

sheet. What are our assets, such as cars and house, worth? Less often, we seek to estimate the current value of more difficult to quantify assets such as our future earnings power or even our liabilities, such as our children's future college costs.

At its core, any estimate of future assets or liabilities is inherently metaphysical and uncertain. Like the number "2," you cannot find the value of a home or the present value of future college costs in space and time. It is a value and always a subjective estimate. Even if our estimate is unbiased, it is subject to wild changes in response to economic events.

For example, selling a home often takes months. Could you sell your home tomorrow? Well, yes, but you would not like the price received. If everyone in your neighborhood decided to sell their houses at the same time and events are such that no one wants to move in, home value estimates would likely tend toward zero.

Successful budgeting requires quality estimates of assets and liabilities that are inherently difficult to determine. Further, if we do not change our actual financial decision-making behavior, then no amount of budgeting logic and budgeting epistemological study will accomplish anything. We must deal with our willingness to actually effect change within the reality of our existence.

As the above case study illustrates, we may believe sincerely that our financial status will improve, but that belief will accomplish nothing if ultimately our future actions do not comport with our present financial plan derived from the budgeting exercise. Note that if we simply are "dancing to our DNA" as secularists would have us believe, then we cannot willingly change. Our brains are simply hard wired to certain behaviors and that's that. Clearly, such a mindset is deeply incoherent with actual life. We can through our will force our minds to comply with our written financial plan. We can choose to rise early and work diligently toward successfully executing the plan to pay off our credit card debts and never carry a positive balance again.

We conclude this section with selected quotes that link

finance with metaphysics.

Quotes Connecting Metaphysics with Finance

We start with selected quotes from Warren T. Brookes.[66]

The most important search of human existence is always teleological and ontological – finding primary causes, instead of thrashing around with superficial effects. (11)

"Wherever the barriers to the free exercise of human ingenuity were removed, man became rapidly able to satisfy ever-widening ranges of desires." F. A. Hayek quoted in Brookes (28)

"Wealth is the progressive mastery of matter by mind." Buckminster Fuller quoted in Brookes (34)

"You cannot bring about prosperity by discouraging thrift. You cannot strengthen the weak by weakening the strong. You cannot help the wage earner by pulling down the wage payer. You cannot help the poor by destroying the rich." Abraham Lincoln quoted in Brookes (50)

Finally, two other quotes are noted that highlight the debate related to the metaphysical nature of finance. Macaulay asserts,

The concept of "pure" or "riskless" interest is metaphysical. The practical contrast is not between "pure" and "impure" but between "promised" or "expected" and "actual" or "realized."[67]

Lipshaw claims the following:

---

[66] See Brookes, *Economy in Mind*.
[67] Frederick R. Macaulay, *Some Theoretical Problems Suggested by the Movements of Interest Rates, Bond Yields and Stock Prices in the United States since 1856*, National Bureau of Economic Research, 38. See https://www.nber.org/system/files/chapters/c6342/c6342.pdf.

(E)conomics is a science in the logical positivist tradition. It ought not try to speculate why things are happening in a metaphysical sense, but simply to explain or predict regularities.[68]

There has been a concerted push in economics and finance to discard the metaphysical "why" and simply explore the physical "what." Specifically, the focus is on positive economics (what is) as opposed to normative economics (what ought to be).

We now address the last pillar of philosophy: ethics.

Ethics

Geisler and Feinberg observe, "Ethics is the study of what is right and what is wrong. Epistemology is concerned with the *true*, and ontology is concerned with the *real*, but ethics with the *good*."[69] Moreland and Craig state, "Ethics can be understood as the philosophical study of morality, which is concerned with our beliefs and judgments regarding right and wrong motives, attitudes, character and conduct."[70]

Ethics can be categorized as social, personal, and normative. Understanding these categories is best understood with an illustration. When a fleet of ships is on the high seas, three questions should be asked by each ship: 1.) How can we keep the ship from bumping into other ships? (Social ethics) 2.) How can we keep the ship from sinking? (Personal ethics) 3.) Why is the ship out there in the first place? (Normative ethics)[71]

We summarize Geisler and Feinberg as follows: the Christian ethic has a superior source—God—and a superior manifestation—Jesus Christ (our complete moral example).

---

[68] Jeffery M. Lipshaw, "The Epistemology of the Financial Crisis: Complexity, Causation, Law, and Judgment," *Southern California Interdisciplinary Law Journal* 19 (2009): 31, doi:10.2139/ssrn.1421837.
[69] Geisler and Feinberg, *Introduction to Philosophy*, 353.
[70] Moreland and Craig, *Philosophical Foundations*, 393.
[71] Source lost. Based on C. S. Lewis, *Mere Christianity*, Book 3 "Christian Behavior," Chapter 1, "The Three Parts of Morality."

Note from a Christian perspective "morality is not a mere legalistic assent to a written code; it is a dynamic relation to a living Person."[72] Further, the Christian perspective has a superior ethical declaration—the Bible—as well as a superior motivation—the love of Christ. Finally, the Christian ethic has a superior justification for ethics: our holy and sovereign God says so.[73] The foundation of the Christian ethic is illustrated in the following two passages.

Romans 8:3–4

[3]For God has done what the law, weakened by the flesh, could not do. By sending his own Son in the likeness of sinful flesh and for sin, he condemned sin in the flesh, [4]in order that the righteous requirement of the law might be fulfilled in us, who walk not according to the flesh but according to the Spirit.

2 Corinthians 5:14–15

[14]For the love of Christ controls us, because we have concluded this: that one has died for all, therefore all have died; [15]and he died for all, that those who live might no longer live for themselves but for him who for their sake died and was raised.

Note that mere knowledge of right and wrong is not enough. Geisler and Feinberg note, "A mirror will show a man the dirt on his face, but it will not wash the dirt away."[74] Obviously, ethics is critical to personal finance. Applied Christian ethics emerge out of a transformed heart not a legalistic adherence to a set of rules. Modifying one's spending habits is straightforward once the heart has been transformed.

Alternative views of right[75]

We briefly note various views of determining what is right.

---

[72] Geisler and Feinberg, *Introduction to Philosophy*, 369.
[73] Ibid.
[74] Ibid., 370.
[75] Several bullet points are from Geisler and Feinberg, *Introduction to Philosophy*. They are noted with GF and page numbers.

- Might is right – "justice is the interest of the stronger party" (Thrasymachus, GF, 353)
- Morals are mores – "Ethics is identified with the ethnic ... 'is-ought' fallacy" (GF, 354)
- "Man is the measure of all things" (Protagoras, GF, 354)
- Race is right – "mankind rather than man is the measure of all things" (GF, 355)
- Right is moderation – "golden mean"
- There is no right – "antinomian" (against-law)
- Right is what brings pleasure – "hedonism claims that what brings pleasure is right and what brings pain is wrong" (GF, 356)
- Right is the greatest good for the race – utilitarianism "the greatest good to the greatest number of persons (in the long run)" (Bentham, GF, 357)
- Good is what is desired for its own sake
- Good is indefinable – known only intuitionally, "ultimacy of 'good' makes it resistant to definition in terms of something else" (GF, 358)
- Good is what God wills – voluntaristic (God wills it), essentialist (God can only will in accordance with His unchangingly good nature)

A Christian View of Right

The Christian view of right is deeply internally coherent, it corresponds well with empirical observation, and it is experientially relevant.
- Origins of the right – "unchanging nature of a God of perfect love and justice," "God's will is subject to His own unchanging nature," (Malachi 3:6, 1 Samuel 15:29, Hebrews 6:18) God is omnibenevolent–God is love (1 John 4:16, John 3:16), morality is based in the unchanging nature of a loving Father who is just (Deuteronomy 32:4), impartial (Romans 2:11), and longsuffering (2 Peter 3:9)
- God's revelation of right in the universe – general revelation (Romans 2:14-15, innate, Tao in *Abolition of*

Man), found in the expectations of the human heart, moral law discovered more by one's reaction than actions
- God's revelation of right in the Bible – the divinely inscripturated truth of God (2 Timothy 3:16-17, noon day Sun), provides more information than general revelation (flash of lightning).
- Absolute nature of the right – an "infinitely perfect God who wills men to be good in accordance with the unchanging perfection of His own nature." (Matthew 5:48)
- Christian ethic is discovered based on God's revelation, not created by men.

We now consider a Code of Ethics provided by the CFA Institute to illustrate the role of ethics within the modern financial markets.

Case Study 3.2: CFA Institute's Code of Ethics[76]

Philosophy always works its way out into practice, often through ethics. The CFA Institute's code of ethics is briefly reviewed here as it is a premier global finance organization and highly respected.

"CFA Institute is a global, not-for-profit organization comprising the world's largest association of investment professionals. With over 100,000 members, and regional societies around the world, we are dedicated to developing and promoting the highest educational, ethical, and professional standards in the investment industry."[77]

---

[76]The code can be found at
http://www.cfapubs.org/doi/pdf/10.2469/ccb.v2010.n14.1.
[77]See http://www.cfainstitute.org/about/strategy/Pages/index.aspx.

THE CODE OF ETHICS

Members of CFA Institute (including CFA charterholders) and candidates for the CFA designation ("Members and Candidates") must:

- Act with integrity, competence, diligence, respect, and in an ethical manner with the public, clients, prospective clients, employers, employees, colleagues in the investment profession, and other participants in the global capital markets.
- Place the integrity of the investment profession and the interests of clients above their own personal interests.
- Use reasonable care and exercise independent professional judgment when conducting investment analysis, making investment recommendations, taking investment actions, and engaging in other professional activities.
- Practice and encourage others to practice in a professional and ethical manner that will reflect credit on themselves and the profession.
- Promote the integrity of and uphold the rules governing capital markets.
- Maintain and improve their professional competence and strive to maintain and improve the competence of other investment professionals.

Note the numerous ethical terms and concepts: (definitions from Mac dictionary)

- Integrity – the quality of being honest and having strong moral principles; moral uprightness
- Competence – the ability to do something successfully or efficiently
- Diligence – careful and persistent work or effort
- Respect – a feeling of deep admiration for someone or something elicited by their abilities, qualities, or achievements
- Ethical manner – a way in which a thing is done or happens
- Others (profession) first
- Reasonable care
- Exercise independent professional judgment
- Uphold the rules
- Professional competence (self and others)

There are also a host of different constituents:

- Public
- Clients
- Prospective clients
- Employers
- Employees
- Colleagues
- Other participants
- Profession
- Capital markets

What worldviews warrant having robust codes of ethics

within professional organizations? Upon what basis can an organization justify codes of ethics like the one given above? As a CFA charterholder since 1991, I have yet to find a published copy of the philosophical foundations for this code.

We turn now from the Code of Ethics of a global finance institute to how ethics influences personal finance.

Ethics and Budgeting

Recall the mechanics of budgeting is deeply logical. The goal is to adjust our numbers so our expenses cease to exceed our revenues. Further, there is concern with the epistemic certainty with which we have estimated our assets and liabilities (explicit and implicit). Also, a financial strategy is sought that is inherently metaphysical, so we modify our financial behavior in such a way as to successfully implement this strategy. Yet the budget is busted, and we failed.

Why? One reason is the lack of personal accountability. Many financial counselors understand this pivotal component. Just like a gym coach, many people benefit greatly from having a financial coach. The key role for the coach is to hold us accountable to fulfill our commitments considering a well-designed budget strategy.

Note that every worldview will have deep influence on the budgeting process. As we move through the remainder of our time together, pay attention to the philosophical foundational issues and how they work themselves out in personal finance. How does our budget-based strategy affect other people (social ethics)? For example, just because we have a bit of financial distress, do we cease all charitable giving? How does our budget-based strategy impact our personal health and well-being? For example, can we still maintain good health? Finally, what is our ultimate objective with our budget-based strategy? Is it to just die rich or is there some other more worthwhile objective?

Ethics plays a dominant role in finance. Once when I was serving on a corporate board, the decision was made to waive significant client fees for a period because the high quality standards were not met due to understandable technical reasons. Most clients never even knew the company took a significant financial loss. The standard for the firm was to place the interests of clients above personal interests.

Our ethical perspective deeply impacts our view of personal finance. Consider the following conclusion reached by Professor Sheldon Solomon in response to understanding death: "I am an infinitesimal speck of carbon-based dust born in a time and place not of my choosing here for an incredible brief amount of time before my atoms are scattered back into the cosmos. That need not be a terrifying thought."[78] If life lacks meaning and purpose and hence there is no moral law — no need to worry, right? There is a more rational alternative: I am an eternal soul of divinely-infused dust created in a time and space of God's choosing here for an incredible brief amount of time before my bodily death and subsequent resurrection where, for all eternity, I will glorify God throughout the cosmos. That is indeed a wonderful thought.

The chosen philosophical foundation drives all aspects of life, including personal finance. We need to carefully decide the foundation upon which to build our lives.

Summary

In this chapter, our quick tour through the field of philosophy was completed. In the last chapter, the first two pillars of logic and epistemology were covered. In this chapter, our brief tour was finished with the final two pillars of metaphysics and ethics.

---

[78] Emma Pattee, "Covid-19 Makes Us Think About Our Mortality. Our Brains Aren't Designed for That." *The Washington Post*, October 7, 2020, https://www.washingtonpost.com/health/covid-thinking-about-death/2020/10/02/1dc0f7e4-c520-11ea-8ffe-372be8d82298_story.html.

Case Study 1: Monte Hall Problem[79]

One well-known logic problem involves picking one of three doors. Behind one door is a valuable prize, such as a new car, and behind the other two doors is nothing. The host knows the door with the valuable prize, but the player does not know. The player picks door one but does not open it. The host then opens door three to reveal nothing. Should the player switch?

Logically, the chance of winning the prize on the original selection of door one is one-third and the chance of winning the prize by selecting doors two or three is two-thirds. If the host opens door three to reveal nothing, then switching to door two has a two-thirds chance of containing the valuable prize. Thus, logically you should switch. Clearly, this game changes if the player has access to information knowable by God and the host.

Case Study 2: Price Discrimination – Informed Versus Uninformed

In business, setting the product price is challenging for a host of reasons. There are many reasons why a company's product may have multiple prices depending on the customer. For example, volume discounts are justifiable. Particularly with financial firms, customers arrive with varying degrees of information. One ethical issue is whether knowledge of a customer's degree of information should influence the quoted price.

Assuming everything else is the same, is it ethical to have two product quote sheets, one for the informed (lower prices) and one for the uninformed (higher prices)?

---

[79]See https://en.wikipedia.org/wiki/Monty_Hall_problem.

Case Study 3: Bond Price, 102% of Par, and Child Temperature[80]

One morning, Kim a trader with the Treasury Department of Bank One needed to sell around $102,000,000 worth of financial instruments to dealers who are accustomed to trading in such large amounts. The standard process is to stage an auction where three to five bids are solicited at say 10:00 a.m. and the high bid accepted by 10:05 a.m. These financial instruments are actively traded, and the expected bids would be around $102,000,000, plus or minus $50,000. Somewhat surprisingly, Bill at Trading Floor C bid 102.5% of par or $102,500,000. What should Kim do?

What Kim did is call Bill and cryptically request that he check his bid. Within thirty seconds Bill call back with the following, "Kim, I am so sorry. I just got off the phone with my wife, and our child is running a fever of 102.5 degrees Fahrenheit, and I inserted that number instead of 102% of par." This act of courtesy saved Bill his job and gained enormous trust from Bill for future transactions.

References

Geisler, Norman L. and Paul D Feinberg, *Introduction to Philosophy A Christian Perspective* (Grand Rapids, MI: Baker Academic, 1980).

Moreland, J. P. and William Lane Craig, *Philosophical Foundations for a Christian Worldview* (Downers Grove, IL: InterVarsity Press, 2003).

Moreland, J. P., *Love Your God With All Your Mind The Role of Reason in the Life of the Soul* (Colorado Springs, CO: NavPress, 1997).

---

[80]This case study was presented by one of my former students to illustrate the importance of personal relationships, even on high-powered trading floors.

Chapter 4. Nature of Information

Learning Objectives

- Understand the nature and limits of data.
- Explore the limits of data analytics.
- Introduce two forms of explanation, mechanism and agency.
- Contrast the syntactic measure of information from the semantic meaning of the information.
- Review selected biblical passages related to information.

Opening Quote

"The most incomprehensible thing about the universe is that it is comprehensible."[81]

Overview

Here the nature of information is examined seeking to understand whether matter generates information or information generates matter. First, four pictures are provided to understand the different types of information. Next, a brief tour is taken through the now popular field of data analysis.

---

[81] Attributed to Albert Einstein. Original quote not found.

Two forms of explanation, mechanism and agency, are introduced. The notion of measuring information syntactically is covered and how that is different from the semantic meaning of the information Finally, an examination is made of several biblical illustrations of information primarily from speech.

Examples of Information

Information is metaphysical in its essence. To motivate this study, four pictures are introduced: nature, cultivated nature, human language, and human emotive communication.

Nature

Figure 4.1 illustrates a typical jungle scene. It is not apparent that there has been any human involvement in its design. What inferences can be made from this picture? Naturalistic evolution or intelligent causation? Clearly, we would need more data to assess the logical arguments involved when comparing these two mutually exclusive propositions.

Figure 4.1. Apparent Uncultivated Jungle Scene[82]

---

[82]Photo by Nathan Ziemanski on Unsplash accessed on July 29, 2024.

Cultivated Nature

Figure 4.2 depicts something clearly different. There must be a gardener. The evidence of cultivation is overwhelmingly clear to anyone, except perhaps an over-trained philosopher. Is it possible that this garden just happened to come into being through naturalistic chance without any human involvement? No. Clearly, an intelligent being was involved in the design and maintenance of the garden depicted in this scene.

Figure 4.2. Cultivated Garden Scene[83]

Clear Communication

Figure 4.3 depicts something entirely different. Human language is a wholly different form of information. What can you infer from this picture assuming, of course, that you can read and understand the English language? Did these numbers just randomly appear in the sand? BBC News reported that Geoff Keys wrote "Help 2807 →" in a sand bank along a river pleading for help on July 28. As an aside, when seeking help, a precisely arranged arrow with rocks is adequate to attract attention.

---

[83]Photo by Parya Tavakoli Tehrani on Unsplash accessed on July 29, 2024.

Figure 4.3. Human Language[84]

Further, the BBC reported,

> *A British man who got lost in a remote part of Australia says a life-saving SOS message he wrote in the sand was 'one of those moments of inspiration'. Geoff Keys sparked a huge search after going missing on his way to a waterfall in Jardine National Park, Queensland. The 63-year-old was rescued after two days, with police saying the written cry for help probably saved his life.*[85]

Case study 4.1: Different Language and Communication

If Geoff Keys was in China, he may have made different marks in the sand as illustrated in Figure 4.4.

---

[84]BBC News reported 8/24/2015, see https://www.bbc.com/news/world-australia-34037852. Photo by engin akyurt on Unsplash.
[85]BBC News reported 8/24/2015, see https://www.bbc.com/news/world-australia-34037852.

Figure 4.4. Alternate Language (Mandarin) for Help

Note that even if one did not understand the foreign language, such unique markings in the sand would prompt the rescue team to look downstream. Clearly, written communication is a unique attribute of being human.

Human Emotive Communication

We illustrate one last form of information, human emotive communication. Figure 4.5 is communication well-understood—gratitude. The BBC News provided a picture of Geoff Keys shaking the hand of Brad Foat, the helicopter pilot who found him. Geoff is clearly communicating information to Brad, specifically deep gratitude.

Figure 4.5. Human Emotive Communication[86]

---

[86]BBC News reported 8/24/2015, see https://www.bbc.com/news/world-australia-34037852. Photo by Nathan Anderson on Unsplash.

Financial Information

By law, financial institutions and corporations communicate vast amounts of information to their stakeholders. For example, publicly traded companies must file a 10-K with the Securities and Exchange Commission each fiscal year. Analysts and investors scrutinize this and other documents for clues regarding the company's prospects. Remember valuation is inherently based on beliefs about the future. It is not based on past performance.

John Maynard Keynes once noted that economists "must study the present in the light of the past for the purposes of the future."[87] The accounting industry is focused primarily on documenting historical transactions whereas the financial industry is focused primarily on making decisions while facing the future. This is a profound difference often missed if you are not careful.

Further, communication goes far beyond sterile data. Many legally required documents contain enormous amount of text. Further, many company executives hold quarterly conference calls to explain past performance as well as further clarify their strategies going forward.

Once, listening on a particular quarterly conference call an analyst asks the chief executive officer if the company was a takeover target. As I recall, I was listening in but working on something else. I really was not paying close attention. When the CEO answered, "No," the tone of the answer was just a bit more forceful and louder than the previous thirty minutes. There clearly was more going on in that answer than simply words. The company was subsequently taken over.

With today's analysis tools, not only are historical numbers carefully examined but there is also textual analysis performed. Thus, communication and even human emotive communication play important roles in understanding finance.

We now dive deeper into understanding the nature of

---

[87] John Maynard Keynes, *Essays in Biography* (New York: Horizon Press, 1951), 140–141. Referenced at https://www.indstate.edu/cas/econ/introduction-economics/jm-keynes-requirements-economist.

information that is deeply relevant to establishing which perspective is true and which perspectives are false. Data analysis is now briefly explored.

Data Analysis

According to Wikipedia, data analysis " ... is a process of inspecting, cleansing, transforming, and modeling data with the goal of discovering useful information, suggesting conclusions, and supporting decision-making."[88]

Information "describes something we now know which we did not know before."[89] Typically, information is used to answer a question of some form. Information helps resolve uncertainty. "The uncertainty of an event is measured by its probability of occurrence and is inversely proportional to that. The more uncertain an event, the more information is required to resolve uncertainty of that event. The bit is a typical unit of information .... For example, the information encoded in one 'fair' coin flip is $\log_2(2/1) = 1$ bit, and in two fair coin flips is $\log_2(4/1) = 2$ bits."[90]

Data analysis seeks to discover previously hidden information for the purpose of explaining something and facilitate better decision-making. Thus, information is used to provide explanations. Unfortunately, many people fail to recognize two primary categories of explanations: mechanism and agency.

Categories of Explanations[91]

There are at least two categories of explanations, mechanism and agency.

---

[88] See https://en.wikipedia.org/wiki/Data_analysis (accessed on July 26, 2020).
[89] John C. Lennox, *God's Undertaker: Has Science Buried God?* (Oxford: Lion, 2009), 148.
[90] See https://en.wikipedia.org/wiki/Information (accessed on July 26, 2020).
[91] Based on Lennox, Chapter 2 "The scope and limits of science."

Mechanism

Mechanism focuses on what it is and/or how it is, but not why it is. Suppose you are examining a Toyota Prius. A Toyota Prius automobile can be explained in terms of fundamental parts and how those parts are assembled, but one is not sure why the engineers at Toyota designed it the way they did unless they choose to reveal it typically in the user's manual and/or other documents.

A more clarifying example used by Lennox is Aunt Matilda's cake. If you observed a cake, you can explain that cake mechanically. You could name its chemical components, infer initial ingredients, and perhaps document its physical dimension. But you will never know for sure why Aunt Matilda baked the cake unless Aunt Matilda chose to tell you. Hence, we always have a second category of explanation.

Agency

Agency focuses on why it is or its purpose. In the examples above, only the design engineers or Aunt Matilda, if they chose to do so, can provide this type of explanation.

Frequently, one makes a category mistake that is driven by a prior philosophical perspective. One cannot infer agency forms of explanations from mechanistic information. Interestingly, atheistic perspectives suggests that mechanism explains agency, whereas the Christian perspective suggests that agency explains mechanism. Data analysis is extremely useful in providing mechanistic explanations but struggles mightily with agency forms of explanations.

For many financial decisions, agency forms of explanations are vital. What is the management team at a particular company (agents) attempting to accomplish? Why are they moving the company in a particular direction? Clearly, agency-based explanations will give you advanced knowledge of where the company is attempting to go rather than rely on mechanistic data that show up later, perhaps in published financial reports.

We now turn our study toward the nature of information

by contrasting syntactic information with semantic information.

Syntactic Information

Syntactic information has nothing to do with meaning. It is simply a measure of information. Syntactic information seeks the number of bits needed to store a certain data structure.

- Information is measured in bits (e.g., a coin flip contains one bit of information).
- Information resolves uncertainty.
- The more uncertain an event, the more information required to resolve its uncertainty.

Semantic Information

Semantic information is derived from the Greek word for a sign. It refers to the meaning of the data. No successful way has been developed to measure semantic information. Semantic information needs context. Figure 4.6 illustrates different street signs. Clearly, there is information communicated by these signs. Imagine, however, a world without cars or any other form of mechanistic transportation. How would the signs in Figure 4.6 be interpreted? Most likely, they would be interpreted incorrectly. When traveling in a foreign country, if you do not read the native language, then it is likely that many signs do not provide you any helpful information.

Figure 4.6. Semantic Information Illustrated with Street Signs[92]

Data analysis is incredibly useful and valuable in human flourishing. In this regard, pursuing a better understanding of our universe's mechanisms can prove beneficial regardless of our fundamental perspective. Developing a love for the truth will aid in removing false claims from our set of beliefs.

Finance is often feared due to the heavy use of mathematics and statistics. Fortunately, many fundamental issues can easily be understood without taking Calculus III or Ordinary Differential Equations, although both classes will aid in developing your ability to be disciplined in your thinking.

---

[92]Photo by Tungsten Rising on Unsplash, accessed on July 29, 2024.

Case Study 4.7: Data Analysis and Bear Stearns Stock Price

Figure 4.7 illustrates the challenge of data analysis applied to finance. This stock price chart represents over 20 percent return for almost 20 years. Clearly, this is an attractive stock based solely on this historical data. It is easy to forget that the past is not an accurate predictor of the future.

Figure 4.7. Data analysis of Bear Stearns stock price

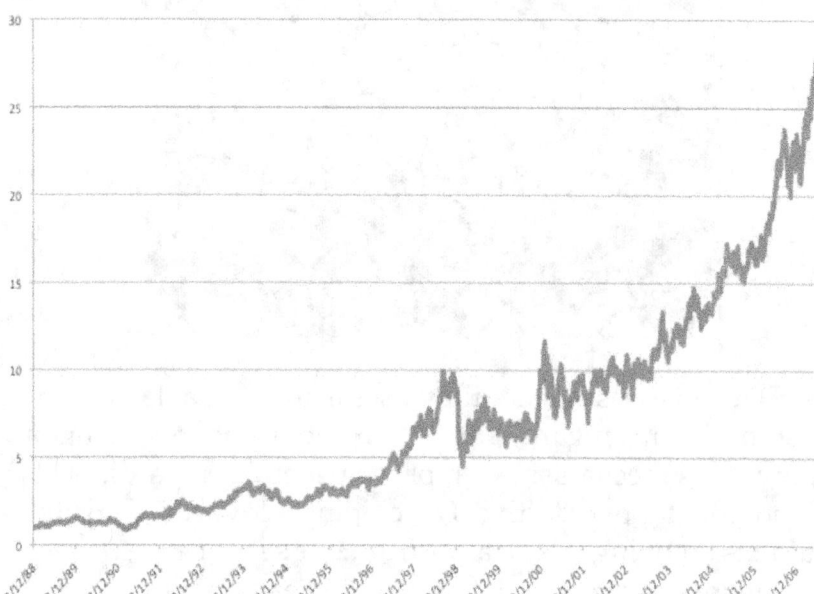

Figure 4.8 provides the rest of the story. Bear Stearns failed spectacularly in March 2008 for a host of reasons. It is clear from these two graphs that data analysis would not have spared you from this financial carnage. It would be nice to believe one would simply bail out when the price faltered, but that is not what people do who have experienced such dramatic gains over such a long period of time.

Figure 4.8. Bear Stearns Stock Price—The Rest of the Story

Do not drive looking in the rearview mirror

Investing based on data analysis of historical data is analogous to driving solely by looking in the rearview mirror. Crashes are inevitable. Is there a better way? Yes, investing based on your foundational perspective or worldview.

We now explore a biblical perspective on the nature of information.

Biblical Perspective on the Nature of Information

From a Christian perspective, information precedes matter or essence precedes existence. In this section, a clear understanding of the biblical claims is sought related to origins. Next, how information is used in making a rational defense of the Christian worldview is examined. Finally, the chapter concludes with several quotes and provocative thoughts related to information.

Role of Information in Questions of Origins

Consider the following passages related to the question of origins. Clearly, agency-related questions are addressed repeatedly. Mechanism questions, however, are not explicitly answered but left to be discovered.

Genesis 1:3, 6, 7, 9, 11, 14, 15, 20, 21, 24, 26

> [3] *And God said, "Let there be light," and there was light. ...*
> [6] *And God said, "Let there be an expanse in the midst of the waters, and let it separate the waters from the waters."* [7] *... And it was so. ...* [9] *And God said, "Let the waters under the heavens be gathered together into one place, and let the dry land appear." And it was so. ...* [11] *And God said, "Let the earth sprout vegetation, plants yielding seed, and fruit trees bearing fruit in which is their seed, each according to its kind, on the earth." And it was so. ...* [14] *And God said, "Let there be lights in the expanse of the heavens to separate the day from the night. ...* [15] *And it was so. ...* [20] *And God said, "Let the waters swarm with swarms of living creatures, and let birds fly above the earth across the expanse of the heavens."* [21] *So God created the great sea creatures and every living creature that moves, with which the waters swarm, according to their kinds, and every winged bird according to its kind. And God saw that it was good. ...* [24] *And God said, "Let the earth bring forth living creatures according to their kinds – livestock and creeping things and beasts of the earth according to their kinds." And it was so. ...* [26] *Then God said, "Let us make man in our image, after our likeness."*

We now know that organic life is driven by information that is represented primarily in DNA. DNA in a human genome contains about 7 billion bits of syntactic information. Smallest proteins possessing biological function involve 100 amino acids, resulting in 10^{130} sequence alternatives. Paul Davies, a renowned physicist summarizes, "We conclude that biologically relevant macromolecules simultaneously possess two vital properties: randomness and extreme specificity. A chaotic process could possibly achieve the former property but would have a negligible probability of achieving the latter."[93]

The spoken word is widely referenced throughout the Bible and a few selected examples are provided below.

Numbers 20:8

[8]"Take the staff, and assemble the congregation, you and Aaron your brother, and tell the rock before their eyes to yield its water. So you shall bring water out of the rock for them and give drink to the congregation and their cattle."

Psalm 19:1–3

[1]The heavens declare the glory of God, and the sky above proclaims his handiwork. [2]Day to day pours out speech, and night to night reveals knowledge. [3]There is no speech, nor are there words, whose voice is not heard.

Matthew 9:6–7

[6]But that you may know that the Son of Man has authority on earth to forgive sins" – he then said to the paralytic – "Rise, pick up your bed and go home." [7]And he rose and went home.

John 18:4–6

[4]Then Jesus, knowing all that would happen to him, came forward and said to them, "Whom do you seek?" [5]They answered him, "Jesus of Nazareth." Jesus said to them, "I am he." Judas, who betrayed him, was standing with them. [6]When Jesus said to them, "I am he," they drew back and fell to the ground.

---

[93]Lennox, *God's Undertaker,* 157. Lennox was quoting Paul Davies.

Colossians 1:16–17

¹⁶*For by him all things were created, in heaven and on earth, visible and invisible, whether thrones or dominions or rulers or authorities – all things were created through him and for him.* ¹⁷*And he is before all things, and in him all things hold together.*

John 1:1–3, 10

¹*In the beginning was the Word, and the Word was with God, and the Word was God.* ²*He was in the beginning with God.* ³*All things were made through him, and without him was not any thing made that was made.* ... ¹⁰*He was in the world, and the world was made through him, yet the world did not know him.*

Psalm 33:6

⁶*By the word of the Lord the heavens were made, and by the breath of his mouth all their host.*

1 Corinthians 8:6

⁶*yet for us there is one God, the Father, from whom are all things and for whom we exist, and one Lord, Jesus Christ, through whom are all things and through whom we exist.*

From these passages, we see that essence clearly precedes existence in contradiction to non-theist worldviews. We find an explicit link between expression and spacio-temporal events. For example, Moses was to speak to the rock and water would subsequently flow.

Role of Information in Defending a Proposition

In the following passages, we find clear reliance on rationality when making a defense of the Christian worldview.

1 Peter 3:13–17

¹³*Now who is there to harm you if you are zealous for what is good?* ¹⁴*But even if you should suffer for righteousness' sake,*

you will be blessed. Have no fear of them, nor be troubled, ¹⁵but in your hearts honor Christ the Lord as holy, always being prepared to make a defense to anyone who asks you for a reason for the hope that is in you; yet do it with gentleness and respect, ¹⁶having a good conscience, so that, when you are slandered, those who revile your good behavior in Christ may be put to shame. ¹⁷For it is better to suffer for doing good, if that should be God's will, than for doing evil.

Acts 22:1–2a

¹"Brothers and fathers, hear the defense that I now make before you." ²And when they heard that he was addressing them in the Hebrew language, they became even more quiet.

Acts 25:16

¹⁶I answered them that it was not the custom of the Romans to give up anyone before the accused met the accusers face to face and had opportunity to make his defense concerning the charge laid against him.

Philippians 1:15–18

¹⁵Some indeed preach Christ from envy and rivalry, but others from good will. ¹⁶The latter do it out of love, knowing that I am put here for the defense of the gospel. ¹⁷The former proclaim Christ out of selfish ambition, not sincerely but thinking to afflict me in my imprisonment. ¹⁸What then? Only that in every way, whether in pretense or in truth, Christ is proclaimed, and in that I rejoice. Yes, and I will rejoice,

(See also 1 Corinthians 9:3, 2 Corinthians 7:11, Philippians 1:7, and 2 Timothy 4:16.)

Biblical Ideas on the Nature of Financial Information

From a biblical perspective, we know that there is objective truth. We also know that humans have a deeply ingrained capacity to misrepresent the truth. Hence, when analyzing investment opportunities or even assessing home refinancing, we need to be ever vigilant to disentangle truth claims out of the mass of financial information.

Many financial industries rely on people not carefully assessing their choices. "Easy payments" just sounds so appealing—especially if I can get something now rather than wait and have delayed gratification. Understanding the foundational nature of semantic information as well as what one's worldview states regarding human nature is one key to successfully navigating the many financial decisions faced every day.

A key to quality financial decision-making is understanding the fundamental difference between historical data and the semantic representations of future expectations. Life's experiences as well as biblical patterns suggest that those things that have never happened in history do. We tend to think we can predict the future better than we can.

James 4:13–14a

> [13] Come now, you who say, "Today or tomorrow we will go into such and such a town and spend a year there and trade and make a profit" — [14] yet you do not know what tomorrow will bring.

With the humble admission that we do not have the capacity to accurately forecast the future, several finance planning strategies change. One simple example is retirement planning. Rather than focus solely on how much to save and where to invest, this inability to forecast leads naturally to focusing on the relationship between invested assets and the fair estimate of the present value of retirement needs.

As interest rates have fallen from the mid-1980s to 2020, the present value of retirement needs has significantly risen. By taking into consideration the way retirement needs rise when interest rates fall naturally suggests investing in a way that accounts for this pattern. One may not have known that rates would fall, but the relationship between rates and retirement needs is well known. Some estimate the losses within the pension industry exceed several trillion dollars just on this one issue.

In response to the massive losses due to the rate decline, many argue that this sharp decline in interest rates was an extremely rare event, often referred to as a black swan. As Nassim Taleb notes, "history teaches us that things that never happened before do happen."[94]

Selected Quotes Regarding Information

We conclude this section with several quotes.[95] Note that one foundational premise of the scientific method is the rational intelligibility of the universe.

> *The very concept of the intelligibility of the universe presupposes the existence of a rationality capable of recognizing that intelligibility. (59)*
>
> *"Science does not explain the mathematical intelligibility of the physical world for it is part of science's founding faith that this is so." (Attributed to John Polkinghorne) (61)*
>
> *The meaning of the message just cannot be determined without prior knowledge of the context. (151)*

Summary

The nature of information was explored in this chapter. The goal is to begin considering whether matter generates information or information generates matter. Four pictures were discussed identifying different types of information. After a brief tour through data analysis, two forms of explanation were introduced: mechanism and agency. Further, two information concepts were examined: syntactic measures of information and semantic meaning of the information. The chapter concludes with several biblical illustrations of information primarily from

---

[94]Nassim Taleb, *Fooled by Randomness: The Hidden Role of Chance in the Markets and in Life* (New York: W. W. Norton, 2001), 108.
[95]Quotes taken from Lennox, *God's Undertaker*.

speech.

Case Study 1: Executive Communication, Earning Call, and Potential Takeover

As previously mentioned, while listening to a quarterly earnings call several years ago, the Chief Executive Officer (CEO) gave an update on the company and spoke softly and in monotone. The CEO clearly was not a public speaker, and I found it difficult to pay attention. As is common, at the end of this quarterly ritual there was a time of question and answer. One analyst asked, "Is your company a target of a takeover?"

There are several ways the CEO can handle this type of question. One common answer is something like, "It is company policy not to discuss topics of this nature." Instead, this CEO said, "NO!" The no was just a bit too loud and with more emphasis than prior communication. What would you conclude? How would you handle this question if you were not legally allowed to disclose ongoing takeover discussions?

Again, it turns out, this company was acquired within six months of this call. Thus, communication is far more than words.

Case Study 2: Mechanism, Agency, and Launching a Startup Business

Recall mechanism focuses on what it is and/or how it is, but not why it is. Agency focuses on why it is or its purpose. New business ventures always begin with an agency explanation. Some founding group cultivates a business idea and typically vets it many ways. Long before any physical assets are acquired, the business idea is formulated.

After this initial exploration, there are typically pilot

products or services crafted. A process is adopted for continuous feedback and improvement. If successful, most business products and services remain somewhat in flux with a willingness to modify as market conditions change. Clearly, in business, mechanism does not beget agency; rather agency begets mechanism. Is there ever a case where mechanism begets agency in business?

Case Study 3: Imago Dei and Political Systems

In Latin, "imago Dei" denotes an image-bearer of God. The idea stems from Genesis 1:26–27.

Genesis 1:26–27

[26]Then God said, "Let us make man in our image, after our likeness. And let them have dominion over the fish of the sea and over the birds of the heavens and over the livestock and over all the earth and over every creeping thing that creeps on the earth." [27]So God created man in his own image, in the image of God he created him; male and female he created them.

Humans have lived under numerous political systems over the centuries. When imago Dei is culturally plausible, what are the implications for political systems? Is unrestrained brutal tyranny justifiable? If not, why?

References

Keynes, John Maynard, *Essays in Biography* (New York: Horizon Press, 1951). Referenced at
https://www.indstate.edu/cas/econ/introduction-economics/jm-keynes-requirements-economist.

Lennox, John C., *God's Undertaker: Has Science Buried God?*

(Oxford: Lion, 2009).

Taleb, Nassim, *Fooled by Randomness: The Hidden Role of Chance in the Markets and in Life* (New York: W. W. Norton, 2001).

Part 2. Theological Soils

Recall the core premise for this book is that financial fruit grows on philosophical roots. In Part 1, the biblically-based philosophical roots were explored. Further, the rational basis for the Christian worldview was established.

Part 2 covers Chapters 5–8 focused on theological soils. To acquire enduring financial fruit, our philosophical roots need the best theological soil. If philosophy is the queen of all sciences, then theology is the king. All philosophical roots ultimately rest in some sort of theological soil.

In Chapter 5, a rational basis for the existence of God is offered. The nature of the theism debate is presented. Further, the implications of atheism and Christianity are contrasted. Finally, a case study is presented of the Apostle Paul's downward spiral of rationality for those who do not honor God found in Romans 1.

In Chapter 6, selected worldviews are explored. After introducing the problem of the criterion, three categories of solution approaches are identified: skepticism, methodism, and particularism. Ultimately, every worldview has particularist claims. With a brief introduction to worldview error types, selected worldviews are discussed.

In Chapter 7, a deeper dive is made into the two prevailing worldviews within western cultures, naturalism and Christianity. Here science's coherence within these two worldviews is carefully addressed. Somewhat surprising to many, science is much more coherent within the Christian worldview than in the naturalistic worldview.

In Chapter 8, one of the hardest challenges that every

worldview must address — the problem of evil — is covered. Within this discussion a contrast is made between the implications from an atheistic and theistic perspective. Given the prevalence of evil, the Christian worldview regarding understanding as well as enduring evil is more coherent and corresponds better with reality.

Chapter 5. Existence of God

Learning Objectives

- Understand the nature of persuasion related to God's existence.
- Demonstrate no contradiction between belief in God's existence and rationality.

Opening Quote

"It is absurd for the Evolutionist to complain that it is unthinkable for an admittedly unthinkable God to make everything out of nothing, and then pretend that it is more thinkable that nothing should turn itself into everything."[96]

Overview

In this chapter, arguments related to the existence of God are introduced. First, the nature of this argument is explored. Next, the atheist's theological problems are scrutinized including no moral laws, that human life lacks meaning, and one has no

---

[96] G.K. Chesterton, *St. Thomas Aquinas* (Grand Rapids, MI: Christian Classics Ethereal Library), 85, https://www.ccel.org/ccel/c/chesterton/aquinas/cache/aquinas.pdf.

hope. A bleak picture, indeed. Although there are numerous arguments favoring the existence of God, Dallas Willard's three-stage approach is followed with some insights drawn from finance. Finally this chapter concludes with a brief exploration into Christianity's theological beauty.

Nature of the Theism Debate

Theology is simply the study of God, his nature, his attributes, and the implications for human experience. Even the belief in the absence of God qualifies as a theology. Atheists have way more faith than theists as G. K. Chesterton notes in the opening quote above. The belief that "… nothing should turn itself into everything" is a non-rational, theologically-based assertion.

God's perfection can be addressed in the following way:
1. God is the only essence in existence, the reason for whose existence is found in Himself.
2. All other essences, entities, or quantities exist by virtue of something else and in that sense God alone is perfect.
3. God alone is:
    a. Uncaused in essence,
    b. infinite in scope, and
    c. an independent being in essence.

How do we address the claim, "God exists," with the counterclaim, "God does not exist"? Recall that an argument is a set of statements that serve as a set of premises leading to a conclusion.[97] The goal of a good argument is to arrive at a conclusion regarding which truth claim is most plausible. One key to making a good argument is to identify the truth claim that ought to bear the burden of proof.

Burden of Proof

With any argument, one should not unknowingly accept the

---
[97] See Moreland and Craig, *Philosophical Foundations*, 29.

burden of proof. That is, is it our responsibility to prove the argument is true, or can we simply sit back and critique the argument letting someone else bear the burden to demonstrate that the argument is true?

It is always easier to be the defendant rather than the prosecutor in a legal case. The prosecutor bares the responsibility to prove the case beyond a reasonable doubt, whereas the defendant simply must rebut the prosecutor's claim to the point of reasonable doubt.

Rather than trying to prove that God exists (take on role as prosecutor), simply challenge the opponent to prove that God does not exist (take on role as defendant). When challenging an opposing truth claim, it is important to distinguish between rebutting and refuting.

Rebuttal and Refutation

A rebuttal demonstrates that an argument does not have the merit to conclude that it is true. For example, the claim, "Black swans do not exist," can be rebutted by simply noting that every location throughout the world where there may be black swans has not yet been searched carefully.

A refutation demonstrates that the argument is wrong — a much higher standard when compared to rebuttal. Recall a rebuttal only requires casting doubt. For example, the claim that "Black swans do not exist" can be refuted by simply producing reasonable evidence that a single black swan exists. Providing evidence for the existence of a black swan could be more challenging than just casting doubt on the original claim that black swans do not exist.

The proposition, "God does not exist," is like the proposition, "Black swans do not exist." Thus, to rebut the proposition, "God does not exist," simply requires noting that one has not examined all the evidence. Therefore, the proposition fails to have the merit to be held absolutely true.

Alternatively, the proposition, "God does exist," is like the proposition, "Black swans do exist." In the case of black swans, it is straightforward to produce a single black swan.

Because God is spirit and not constrained by space and time, producing space-time evidence in favor of this proposition is a bit more challenging. Although ample empirical evidence will be provided supporting the existence of the God referenced in the Bible, it cannot by setup reach epistemic certainty.

God's Existence Is Properly Basic Belief

Ronald Nash asserts the following:

> *Belief in God is properly basic; so far as the rationality of the Christian's personal faith is concerned, the discovery of proofs or arguments is not necessary. When it comes to challenging the rationality of Christian faith, the burden of proof rests with the atheologian.*[98]

An atheologian is "one who is opposed to a theologian."[99] Note Nash is specifically denying the burden of proof.

Alvin Plantinga notes this:

> *The Christian philosopher has a perfect right to the point of view and prephilosophical assumptions he brings to philosophic work; the fact that these are not widely shared outside the Christian or theistic community is interesting but fundamentally irrelevant.*[100]

Properly basic beliefs are those that are reasonable even though they are not inferred from other truth claims.

---

[98] Ronald Nash, *Faith and Reason* (Academie Books, 1988), 105.
[99] See Noah Webster, American Dictionary of the English Language, 1828 or http://webstersdictionary1828.com/Dictionary/atheologian.
[100] See Alvin Plantinga, *Where the Conflict Really Lies: Science, Religion, and Naturalism* (Oxford: Oxford University Press) 2011. Quote found at https://www.goodreads.com/quotes/704625-the-christian-philosopher-has-a-perfect-right-to-the-point.

Case Study 5.1: Challenging the Internal Logic of the Atheist

How would one prove that the atheist's premise that the assertion, "God does not exist," is rational and properly basic?

If it is immoral to believe anything without proof, then the atheist must prove this premise! There is no proof for the statement, "God does not exist." The empirical evidence, however, favors theism overwhelmingly. So, either the ground rules are false, or approaching theism in this fashion is irrational.

Many atheists are deeply skeptical. A skeptic is generally a person who denies that other people have rationally justified beliefs or knowledge. There are at least two kinds of skeptics. The global skeptic applies his skepticism to all truth claims. The local skeptic applies his skepticism only to certain knowledge categories, such as religious claims.

We follow a general approach in addressing God's existence.[101]

Atheism's Theological Problems

Atheism and its cousin agnosticism suffer from numerous severe theological problems. Three major characteristic statements: There are no moral laws. Life is meaningless. And there is no hope beyond our present existence.

There Are No Moral Laws

The logical argument is straightforward:

Premise >   Evil exists.

---

[101]See https://www.youtube.com/watch?v=mRRuKDXT7Kg. We expand on several points.

Premise >   Therefore, good exists.
Premise >   Therefore, there must be a law to decide (Criterion)
Conclusion > There must be a lawgiver

The rational atheist therefore assumes as a premise that God does not exist as follows.

Premise >   God does not exist.
Premise >   Therefore, there is no lawgiver.
Premise >   Therefore, there is no law to decide (Criterion)
Conclusion > Therefore, good and evil categories do not exist.

Numerous leading atheistic philosophers come to this same conclusion. The moral outrage on any given day to the human experience of injustice evidences that the vast majority implicitly believe God exists due to their belief that evil exists. According to Richard Dawkins, without God, there is "no evil and no good. Nothing but blind, pitiless indifference."

Kai Nielsen notes, "Pure practical reason, even with a good knowledge of the facts, will not take you to morality."[102]

Logically, if God does not exist, then there are no immutable moral laws—a very impractical perspective for addressing life's challenging problems. Without anchoring one's life in immutable moral laws, the desire for more wealth has led many to destruction. Often financial violations of actual laws started with minor ethical violations of standard financial practice. As is common, a particular corporate executive began to slightly increase the quarterly earnings numbers with deceitful intensions to make the company look just a bit better. Let us say that this decision was all within what is legally allowed. Over time, however, this same executive found himself in federal prison due to criminal violations of financial laws.

We now turn to the meaningfulness of life.

---

[102]See Kai Nielson, "Why Should I Be Moral?" *American Philosophical Quarterly* 21, (1984): 90. Quoted in William Lane Craig, *Reasonable Faith Christian Truth and Apologetics*, 3rd ed (Wheaton, IL: Crossway, 2008), 75.

Life Lacks Meaning

Frederich Nietzsche was an atheistic nihilist who concluded life has no meaning. He popularized the notion that God is dead and that the philosophers killed him lamenting the loss of the philosophical foundation of Western civilization. Niccolò Machiavelli is often credited with the assertion that might makes right. He asserts,

> *People should either be caressed or crushed. If you do them minor damage they will get their revenge; but if you cripple them there is nothing they can do. If you need to injure someone, do it in such a way that you do not have to fear their vengeance.*[103]

Without God, there is no meaning in the quest for meaning. Yet most normal humans find life deeply meaningful. It is only after much bad education does one conclude life is meaningless. Stephen Jay Gould concludes,

> *We are here because one odd group of fishes had a peculiar fin anatomy that could transform into legs for terrestrial creatures; because the earth never froze entirely during an ice age; because a small and tenuous species, arising in Africa a quarter of a million years ago, has managed, so far, to survive by hook and by crook. We may yearn for a "higher answer"– but none exists.*[104]

Without meaning, why should you be charitable especially to those from whom no possible benefit will ever come your way? Life will quickly reduce to mere transactional existence. Quid pro quo everywhere you go. We intuitively know that transactional existence is dysfunctional as we overvalue what we provide and undervalue what is provided to us. It leads quickly to hopelessness.

---

[103] Quoted in *The Prince*, 1513. See https://libquotes.com/niccolò-machiavelli/quote/lbg2w6u.
[104] See Richard Kinnier, ed., *The Meaning of Life* (Palazzo Editions, 2007), 108.

Humans Have No Hope

Humans exhibit great hope in life, yet the atheistic philosophers conclude that they are deluded as there is no hope. Life just is and when you die it is no more. A thousand years from now, there will be no meaning from your life; hence, life today lacks any hope. Atheists have nothing to offer a world that is longing for hope. This perspective just does not accord with life's actual experience.

Investing is anchored solidly in hope. If you invest $10,000 in an exchange-traded fund, such as a stock index fund, what is it you seek? Is your objective to assist in human flourishing by providing the necessary capital for companies to function so they can provide benefits to the many employees, customers, and suppliers? Perhaps, but it is my belief that most people do not think this way regarding investment decisions. Rather, one invests in the hope that your $10,000 investment will one day be worth significantly more and perhaps provide resources for your family when you are in retirement. Hope is a key element within financial decisions. Without hope, all that is left is to eat, drink, and be merry for soon we die.

We now turn to consider the question of God's existence based, in part, on Dallas Willard's three stages.

Willard's Three-Stage Approach to God's Existence[105]

The approach taken here benefitted greatly from the article by Dallas Willard, "Language, Being, God, and the Three Stages of Theistic Evidence." The errors, however, are mine as I am not as systematic in presenting these kinds of arguments as trained

---

[105] See Dallas Willard, "Language, Being, God, and the Three Stages of Theistic Evidence." Available at http://www.dwillard.org/articles/individual/language-being-god-and-the-three-stages-of-theistic-evidence. Willard's framework is used and expand in several ways.

philosophers. Thank you for your patience.

Stage 1: No Physical Quantity Completely Explains Its Own Existence

Physical realities and the nature of them, regardless of how partitioned, owe their existence to something that preexisted it, but it does not explain it fully. A blueberry from my blueberry tree does not explain its own existence. Further, there are no known physical realities that explain its self-existence.

Further, there are no known infinite series of causes. Theoretically, if we found an infinite series of integers showing on our computer every second (e.g., –10, –9, and so forth), then we would never arrive at any stated number. Logically, the computer would have failed a long time ago. A common example is noting that with a series of falling dominos, we would never arrive at any given current domino. Alternatively, consider a very long coal train. Clearly, the observation of a series of moving coal train cars logically suggests the existence of an engine car often being at the front of the train.

Thus, there must be an initial uncaused cause. There can only be one self-existent cause which is not concurrently within existence.

Stage 2: Argument From and To Design

As Lennox notes, one of the foundational premises of the scientific method is the rational intelligibility of the universe. He states,

> *The very concept of the intelligibility of the universe presupposes the existence of a rationality capable of recognizing that intelligibility.*[106]

He quotes John Polkinghorne,

---
[106] Lennox, *God's Undertaker*, 59.

> *"Science does not explain the mathematical intelligibility of the physical world for it is part of science's founding faith that this is so."*[107]

We explore the role of science in more detail in Chapter 7.

For now, let us consider the design evidence approach from two perspectives, from design to a designer and to design because of a designer. Although similar, these two approaches provide unique insights.

Argument from Design[108]

J. P. Moreland when addressing the question of God, documents the famous atheist Anthony Flew upon his conversion to theism, noted

> *… if the arguments and evidence for God had been known fifty years ago, he and other prominent atheists of the twentieth century would have become believers decades ago. (173)*

Moreland notes,

> *In fact, the evidence for God from design is most likely the most popular argument for God. (174)*

Recall from Chapter 4, Lennox identifies two forms of explanation, mechanism and agency. Mechanism-based explanations involve impersonal causes, conditions, and the laws of nature. Agency-based explanations involve motives, intentions, and purposes. Citing evidence from the human eye (2 million working parts), human ear (discriminate between 400,000 different sounds), and the human heart (pumps more than 3 supertankers of blood over a lifetime), Moreland notes,

---

[107] Ibid., 61.
[108] This section draws heavily from J. P. Moreland, Revised and Updated *Love Your God with All Your Mind: The Role of Reason in the Life of the Soul* (Colorado Springs, CO: NavPress, 2012).

Certain facts about the world cannot be adequately explained by impersonal causes, conditions, and the laws of nature. But they can be adequately explained by a personal explanation. There is no reason to treat these facts about the world as unexplainable brute facts. It is better to use a form of explanation – personal explanation – to explain them. Moreover, some of these facts have characteristics that clearly indicate that only come from intelligent agents. So the intelligent action of a Designing Person is the best explanation for these facts. (175)

The notion that you can discern the difference between chance and design is ancient. In Dembski's book *The Design Inference*, he opens with a quote from Cicero.[109]

Cicero (46 BC, p. 213) remarked, "If a countless number of copies of the one-and twenty letters of the alphabet, made of gold or what you will, were thrown together into some receptacle and then shaken out on to the ground, [would it] be possible that they should produce the Annals of Ennius? ... I doubt whether chance could possibly succeed in producing even a single verse." (1)

Now consider Michelangelo's famous painting, *The Creation of Adam*, on the Sistine Chapel created somewhere around 1508–1512. One can easily infer that the Sistine Chapel ceiling itself was designed as well as the painting it portrays.

Moreland notes that the "ubiquitous existence of stunning, gratuitous beauty" is evidence of design. He notes that beauty comes from artists, beauty is intrinsically good and valuable, and humans can recognize it. Moreland concludes, "The world is teeming with overwhelming beauty" (Love Your God, 175).

Moreland follows Behe in identifying another type of design termed irreducible complexity.

---

[109]See William A. Dembski, *The Design Inference: Eliminating Chance Through Small Probabilities*, Cambridge University Press, 1998.

An irreducibly complex system is a system containing several well matched, interacting parts that contribute to its basic function, and where the loss of any single part causes the system to cease functioning. (Love Your God, 177)

The human body is comprised of numerous irreducibly complex systems, such as the eye, ear, and heart mentioned above.

Moreland follows Dembski in identifying a third type of design termed specified complexity where some phenomenon is most likely caused by "a purposive, intelligent act by an agent" (179).

Something is intentional if

*(1) **the event was contingent, that is, even though it took place, it did not have to happen, no law of nature requires that the event happened** (unlike water, which, given the laws of nature, must freeze at a certain temperature); (2) **the event had a small probability of happening;** and (3) **the event is capable of independent specified ability** (capable of being identified as a special occurrence beside the simple fact that it did, in fact, happen). (179) (Bold was italics in original)*

Scientists have documented over thirty independent basic constants of nature required to sustain life in this universe. These constants were set in the first picosecond (one trillionth of a second or the approximate amount of time it takes for light to travel across a single strand of hair)[110] of the universe's creation.

Moreland concludes, "The universe is a razor's edge of precisely balanced life-permitting conditions" (181). Note that each of these constants could have been different and the likelihood of this precise balance is very unlikely. Finally, each constant must hold in combination with the other factors. Thus, our universe appears to exhibit specified complexity of the sort that suggests design.

It goes without saying that biological life is complex

---

[110]See https://en.wikipedia.org/wiki/Picosecond.

beyond normal human reasoning. The discovery of DNA screams of creative beauty, irreducible complexity, as well as specified complexity. There are about 3 billion bits of information contained in a single strand of human DNA. Francis Collins, who has been instrumental in DNA research, is reported to have used a spectacular figure showing geometric intricacies in a talk he gave.[111] This picture is a view down the long axis of genetic material, the β DNA double helix (common in human cells).

Side-by-side in Collins' talk was a picture of the Rose Window at York Minster in England. Clearly, Rose Window was painstakingly created, designed, and built. It is rational to conclude that the DNA involves a being even more creative to design and construct it.

We now turn to a similar yet distinct approach to the argument from design—the argument to design.

Argument to Design

The argument to design is explained as the

> ... configuration and coalescing of intelligent entities and quantities that pre-disposed the possibility of the resultant entity that came into being.[112]

It is important to note that the starting point for the atheist is very unnatural. As the opening quote by G. K. Chesterton points out, it is rationally absurd that "nothing should turn itself into everything."

From a Christian perspective, the universe and all that it contains was both created from design as well as being continuously created to design. From the passages given below,

---

[111]Francis Collins served as the 16th Director of the National Institutes of Health who provided numerous discoveries and provided leadership to the Human Genome Project. See, https://www.nih.gov/about-nih/who-we-are/nih-director/biographical-sketch-francis-s-collins-md-phd. Collins presents these two pictures in his talks related to faith and science, see for example, https://religionnews.com/2018/06/19/christian-geneticist-francis-collins-ponders-promise-peril-of-biotechnology/.
[112]See https://www.youtube.com/watch?v=mRRuKDXT7Kg.

we see that all things were created by Jesus Christ and for His purposes.

Colossians 1:16–17

> [16] For by him [Jesus Christ] all things were created, in heaven and on earth, visible and invisible, whether thrones or dominions or rulers or authorities – all things were created through him and for him. [17] And he is before all things, and in him all things hold together.

John 1:1–3, 10

> [1] In the beginning was the Word, and the Word was with God, and the Word was God. [2] He was in the beginning with God. [3] All things were made through him, and without him was not any thing made that was made. ... [10] He was in the world, and the world was made through him, yet the world did not know him.

Psalm 33:6

> [6] By the word of the Lord the heavens were made, and by the breath of his mouth all their host.

1 Corinthians 8:6

> [6] yet for us there is one God, the Father, from whom are all things and for whom we exist, and one Lord, Jesus Christ, through whom are all things and through whom we exist.

We conclude this section on design with two parables. In 1955, Anthony Flew when he was still an atheist wrote the following parable:

> Once upon a time two explorers came upon a clearing in the jungle. In the clearing were growing many flowers and many weeds. One explorer says, "Some gardener must tend this plot." The other disagrees, "There is no gardener." So they pitch their tents and set a watch. No gardener is ever seen. "But perhaps he is an invisible gardener." So they set up a barbed-wire fence.

They electrify it. They patrol with bloodhounds. (For they remember how H. G. Wells's The Invisible Man could be both smelt and touched though he could not be seen.) But no shrieks ever suggest that some intruder has received a shock. No movements of the wire ever betray an invisible climber. The bloodhounds never give cry. Yet still the Believer is not convinced. "But there is a gardener, invisible, intangible, insensible, to electric shocks, a gardener who has no scent and makes no sound, a gardener who comes secretly to look after the garden which he loves." At last the Skeptic despairs, "But what remains of your original assertion? Just how does what you call an invisible, intangible, eternally elusive gardener differs from an imaginary gardener or even from no gardener at all?"[113]

In a masterful response, John Frame counters with this revised parable.[114]

Once upon a time two explorers came upon a clearing in the jungle. A man was there, pulling weeds, applying fertilizer, trimming branches. The man turned to the explorers and introduced himself as the royal gardener. One explorer shook his hand and exchanged pleasantries. The other ignored the gardener and turned away: "There can be no gardener in this part of the jungle," he said; "this must be some trick." They pitch camp. Every day the gardener arrives, tends the plot. Soon the plot is bursting with perfectly arranged blooms. "He's only doing it because we're here – to fool us into thinking this is a royal garden." The gardener takes them to a royal palace, introduces the explorers to a score of officials who verify the gardener's status. Then the skeptic tries a last resort: "Our senses are deceiving us. There is no gardener, no blooms, no palace, no officials. It's still a hoax!" Finally, the believer despairs: "But what remains of your original assertion? Just how does this mirage, as you call it, differ from a real gardener?"

---

[113]See https://en.wikipedia.org/wiki/Parable_of_the_Invisible_Gardener.
[114]John M. Frame, "God and Biblical Language: Transcendence and Immanence," in *God's Inerrant Word*, ed. J. W. Montgomery (Minneapolis: Bethany Fellowship, 1974), 171. Quoted at https://www.thegospelcoalition.org/blogs/justin-taylor/the-invisible-vs-the-constant-gardener-parables-for-and-against-atheism/.

Willard concludes his second stage,

> "We have established that not all order is evolved and that relative to our data there is a probability of zero that order should emerge from chaos or from nothing into the physical world."[115]

We now explore the last stage with a focus on human events.

Stage 3: Human Events

In Willard's third stage, he considers

> the course of human events – historical, social and individual – within the context of a demonstrated extra-naturalism (stage one) and of a quite plausible cosmic intellectualism (stage two). ... We know, most importantly, that human minds standardly create for a purpose, and that they retain an active interest in, feel intimately invested in, what they create – and all the more so the greater the originality or "creativity" involved.[116]

These stages can be exemplified in every new business venture as it is itself a deeply creative human activity. The entrepreneurs involved in its creation nurture it often with deep care. It requires continuous creativity, innovation, and adaptation over time. There does not have to be something flawed in the creation of the business for future creative acts to occur. At times, this deep investment of one's life in the new business blinds folks from seeing lethal defects. Many businesses ultimately fail. From a theist perspective, it is reasonable to infer that our universe is in a process of continual

---

[115] See Dallas Willard, "Language, Being, God, and the Three Stages of Theistic Evidence." Available at http://www.dwillard.org/articles/individual/language-being-god-and-the-three-stages-of-theistic-evidence.

[116] See Dallas Willard, "Language, Being, God, and the Three Stages of Theistic Evidence." Available at http://www.dwillard.org/articles/individual/language-being-god-and-the-three-stages-of-theistic-evidence.

creation from a living and active God.

God's ongoing creation may well include redemption. Though known from eternity past, God intervenes on behalf of humans who have self-inflicted lethal defects commonly known as sin.

It is obvious from human history that something has gone terribly wrong. With numerous examples of brutal dictators, such as Hitler and Stalin, we intuitively know that certain actions are wrong. There is a convergence of ethics, justice, love, and forgiveness uniquely found at the cross of Jesus Christ. From the brutal crucifixion of Jesus Christ followed by the affirmed resurrection, we have beauty.

Christianity's Theological Beauty

There are intense benefits — the immutable moral law, a deeply meaningful life, and satisfying hope — arising from the affirmation of God's existence within the Christian worldview.

Immutable Moral Law

Psalm 19 depicts the beauty of God's moral law when embraced with gratitude. Hence, this psalm of David attributes more economic value to this law than fine gold and more desirability than the sweetest honey. When first confronted with biblical commands, however, one typically bristles at its strictness. Over time, the deep wisdom and truthfulness of God's law becomes overwhelming.

Psalm 19:7–11

> 7*The law of the Lord is perfect, reviving the soul; the testimony of the Lord is sure, making wise the simple;* 8*the precepts of the Lord are right, rejoicing the heart; the commandment of the Lord is pure, enlightening the eyes;* 9*the fear of the Lord is clean, enduring forever; the rules of the Lord are true, and righteous altogether.* 10*More to be desired are they than gold, even much fine gold; sweeter also than honey and drippings of the*

honeycomb. *[11]Moreover, by them is your servant warned; in keeping them there is great reward.*

Deeply Meaningful Life

There are several passages in the Bible that are indicative of human life being deeply meaningful. We find references to our Christian identity being expressed as God's own possession with a commission to serve as an ambassador. The following verses are just a few.

1 Peter 2:9

[9]But you are a chosen race, a royal priesthood, a holy nation, a people for his own possession, that you may proclaim the excellencies of him who called you out of darkness into his marvelous light.

Colossians 1:16

[16]For by him all things were created, in heaven and on earth, visible and invisible, whether thrones or dominions or rulers or authorities — all things were created through him and for him.

Romans 8:28

[28]And we know that for those who love God all things work together for good, for those who are called according to his purpose.

Psalm 139:13–14

[13]For you formed my inward parts; you knitted me together in my mother's womb. [14]I praise you, for I am fearfully and wonderfully made. Wonderful are your works; my soul knows it very well.

A Satisfying Hope

As countless Christians will testify, Jesus Christ provides a satisfying hope way beyond what mere transitory wealth promises. We know that God's plan for us is a future and hope that satisfies our deepest longings as illustrated in the following passages.

Jeremiah 29:11

> ¹¹For I know the plans I have for you, declares the Lord, plans for welfare and not for evil, to give you a future and a hope.

1 Timothy 6:17

> ¹⁷As for the rich in this present age, charge them not to be haughty, nor to set their hopes on the uncertainty of riches, but on God, who richly provides us with everything to enjoy.

The realization that life is deeply meaningful within the context of a loving God provides deep context and purpose of expressing one's God-given creativity. Further, the physical, bodily resurrection of Jesus Christ give us an eternal hope even when life's experiences are deeply painful and discouraging.

Case Study 5.2: God's Existence and Personal Finance

The reality of God's existence has a profound influence on personal financial management. If the Christian worldview is true, then according to the Apostle Paul, there exists an unavoidable downward spiral facing those who choose an alternative worldview as illustrated in Figure 5.1.

Figure 5.1. Illustration of Downward Spiral Described in the Book of Romans[117]

Paul in Romans 1:18–32 expresses this downward spiral.

Romans 1:18–32

[18]For the wrath of God is revealed from heaven against all ungodliness and unrighteousness of men, who by their unrighteousness suppress the truth. [19]For what can be known about God is plain to them, because God has shown it to them. [20]For his invisible attributes, namely, his eternal power and divine nature, have been clearly perceived, ever since the creation of the world, in the things that have been made. So they are without excuse. [21]For although they knew God, they did not honor him as God or give thanks to him, but they became futile in their thinking, and their foolish hearts were darkened. [22]Claiming to be wise, they became fools, [23]and exchanged the glory of the immortal God for images resembling mortal man and birds and animals and creeping things.

[24]Therefore God gave them up in the lusts of their hearts to impurity, to the dishonoring of their bodies among themselves, [25]because they exchanged the truth about God for a lie and worshiped and served the creature rather than the Creator, who is blessed forever! Amen.

---

[117]Photo by Elijah G on Unsplash. Accessed October 22, 2024.

> ²⁶*For this reason God gave them up to dishonorable passions. For their women exchanged natural relations for those that are contrary to nature;* ²⁷*and the men likewise gave up natural relations with women and were consumed with passion for one another, men committing shameless acts with men and receiving in themselves the due penalty for their error.*
>
> ²⁸*And since they did not see fit to acknowledge God, God gave them up to a debased mind to do what ought not to be done.* ²⁹*They were filled with all manner of unrighteousness, evil, covetousness, malice. They are full of envy, murder, strife, deceit, maliciousness. They are gossips,* ³⁰*slanderers, haters of God, insolent, haughty, boastful, inventors of evil, disobedient to parents,* ³¹*foolish, faithless, heartless, ruthless.* ³²*Though they know God's righteous decree that those who practice such things deserve to die, they not only do them but give approval to those who practice them.*

Baucham suggests seven phases in this downward spiral.[118] First, someone rejects God's general revelation (v. 18-20). Second, this person refuses to honor the God they know (v. 21a). Third, he becomes futile in his thinking and his heart is darkened (v. 21b-22). Fourth, he exchanges the glory of God for various idols (v. 23). Fifth, God releases them, and he gives into his lustful desires (v. 24-25). Sixth, he shatters the image he bears (v. 26a). Finally, he loses his mind. Clearly, a darkened and lost mind will make poor financial choices (v. 26b-32).

Since God does exist, what are the implications of this downward spiral for personal financial management? Regardless of one's intellectual, physical, emotional, spiritual training, poor financial decisions will be made by those who lose their minds.

Summary

In this Chapter, the unique nature of challenges to the existence

---

[118]Baucham, *Expository Apologetics*, 50–56.

of God is identified. There is no reason why a theist must bear the burden of proof. Next, atheism's bleak implications are exposed. It lacks any rational basis for moral laws and concludes life is meaningless and without hope. Dallas Willard's three-stage approach is followed with some insights drawn from finance. Finally, the opposing view is considered and conclude the Christian perspective results in intense beauty.

Case Study 1: God, Finance, and Fiduciaries

A fiduciary is typically a person in a trust position with another person(s), who is held to the highest legal standard to seek the beneficiary's best interest. Frequently, financial advisors have a legal fiduciary duty to their clients. For example, a trust (pool of funds) managed on behalf of a child places the fund's manager in a fiduciary position. Although clearly non-theists can behave ethically and fulfill their fiduciary duties, how does belief in a living, personal, omniscient God influence fiduciary behavior?

Case Study 2: Christian Worldview, Finance, and Meaning

From a Christian worldview, our lived experience is deeply meaningful as God-created beings. Based on Ephesians 2:8–10, is life meaningful? If so, how does this passage portray our lived experience?

Ephesians 2:8–10

> [8]*For by grace you have been saved through faith. And this is not your own doing; it is the gift of God,* [9]*not a result of works, so that no one may boast.* [10]*For we are his workmanship, created in Christ Jesus for good works, which God prepared beforehand, that we should walk in them.*

Case study 3: DNA-Dancing, Dancing Before God, and Finance

There are two perspectives on existence: 1) God exists. 2) God does not exist. In 2 Samuel 6:14–16 we see a vivid display of King David's behavior considering a living and personal God.

2 Samuel 6:14–16

> *14And David danced before the LORD with all his might. And David was wearing a linen ephod. 15So David and all the house of Israel brought up the ark of the LORD with shouting and with the sound of the horn. 16As the ark of the LORD came into the city of David, Michal the daughter of Saul looked out of the window and saw King David leaping and dancing before the LORD, and she despised him in her heart.*

The two quotes below from Richard Dawkins, illustrate the alternative perspective.

> *In a universe of electrons and selfish genes, blind physical forces and genetic replication, some people are going to get hurt, other people are going to get lucky, and you won't find any rhyme or reason in it, nor any justice. The universe that we observe has precisely the properties we should expect if there is, at bottom, no design, no purpose, no evil, no good, nothing but pitiless indifference.*[119]
> *DNA neither cares nor knows. DNA just is. And we dance to its music.*[120]

---

[119]See https://www.goodreads.com/work/quotes/1121858-river-out-of-eden-a-darwinian-view-of-life. Quoted from Richard Dawkins, *River Out of Eden: A Darwinian View of Life*.
[120]See https://www.goodreads.com/quotes/496577-dna-neither-cares-nor-knows-dna-just-is-and-we. Quoted from Richard Dawkins, *River Out of Eden: A Darwinian View of Life*.

Given the stark contrast between these two perspectives, how does one's management of their personal finances change when shifting say from Dawkins' atheistic perspective to King David's theistic perspective?

References

Baucham, Jr., Voddie, *Expository Apologetics: Answering Objections with the Power of the Word* (Wheaton, IL: Crossway, 2015).

Chesterton, G.K., *St. Thomas Aquinas* (Grand Rapids, MI: Christian Classics Ethereal Library), available at https://www.ccel.org/ccel/c/chesterton/aquinas/cache/aquinas.pdf.

Craig, William Lane, *Reasonable Faith Christian Truth and Apologetics*, 3rd ed (Wheaton, IL: Crossway, 2008).

Dembski, William A., *The Design Inference: Eliminating Chance Through Small Probabilities*, Cambridge University Press, 1998.

Flew, Anthony, "Parable of the Invisible Gardener," https://en.wikipedia.org/wiki/Parable_of_the_Invisible_Gardener.

Frame, John M., "God and Biblical Language: Transcendence and Immanence," in *God's Inerrant Word*, ed. J. W. Montgomery (Minneapolis: Bethany Fellowship, 1974), 171. Quoted at https://www.thegospelcoalition.org/blogs/justin-taylor/the-invisible-vs-the-constant-gardener-parables-for-and-against-atheism/.

Kinnier, Richard, ed., *The Meaning of Life* (Palazzo Editions, 2007).

Moreland, J. P., Revised and Updated *Love Your God with All Your Mind: The Role of Reason in the Life of the Soul* (Colorado Springs, CO: NavPress, 2012).

Nash, Ronald, *Faith and Reason* (Academie Books, 1988).

Plantinga, Alvin, *Where the Conflict Really Lies: Science, Religion, and Naturalism* (Oxford: Oxford University Press) 2011.

Willard, Dallas, "Language, Being, God, and the Three Stages of

Theistic Evidence." Available at http://www.dwillard.org/articles/individual/language-being-god-and-the-three-stages-of-theistic-evidence.

Chapter 6. Competing Worldviews

Learning objectives

- Define and review worldviews.
- Introduce three categories of worldviews: skepticism, methodism, and particularism.
- Understand errors made when adopting a worldview.
- Review several worldviews.
- Identify characteristics of beliefs.

Opening quote

"We must believe something before we can know anything."
Augustine (AD 354-430)

Overview

After defining carefully what is meant by worldview, three categories of worldviews are identified: skepticism, methodism, and particularism. Although particularism is somewhat new, every worldview ultimately contains particularist elements. When evaluating various worldviews, common errors are highlighted. Finally, a review is made of several worldviews as well as unique characteristics of beliefs identified.

Worldview Explained

A worldview is simply a conceptual arrangement by which we fit everything we believe and through which we interpret and judge reality. Recall from Chapter 2 that a worldview is a set of ordered propositions that one believes, especially propositions about life's most important questions.[121]

Myers and Noble define worldview in the following way.

> *Worldview is a pattern of ideas, beliefs, convictions, and habits that help us make sense of God, the world, and our relationship to God and the world.*[122]

Habits are essential for life. We do many things in a habitual fashion. Some people habitually purchase goods on impulse whereas others analyze each purchase carefully. Although often an initial struggle, many people can change their habits.

Clearly, flourishing financially depends on one's patterns or habits. In the same way, one's core ideas flow in patterns, and they are typically easy to recognize by yourself and others. It is often said, "Show me a person's financial statement, and I can tell you what they really believe." How we spend money is a powerful resource for understanding our core ideas, beliefs, convictions, and habits.

Patterns are also studied by finance professionals. The better an analyst understands the habits of customers, suppliers, and competitors, the more likely the analyst will make the best decisions. Although it is impossible to perfectly forecast the future, often you can understand the times as illustrated in Chronicles.

---

[121] Moreland and Craig, *Philosophical Foundations*, 13.
[122] Jeff Myers and David Noble, *Understanding the Times*, (Colorado Springs, CO: David C Cook, 2015), 11.

1 Chronicles 12:32

> ³²Of Issachar, men who had understanding of the times, to know what Israel ought to do, 200 chiefs, and all their kinsmen under their command.

The ability to understand and explore numerous different worldviews requires one to identify core patterns as well as create broad categories. We can in fact discern between entire categories of worldviews that are plausible and ones that are false. Thus, we can, as Paul states in Corinthians, arrive at the truth.

2 Corinthians 10:5

> ⁵We destroy arguments and every lofty opinion raised against the knowledge of God, and take every thought captive to obey Christ...

The propositions within worldviews tend to be presuppositions. They are implicit assumptions about the world for it to make sense. These presuppositions are often core to any argument to posit a worldview. One's worldview is like a pair of glasses.

Recall Chapter 1. There were three tests for truth and four questions to be answered when exploring worldviews. The tests for whether a worldview is true are the following: Is the worldview logically consistent? Is the worldview empirically adequate? And is the worldview experientially relevant? The four questions a worldview must answer are the following: Where did we come from? Is life meaningful? Are there immutable moral laws? And where am I going?

Within this framework, there are several ways to test the legitimacy of a worldview. First, we can test the reasonableness of the worldview. Is it internally coherent? For example, how well does it answer these four questions? Further, we can explore how the worldview comports with our actual personal experience. How well does it explain yourself? For example, can it address why I do things I believe I should not do? Finally, we can consider how the worldview aligns with scientific experience. Does it explain empirical observations well? For example, why is the Bible the world's bestselling book, year after year? Finally, we can gauge how the worldview results in personal practice. Does it lead to a fulfilled life? For example, can it provide answers to the purpose of life?

There are numerous different worldviews that have been proposed. To sort them all, here we explore three general categories of worldviews as a potential solution for the problem of the criterion.

Skepticism, Methodism, and Particularism

The objective here is to introduce alternative worldviews with the intention of framing the rational approach to the Christian worldview. First, the problem of the criterion is sketched.

Problem of the Criterion

The following three steps develop the problem of the criterion. Step 1 illustrates two mutually exclusive declarative propositions—truth bearers. For example, let THIS denote "Jesus Christ is God's Son Sacrificed" and let Not THIS denote "Jesus Christ is *not* God's Son Sacrificed."

Step 1:

Clearly, we need some sort of criterion to evaluate these two truth-bearers (Step 2). If the criterion is scientism, then, based on this criterion, the scientific evidence for this claim is evaluated.

Step 2:

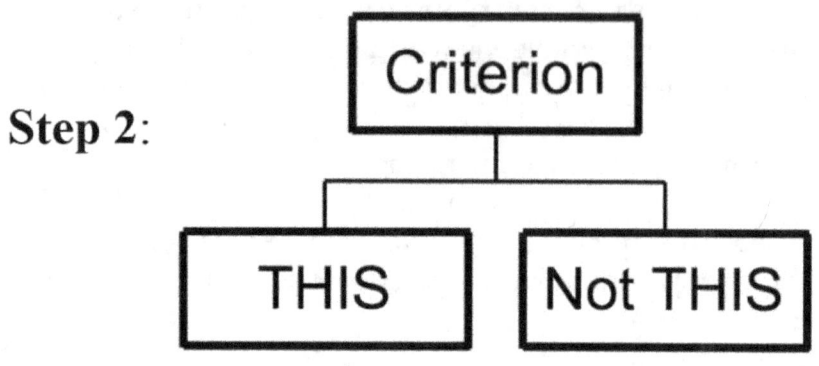

One may object to that criterion and offer an alternative criterion. For example, an alternative criterion is rationalism — that is, the reasonableness of this claim is evaluated. You may object and offer some criterion to evaluate competing criterion (Step 3 below), and off we go down an infinite regress.

Step 3:

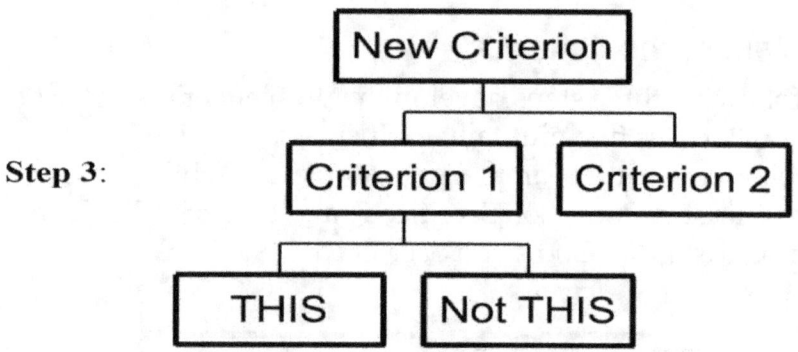

Thus, we have the problem of the criterion. There are three categories of potential solutions:
- Skepticism – placing one's faith in the fact that one can never know the appropriate criterion,
- Methodism – placing one's faith in a particular method to make the choice, and
- Particularism – placing one's faith in selected declarative propositions that you believe you have warrant to be held true.

We now investigate each potential solution with an emphasis on key perspectives within each potential solution.

Skepticism

The worldview category of skepticism is widely held among academics; however, most academics are not global skeptics, rather they are local skeptics — say skeptics of any religious claims. Some skeptics make the following argument:

> *Premise 1*: I believe I know some claims are true.
> *Premise 2*: I do not know every true claim.
> *Observation*: Some claim presently unknown, may prove that what I believed as true in Premise 1 is, in fact, false.
> *Conclusion*: Therefore, I cannot know any claim is true.

Thus, all knowledge claims start with some core beliefs. Given we do not know if the core beliefs are true, then we do not know if any claims are true.

Methodism

Methodism is much more popular and often ardently held without much thought. From my interactions, it appears that many people have adopted a culturally plausible worldview without careful examination. For example, some methodists seemingly have not grounded their conversion with any criterion. Further, over time they become deeply faithful to their adopted worldview.

Another example in this line of thought is that of scientism. It is popular in academic circles as it asserts that one should only believe truth claims that are supported by scientific evidence. As seen later, there is no scientific evidence for scientism's core truth claim.

Particularism

The only remaining category of worldviews is the lesser known particularism. Particularism asserts that selected declarative propositions have warrant to be held true. For example, across most cultures, it is held that harming a defenseless child is wrong. The empirical evidence favoring this idea is sketchy at best, but it is wrong. Thus, the particularist would say that the widely held human virtues (for example, prudence, justice, temperance, and courage) are rationally held even if adequate scientific evidence is not available or is not supportive.

Note that both skepticism and methodism rely on particularism to justify their existence. For example, the skeptic who asserts he is certain that you cannot discern between mutually exclusive ideas has just asserted the truthfulness of an idea (skepticism) and hence his skepticism has a defeater.

Particularism provides the rational basis for the Christian worldview when compared to various other methodist worldviews, such as scientism, positivism, rationalism, logical positivism, and so forth. The natural question that arises is what are the foundational claims?

A particularist asserts that humans are equipped with belief-forming mechanisms to account for ways we think in the presence of certain experiences. For example, holding a cup of coffee is fundamentally different from the idea of holding a cup of coffee. That is, the idea (abstract) is different from actual cup (concrete).

How do we know that the idea (abstract, truth bearer) in our minds correspond to actual reality (concrete, truth maker)? We naturally assume reality corresponds to our ideas of reality. The Christian particularist would therefore claim we are created in such a way that we cannot help but think that in this manner (a particular knowledge claim).

Biblical Particularism

The Christian worldview is easily categorized with particularism. The following passages illustrate core particular claims.

2 Timothy 3:16–17

16All Scripture is breathed out by God and profitable for teaching, for reproof, for correction, and for training in righteousness, ¹⁷that the man of God may be complete, equipped for every good work.

Genesis 1:1

¹In the beginning, God created the heavens and the earth.

Psalms 1:1–6

¹Blessed is the man who walks not in the counsel of the wicked, nor stands in the way of sinners, nor sits in the seat of scoffers; ²but his delight is in the law of the LORD, and on his law he meditates day and night. ³He is like a tree planted by streams of water that yields its fruit in its season, and its leaf does not wither. In all that he does, he prospers. ⁴The wicked are not so, but are like chaff that the wind drives away. ⁵Therefore the wicked will not stand in the judgment, nor sinners in the congregation of the righteous; ⁶for the LORD knows the way of the righteous, but the way of the wicked will perish.
See also Deuteronomy 11:13–15 and Joshua 1:8–9.

Luke 9:23–24

²³And he said to all, "If anyone would come after me, let him deny himself and take up his cross daily and follow me. ²⁴For whoever would save his life will lose it, but whoever loses his life for my sake will save it.

John 15:9–11

⁹As the Father has loved me, so have I loved you. Abide in my love. ¹⁰If you keep my commandments, you will abide in my love, just as I have kept my Father's commandments and abide in his love. ¹¹These things I have spoken to you, that my joy may be in you, and that your joy may be full.
See also John 8:31–36.

Luke 6:46–49

⁴⁶"Why do you call me 'Lord, Lord,' and not do what I tell you? ⁴⁷Everyone who comes to me and hears my words and does them,

I will show you what he is like: ⁴⁸*he is like a man building a house, who dug deep and laid the foundation on the rock. And when a flood arose, the stream broke against that house and could not shake it, because it had been well built.* ⁴⁹*But the one who hears and does not do them is like a man who built a house on the ground without a foundation. When the stream broke against it, immediately it fell, and the ruin of that house was great."*

1 Corinthians 3:10–11

¹⁰*According to the grace of God given to me, like a skilled master builder I laid a foundation, and someone else is building upon it. Let each one take care how he builds upon it.* ¹¹*For no one can lay a foundation other than that which is laid, which is Jesus Christ.*

2 Timothy 2:15

¹⁵*Do your best to present yourself to God as one approved, a worker who has no need to be ashamed, rightly handling the word of truth.*

People can and do change their worldview. It is extremely disingenuous to assert that people are born with a worldview. Clearly, we are all born into families and cultures with predominant worldviews. Our families and local cultures do influence our perspectives.

As a professor for many decades, I have observed that college students often do drastically change their worldviews. This is most dramatically seen with students from statist countries, such as Marxist-based, that impose their worldview by force. When considering changing our worldview, say from naturalism to Christianity, one must consider the potential for error.

Error Analysis Related to Worldviews

Without a doubt, the stakes are very high when deciding to change our worldview. One can go to two different extremes when appraising a worldview—tight and loose.

Tight (Intolerant, Dogmatism)

At this extreme, one is intolerant to new ideas. For example, some investment professionals have adopted an investment philosophy based on what was established many years ago despite the significant, mounting evidence concerning its truthfulness. Professors teach what they were taught many years ago regardless of new evidence. To illustrate, there is mounting evidence that investment professionals lack the ability to forecast financial instrument prices. Unfortunately, being either delusional or deceptive, they continue to claim they have this skill.

Loose (Overly Tolerant, Relativism)

At this extreme, one is overly tolerant of new ideas. For example, with some investment professionals, their adopted investment philosophy is based on whatever is presently in fashion, independent of any contrary evidence. Some professors may teach any expressed idea as if it has equal merit regardless of evidence, an approach very popular position among investment professionals. As an illustration, trend-following is very popular where the investment professional promotes whatever trading strategy seemed to be successful during the recent past.

Foundational ideas coalesce to form our worldview. Two categories of error are explored when applying different worldviews.

Type I and Type II Error

The following table is widely used in statistical analysis but can also be applied in logical assessments of various assertions. For example, the assertion, "God does not exist," and its contrary "God does exist." The following generic table lays out the possibilities.

Types of Errors	Logical or Empirical Assertion is:	
Decision Regarding Assertion:	True	False
Fail to Reject	Correct inference (True negative)	False negative (Type II Error)
Reject	False positive (Type I Error)	Correct inference (True positive)

Applying this type of error analysis, one could apply probabilities to each of the four potential outcomes. For example, some analysis of the assertion "God does not exist" might fail to reject it. If, in fact, "God does not exist" is true, then failing to reject this assertion is a correct inference. If, however, "God does exist" is true, then the assertion "God does not exist" is false. This is labeled a Type II error as it is a false negative or an error in omission.

If, however, we reject the assertion "God does not exist" and it turns out to be true, then a Type I error is committed as it is a false positive or an error of commission. Finally, if the assertion "God does not exist" is false, then clearly "God does exist" is true. The correct inference is made if we reject "God does not exist" when, in fact, the assertion "God does exist" is true.

Case Study 6.1: Error Types and Eternity

The Christian worldview is either true or false. If true, then humans are eternal beings with two destinations. If false, then some other worldview is likely true. Although covered in detail later, consider the implications of the error analysis of the assertion, "Christian worldview is true" and its contrary "Christian worldview is false."

Types of Errors	Christian Worldview	
Decision Regarding Assertion:	True	False
Embrace	Eternal life with God	Most pitied in this life
Reject	Eternal life separated from God	Not sure

Explain the relative weight of the consequences of Type I and Type II errors.

Note that tight worldviews have a high type I error potential whereas loose worldviews have a high type II error potential. Both errors are of deep concern as the more truth claims are discarded and false claims are adopted, the more detrimental this can be to human flourishing.

Brief Review of Selected Worldviews

We now review a few selected worldviews. The two most popular worldviews—naturalism and Christianity—will be explored in detail in the next Chapter. Note that skepticism and methodism were previously covered. Most worldviews contain defeaters. That is, if the worldview itself is evaluated by its own claim, then it cannot be shown to be true.

Scientism

Scientism can be roughly stated as a worldview where no declarative proposition will be asserted true absent scientific evidence. Clearly, scientism itself contains a defeater because its own definition fails to allow for the scientism belief. Scientism is a statement of theology or philosophy; hence there is no scientific evidence for it. The only way to rationally hold to scientism is through particularism. Importantly, it fails to give satisfactory answers to the four questions related to origins, meaning, morality, and destiny. Scientism leaves one with no explanation for how nothing became something. Further, in the end, scientism leads one to conclude that life is meaningless, there are no moral laws, and there is no ultimate destiny.

Positivism

Positivism (also known as logical positivism) is "a philosophical system that holds that every rationally justifiable assertion can be scientifically verified or is capable of logical or mathematical proof, and that therefore rejects metaphysics and theism."[123] Again, positivism's assertion is self-refuting. That is, the positivism worldview cannot scientifically verify or logically prove itself.

Verificationism

"Verificationism is the doctrine that a proposition is only cognitively meaningful if it can be definitively and conclusively determined to be either true or false (i.e., verifiable or falsifiable). ... Verificationism is often used to rule out as meaningless much of the traditional debate in areas of Philosophy of Religion, Metaphysics, and Ethics, because many philosophical debates are made over the truth of unverifiable sentences. It is the concept underlying much of the doctrine of Logical Positivism, and is an important idea in Epistemology, Philosophy of Science and Philosophy of Language."[124] Again, the verificationism doctrine itself would be deemed false under its own criterion.

Post-Modernism

Post-modernism (PM) allows for only "local" truths. With this view, the justification standard is set low so that all true claims

---

[123] Mac Dictionary, Apple, Inc., 2.3.0 (268), 2020.
[124] See http://www.philosophybasics.com/branch_verificationism.html.

are validated. The PM worldview appears among many professionals to be the prevailing investment worldview today. For example, modern data mining exercises, such as artificial intelligence, lead to numerous truth claims related to investment strategies.

Critical Realism

Critical realism (contemporary or modern empiricist) is a blend of critical pluralism (open to new theories but apply critical scrutiny) and scientific realism (the evidence supports the new theory better than the old).

Thus, there are many different worldviews each with different competing claims. Eventually, one must decide what to believe. Belief itself, however, is difficult to understand. Thus, let us take a careful look at the nature of belief.

Nature of Beliefs[125]

Beliefs provide the framework for living and are heavily influenced by culture. Three observations about beliefs are made.

First, beliefs have at least three characteristics: content, strength, and centrality. When we appraise the content within a particular belief truth claim, it is vital to addresses the question, "Is it true?" What we believe matters. It shapes the very contours of our lives. We quickly realize that reality is indifferent to the sincerity of our beliefs, particularly if it is not true. For example, I may sincerely believe that my car flies, but that makes no difference in the behavior of my car. Clearly, we are responsible for the content of our beliefs.

The degree to which we are convinced a belief is true is relative to its strength. We must be more than fifty percent convinced compared with the converse. Strength degrees include plausibility, such as likely, fairly likely, quite likely,

---

[125] This section draws heavily on Moreland and Craig, *Philosophical Foundations*.

beyond reasonable doubt, and completely certain. As we gain evidence, our belief will strengthen. The more certain we are of the belief, the more we will rely on it, and it becomes a part of our very soul. Figure 6.1 illustrates a strengthening belief in the Christian worldview. Philosophy is often useful in migrating the Christian worldview from absurd to remotely possible. Christian apologetics aids in moving from implausible or remotely likely to a core basis belief.

Figure 6.1 Illustration of the Migration of Belief in the Christian Worldview

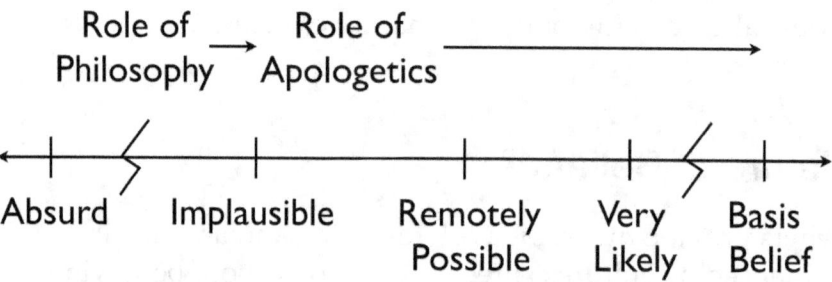

Belief centrality addresses the degree of importance the belief plays in our entire set of beliefs. How important is this particular belief's role in our worldview. For example, my belief that blueberries are good for me is true, but it is not central whereas my belief in moral absolutes is central to me. Note that as you grow, a belief's centrality may change.

Second, beliefs can be changed. Remember we are responsible for our beliefs. Life's experiences teach us that we cannot change beliefs by direct effort. For example, even if offered a large sum of money, most people cannot believe there is presently a crimson elephant in the room. We can, however, change our beliefs indirectly. Through study, meditation, and reflection, we can identify false beliefs and thus change the content, strength, and centrality of various beliefs. Activities of the mind can change the characteristics of beliefs that transform our personality and beliefs.

Finally, beliefs are heavily influenced by the plausibility structure of a culture. Namely, the set of ideas a person is or is not willing to entertain as plausible. For example, you are most likely unwilling to attend a flat earth convention. Whether a proposition is plausible is a function of the beliefs one already has and the prior conditions of the human mind. For the proposition to become plausible, one must create favorable conditions for it. For example, the proposition that theology matters in personal finance may have been implausible prior to examining this material.

Worldview and Personal Finance

Beliefs are entrenched into personality in a variety of ways, including repetition, practice, and training. For a young couple to manage their money well, they should focus heavily on discovering the correct worldview. Anchoring on the true worldview will naturally result in a lifestyle that can maintain right beliefs. Right beliefs naturally flow to improved decision-making and hence better financial health.

C. S. Lewis notes the following:

> *For the wise men of old the cardinal problem had been how to conform the soul to reality, and the solution had been knowledge, self-discipline, and virtue. For magic and applied science alike the problem is how to subdue reality to the wishes of man: the solution is a technique; and both, in the practice of this technique, are ready to do things hitherto regarded as disgusting and impious – such as digging up and mutilating the dead.*[126]

Peter Kreeft, writing on this assertion by C. S. Lewis notes,

---

[126] C. S. Lewis, *The Abolition of Man* (New York: The Macmillan Company, 1973), 88.

Science and religion both aim at conforming the mind to objective truth, objective reality (science conforms our mind to the nature of the universe, and religion conforms our mind to the mind of God and our will to the will of God). Magic and technology, on the other hand, try to conform objective reality to the human will. That is why they both arose at the same time — not the Middle Ages but the Renaissance, not the Age of God but the Age of Man. Both are Faustian, Promethean. The difference is, of course, that technology works while magic doesn't (usually). But their end, their goal, the purpose behind them, the human values and desires and state of soul that set them in motion, are the same.[127]

Remember that we all are in the process of conforming our minds to some chosen worldview. Clearly, if the chosen worldview is fundamentally wrong, then our entire philosophical framework is misaligned and subsequent decisions will be deeply impacted, particularly financial decisions. Figure 6.2 illustrates what happens when the foundation is flawed. The Piazza del Duomo is unique and a spectacle to see; the building just cannot function as the original designers intended.

---

[127] Peter Kreeft, *C. S. Lewis for the Third Millennium: Six Essays on the Abolition of Man* (San Francisco: Ignatius, 2011). Quoted by Justin Taylor at https://www.thegospelcoalition.org/blogs/justin-taylor/these-three-sentences-by-c-s-lewis-are-worth-at-least-an-hour-of-meditation/.

Figure 6.2. Illustration of the Consequences of Faulty Worldview[128]

Case Study 6.2: Views on Personal Debt

One key area where worldview deeply impacts personal finance is one's view of debt. There seems to be an incessant need to linearly extrapolate past financial patterns into future expectations. For example, the decision to buy a bigger house based on the assumption that our wages will continue to increase and we can grow our income to be able to make the mortgage payments. Empirically, future financial outcomes rarely follow historical averages. Like the Piazza del Duomo, a faulty worldview may be pretty to look at but results in dysfunction and often significant human suffering. From never borrowing money, even for a house, to maxing out available

---

[128]Piazza del Duomo, 56126 Pisa PI, Italy, Pisa. Photo by Michael Hamments on Unsplash.

credit cards, how does one's worldview influence personal debt choices?

Summary

In this Chapter, several definitions for worldview are given and three categories of worldviews are reviewed, skepticism, methodism, and particularism. Every worldview ultimately contains particularist elements. When selecting a worldview, a caution was given against two types of errors—type I and II. Several worldviews were reviewed, and this chapter concludes with identifying unique characteristics of beliefs.

Case Study 1: Paul's Particularist Claim

Based on 1 Corinthians 3:10-11, what claim does Paul make regarding the core presupposition of the Christian worldview?

> *1 Corinthians 3:10-11*
> [10]*According to the grace of God given to me, like a skilled master builder I laid a foundation, and someone else is building upon it. Let each one take care how he builds upon it.* [11]*For no one can lay a foundation other than that which is laid, which is Jesus Christ.*

Case Study 2: Atheism, AI, and Economic Forecasting

Bill is an atheist and believes humans are simply dancing to their DNA. Based on this perspective, Bill asserts that economic forecasting based on artificial intelligence (AI) will soon be so accurate as to essentially remove uncertainty from financial management. What would be a Type I error regarding the assertion, "Economic forecasting will be nearly precise due to AI"? What would be a Type II error for this assertion?

Types of Errors	Logical or Empirical Assertion is:	
Decision Regarding Assertion:	True	False
Fail to Reject	Correct inference (True negative)	False negative (Type II Error)
Reject	False positive (Type I Error)	Correct inference (True positive)

Case Study 3: Christianity, AI, and Economic forecasting

Jan is a wholly devoted follower of Jesus Christ. Biblically, Jan knows the providential God and that humans are solely "imago Dei" (God's image-bearers). Based on this perspective, Jan asserts that economic forecasting based on artificial intelligence (AI) will never be so accurate as to essentially remove uncertainty from financial management. What would be a Type I error regarding the assertion, "Economic forecasting will remain extremely imprecise even with AI"? What would be a Type II error for this assertion?

Types of Errors	Logical or Empirical Assertion is:	
Decision Regarding Assertion:	True	False
Fail to Reject	Correct inference (True negative)	False negative (Type II Error)
Reject	False positive (Type I Error)	Correct inference (True positive)

References

Kreeft, Peter, *C. S. Lewis for the Third Millennium: Six Essays on the Abolition of Man* (San Francisco: Ignatius, 2011).

Lewis, C. S., *The Abolition of Man* (New York: The Macmillan Company, 1973).

Moreland, J. P. and William Lane Craig, *Philosophical Foundations for a Christian Worldview* (Downers Grove, IL: InterVarsity Press, 2003).

Myers, Jeff and David Noble, *Understanding the Times*, (Colorado Springs, CO: David C Cook, 2015).

Chapter 7. Naturalism, Christianity, and Science

Learning Objectives

- Carefully define naturalism and Christianity as well as their major implications.
- Introduce science and its relationship with naturalism and Christianity.

Opening Quote

"(T)here is superficial conflict but deep concord between science and theistic religion, but superficial concord and deep conflict between science and naturalism."[129]

Overview

Two dominant worldviews are addressed here, naturalism and Christianity. Of particularly interest is which worldview is most compatible with science in general and personal finance in

---

[129] Alvin Plantinga, *Where the Conflict Really Lies: Science, Religion, & Naturalism*, (New York: Oxford University Press, 2011), *ix*.

particular. These two worldviews are briefly introduced with selected personal finance connections.

Naturalism

Naturalism is frequently defined as

> *the philosophical belief that everything arises from natural properties and causes, and supernatural or spiritual explanations are excluded or discounted.*[130]

Naturalism is

> *physicalist in flavor ... reality is exhausted by the spatiotemporal world of physical objects accessible is some way to the senses and embraced by our best scientific theories.*[131]

That is,

> *Nothing exists outside the material, mechanical (that is, nonpurposeful), natural order.*[132]

Clearly, naturalism implies atheism, but atheism does not imply naturalism. Plantinga notes,

> *Naturalism is stronger than atheism: you can be an atheist without rising to the full heights (sinking to the lowest depths?) of naturalism; but you can't be a naturalist without being an atheist.*[133]

In 1911, Dubray states,

---

[130] See, for example, https://www.naturalnavigator.com/news/2012/07/meaning-of-the-word-naturalism/.
[131] Ibid.
[132] Moreland and Craig, *Philosophical Foundations*, 184.
[133] Plantinga, *Where the Conflict Really Lies*, ix.

Naturalism is not so much a special system as a point of view or tendency common to a number of philosophical and religious systems; not so much a well-defined set of positive and negative doctrines as an attitude or spirit pervading and influencing many doctrines. As the name implies, this tendency consists essentially in looking upon nature as the one original and fundamental source of all that exists, and in attempting to explain everything in terms of nature. Either the limits of nature are also the limits of existing reality, or at least the first cause, if its existence is found necessary, has nothing to do with the working of natural agencies. All events, therefore, find their adequate explanation within nature itself. But, as the terms nature and natural are themselves used in more than one sense, the term naturalism is also far from having one fixed meaning.[134]

Schafersman further clarifies:

According to Steven Schafersman, naturalism is a philosophy that maintains that;
1. *"Nature encompasses all that exists throughout space and time;*
2. *Nature (the universe or cosmos) consists only of natural elements, that is, of spatio-temporal physical substance — mass–energy. Non-physical or quasi-physical substance, such as information, ideas, values, logic, mathematics, intellect, and other emergent phenomena, either supervene upon the physical or can be reduced to a physical account;*
3. *Nature operates by the laws of physics and in principle, can be explained and understood by science and philosophy;*
4. *The supernatural does not exist, i.e., only nature is real. Naturalism is therefore a metaphysical philosophy opposed primarily by supernaturalism."*

---

[134]See https://en.wikipedia.org/wiki/Naturalism_(philosophy) quoting *Dubray 1911*.

Or, as Carl Sagan succinctly put it: "The Cosmos is all that is or ever was or ever will be."[135]

We now turn to explore the link between naturalism and personal finance.

Naturalism and Personal Finance

If naturalism is true, then we would not expect human choice to cause artificial intelligence or data analytics any significant problems. Humans should be as predictable as cattle on the farm. We should simply be able to study historical financial data and infer deep insights into future financial prices.

There has been enormous effort in this pursuit for the simple reason that the ability to forecast future prices leads to vast acquisition of wealth. An abundance of empirical evidence has accumulated to suggest that active trading results in lower average returns and higher risk, neither of which is attractive to investors. The future does appear to cast its shadow in financial markets, but it remains deeply elusive as human choice and future uncertainties clash.[136]

Naturalism is like having your feet firmly planted in midair. If we are solely sensate animals, then all we must do is determine what makes us most happy and pursue financial transactions that facilitate this happiness. Like animals in the wild, if another person is harmed or worse, there is no morally-based consequence. The Golden Rule does not have any foundation and would be abandoned.

We now turn to carefully consider the Christian worldview.

---

[135]See https://en.wikipedia.org/wiki/Naturalism_(philosophy).
[136]For an exploration of the link between economic forecasting and the worldviews, see Op-Ed 24-O3 *Economic Prediction and the Christian Worldview* available at https://robertebrooks.org/project/opinion-editorials/.

Christianity

There are many ways to define Christianity. Plantinga's definition is adopted here:

> *Human beings and the universe in which they reside are the creation of the God who has revealed himself in Scripture ... [or] [the] rough intersection of the great Christian creeds ... the result would be something like the 'Mere Christianity' of which C. S. Lewis spoke.*[137]

At the core of Christianity is the gospel of Jesus Christ. Paul provides a concise summary in Corinthians.

1 Corinthians 15:1–5

> ¹*Now I would remind you, brothers, of the gospel I preached to you, which you received, in which you stand,* ²*and by which you are being saved, if you hold fast to the word I preached to you — unless you believed in vain.* ³*For I delivered to you as of first importance what I also received: that Christ died for our sins in accordance with the Scriptures,* ⁴*that he was buried, that he was raised on the third day in accordance with the Scriptures,* ⁵*and that he appeared to Cephas, then to the twelve.*

We make the following assertions within the Christian worldview:
- Human beings and the universe in which they reside are the creation of the God who has revealed Himself in Scripture.
- Jesus Christ is God's Son sacrificed.

The Christian symbol is often a fish. The Greek rendering of the statement, "Jesus Christ is God's Son savior" is the following (with the English rendering below it):

---

[137]Plantinga, *Where the Conflict Really Lies*, 8.

Ιησους Χριστου Θεος υιος σοτερ
Jesus   Christ   God's son savior

The first letter of each Greek word, Ιχθυς, spells fish in the Greek. Figure 7.1 illustrates this commonly observed symbol.

Figure 7.1 Christianity's Symbol

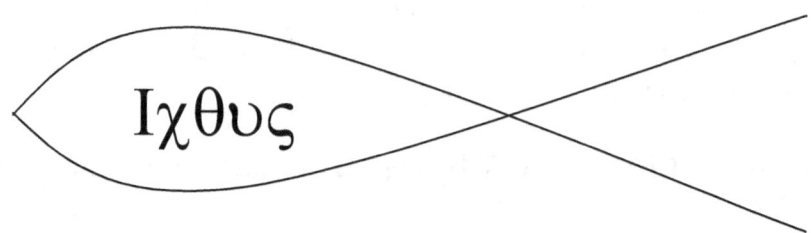

    The resurrection of Jesus Christ validates his teaching, including finance-related. Humans are more than simply sensate animals. Life is more than determining what makes us most happy and pursuing financial transactions that facilitate this happiness. We are higher than the animals in the wild. Again, there are clearly moral absolutes, and if another person is present, there are morally-based consequences. Financial decisions are not reduced to simply advancing one's own narcissistic goals regardless of who may be hurt. The Golden Rule has a rational foundation and is worthy to be pursued.
    Ideation, the formation of ideas, is preeminent over simple sensate beings. We are more than simply sensate animals seeking our own self-interest. There exist immutable, metaphysical ideas that are foundational to all decision-making, especially personal financial decisions.
    Based on the three tests and four questions, the Christian worldview is the most coherent.

Table 7.1. Three Tests and Four Questions Answered

Three tests for truth	Christian worldview	Naturalist
Logically consistent	Yes, deep coherence	Vacuous by definition
Empirically adequate	Yes, human nature explained well	Discord with observations
Experientially relevant	Yes, peace and joy even in suffering	Hopelessness reigns
Four questions	**Christian worldview**	**Naturalist**
Where did I come from?	Created by God	Don't know
Is life meaningful?	Yes, we are to glorify God	Don't know
Immutable moral laws?	Yes, clearly provided	Let me think about it
Where am I going?	Heaven	Don't know

One interesting test of different worldviews is what you would say to someone on the verge of suicide.

Case Study 7.1: Christian Worldview and Suicide

It is unclear what a naturalist would say other than go ahead if you feel like it. It really will not matter in a thousand years. The Christian plea, being in opposition to the naturalist, would be to seek and rescue this person found in such a hopeless state. The Christian answer is clearly to seek and rescue this person. The answer is never to end your temporal existence and start one's eternal life sooner. There is always hope. A few biblical passages are documented here. According to biblical Christianity, there does exist an entity seeking to destroy but there also exists a rescuer who is the Truth.

John 10:10

> ¹⁰The thief comes only to steal and kill and destroy. I came that they may have life and have it abundantly.

John 14:6

> ⁶Jesus said to him, "I am the way, and the truth, and the life. No one comes to the Father except through me."

Pilate asked the perfect question to the perfect person but did not wait around for the answer.

John 18:33–38

> ³³So Pilate entered his headquarters again and called Jesus and said to him, "Are you the King of the Jews?" ³⁴Jesus answered, "Do you say this of your own accord, or did others say it to you about me?" ³⁵Pilate answered, "Am I a Jew? Your own nation and the chief priests have delivered you over to me. What have you done?" ³⁶Jesus answered, "My kingdom is not of this world. If my kingdom were of this world, my servants would have been fighting, that I might not be delivered over to the Jews. But my kingdom is not from the world." ³⁷Then Pilate said to him, "So you are a king?" Jesus answered, "You say that I am a king. For this purpose I was born and for this purpose I have come into the world — to bear witness to the truth. Everyone who is of the truth listens to my voice." ³⁸Pilate said to him, "What is truth?" After he had said this, he went back outside to the Jews and told them, "I find no guilt in him."

Life is meaningful. Thus, artificially terminating this temporal existence is wrong.

We now examine selected personal finance issues through the lens of Christianity.

Christianity and Personal Finance

The key objective from a Christian worldview is to conform ourselves to the reality around us. The cosmos in which we reside is living and abundant—teeming with abundance created as well as sustained by God.

Further, we know that humans are deeply flawed. We were created within a moral universe with an ingrained sense of right and wrong. Unfortunately, we have a never-ending pull toward what is wrong, known as sin. Absent God's grace and mercy, we are destined for sin and destruction.

Deep within our being is the desire to align what we observe empirically with what we infer ought to be. We naturally seek the normative reason why. Once while working with a particular financial institution, this institution was requesting a significant allocation—say $50 million—from an another entity managing over $100 billion. It was interesting to me that the analysts minimized the importance of our historical performance and sought to understand the normative reason why our portfolio management strategy had been historically successful. There was a deep desire to understand the normative foundation for the performance.

We should restructure our worldview to make personal financial decisions that lead to deep contentment regardless of extremely negative future financial events. History is filled with Christians who have suffered both physically as well as financially, but they have remained deeply contented due to their personal relationship with God.

We now examine science through the lens of naturalism and Christianity.

Science

Science is an international enterprise, involving numerous people with a wide array of worldviews and presuppositions. Scientific activities usually focus on that which is repeatable, but the repeatability standard is not applicable in many areas, such as cosmology, biogenesis, and finance.

Interestingly, in most social science fields such as finance, it is often impossible to conduct repeatable events. Every day is unique, and humans are constantly learning and changing. For example, the 2019–2020 pandemic has changed numerous financial models. It has clearly changed the way people view the safety of their retirement accounts.

According to Michael Ruse, science "deals only with the natural, the repeatable, that which is governed by law."[138] Thus, it is too limiting as it rules out cosmology and many other disciplines including finance. According to John C. Lennox, science is a "method of inference to the best explanation."

There are three formal reasoning methods that can be applied. According to Merriam-Webster,

> *Deductive reasoning, or deduction, is making an inference based on widely accepted facts or premises. If a beverage is defined as "drinkable through a straw," one could use deduction to determine soup to be a beverage. Inductive reasoning, or induction, is making an inference based on an observation, often of a sample. You can induce that the soup is tasty if you observe all of your friends consuming it.*
>
> *Recall abductive reasoning, or abduction, is making a probable conclusion from what you know. If you see an abandoned bowl of hot soup on the table, you can use abduction to conclude the owner of the soup is likely returning soon.*[139]

Scientific activity best falls within abductive reasoning; especially within the social science fields such as finance.

There are two broad categories of science, observation-and-prediction-based or problem-and-explanation-based. As an aside, naturalists are trying to determine apparent design whereas theists are trying to determine the Creator's actual

---

[138]Michael Ruse, *Darwinism defended: A guide to the evolution controversies.* (Reading, MA: Addison-Wesley, 1982), p. 322.
[139]See https://www.merriam-webster.com/words-at-play/deduction-vs-induction-vs-abduction.

design. Interestingly, you end up with the same conclusion. According to Lennox, it is probably better to avoid this type of terminology. Further Lennox acknowledges that many areas of science are not impacted by philosophical commitments although some areas of science are.

Lennox has several deep insights related to science. A few quotes are provided here.[140]

> *(S)cience done on atheistic presuppositions will lead to the same results as science done on theistic presuppositions. (36–7)*
>
> *(E)ssence of true science–that is, a willingness to follow empirical evidence, wherever it leads. (38)*
>
> *Two extremes: (1) Relationship between science and religion can only be viewed in terms of conflict. (2) All science is philosophically or theologically neutral. (39)*
>
> *The statement that only science can deliver knowledge is self-refuting. (40)*
>
> *"Science is powerless to answer questions such as 'Why did the universe come into being?' 'What is the meaning of human existence?' 'What happens after we die?'" Francis Collins, Director of the Human Genome Project (42)*
>
> *(W)e should not confuse the mechanism by which the universe works either with its cause or its upholder. (45)*
>
> *"(T)here is no logical conflict between reason-giving explanations which concern mechanisms, and reason-giving explanations which concern the plans and purposes of the agent, human or divine." Michael Poole (45)*

---

[140]Lennox, *God's Undertaker*.

Science and Personal Finance

Personal financial management is an interesting combination of observation-and-prediction-based (OaP) or problem-and-explanation-based (PaE) analysis. Many people enjoy the hobby of predicting financial instrument prices based on historical financial data. Very few people have a documented record of success; in fact, less than what you would expect if completely random. For example, if 1,024 people entered a coin flipping contest to see who the best at landing on heads is each time without exception, then it is expected that only one would flip 10 heads in a row. Thus, this person would appear particularly skilled.[141]

Although vast amounts of time and effort are placed on OaP, the significant gains in personal finance will be found in PaE. Having a correct understanding of what it means to be human aids in creating flourishing cultures and effective strategies. For example, understanding the reality of peoples' total depravity, including our own, aids in developing appropriate financial guardrails.

OaP struggles with financial data because it involves human feedback. Performativity is the concept that beliefs about financial prices change financial prices. Note that beliefs about physical systems, such as gravity, do not change the behavior of gravity. There is ample evidence that beliefs about financial prices deeply impact observed financial prices. Most people fail to grasp the core reasons why their financial predictions fail. Many famous scientists have taken their analytical skills into various financial markets only to suffer massive financial losses.

From a Christian worldview, if one is encouraged early in their Christian life to engage in a deep dive into what the Bible says about personal finance, then one will likely have in a different perspective on debt as well as perhaps financial risk-taking. Finding no encouraging passages on debt and many warning passages will enhance one's aversion to borrowing. Delayed gratification will be much sweeter.

---

[141] The probability of flipping 10 heads in a row is 1 in 1,024 (= 2^{10}).

Interestingly, one may increase financial risk-taking for several reasons. Given the vast number of Christians who have been martyred for their faith, taking a bit of financial risk seems rather benign. For example, a Christian who followed biblical financial principles may well be eighty percent equity at eighty years old—a very contrary position to modern financial orthodoxy. Why? The Christian is seeking to leave an inheritance to her children's children.[142] Generation skipping justifies a more long-term view, especially since their present financial needs have been adequately planned and supplied. The long-term view allows the "miracle" of compound interest. As the often attributed Albert Einstein quote, "Compound interest is the eighth wonder of the world. He who understands it, earns it ... he who doesn't ... pays it." The long-run view allows for this most powerful force.[143]

We now turn to examine the relationships between naturalism, Christianity, and science.

Naturalism, Christianity, and Science

Christianity and science are often portrayed as being in deep discord whereas naturalism and science as being in complete concord. For example, Peter Atkins, a chemist and prolific writer, asserts

> *Humanity should accept that science has eliminated the justification for believing in cosmic purpose, and that any survival of purpose is inspired only by sentiment. ... There is no reason to suppose that science cannot deal with every aspect of existence.*[144]

---

[142]Proverbs 13:22 A good man leaves an inheritance to his children's children, but the sinner's wealth is laid up for the righteous.
[143]Albert Einstein is often given credit for various quotes related to compound interest. The evidence is unclear. See, for example, https://skeptics.stackexchange.com/questions/25330/did-einstein-ever-remark-on-compound-interest.
[144]See https://todayinsci.com/A/Atkins_Peter/AtkinsPeter-Quotations.htm.

Exploring the Philosophical Roots that Influence Financial Fruit

Science has nothing to say regarding cosmic purpose. Cosmic purpose is simply not within the science domain. Again, Atkins is conflating naturalism with science. Recall Alvin Plantinga asserts

> *There is superficial conflict but deep concord [agreement] between science and theistic religion, but superficial concord and deep conflict between science and naturalism.*[145]

Figure 7.2 illustrates the key assertion in this section. Specifically, there is deep concord (✓) between Christianity and science whereas there is deep discord (X) between naturalism and science. Further, naturalism and Christianity cannot both be true.

Figure 7.2. Naturalism, Christianity, and Science

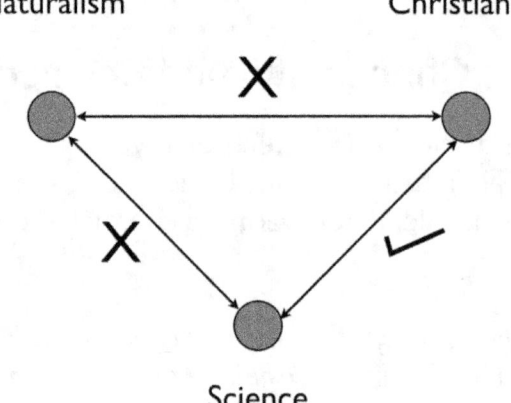

Selected observations by Lennox [146] are quoted or paraphrased here:

> *Naturalist thinkers tell us that science has eliminated God whereas scientists who are theists tell us that science confirms their faith in God. (20)*

---
[145]Plantinga, *Where the Conflict Really Lies*, ix.
[146]Lennox, *God's Undertaker*.

Science is based on the conviction that the universe is orderly. This comes from the conviction that the universe is governed by a single God and not by the whims of many gods. (20)

The medieval thinkers insisted on the rationality of God. Many of the fathers of modern science were theists (for example, Galileo, Pasteur, Newton, Copernicus, Maxwell, Faraday, Heisenberg, Planc, A. Eddington, Leeuwenhoek, Kepler, and Mendel). They expected laws of nature because they believed in a lawgiver. Science freed from Aristotelian method of deducing from fixed principles of how the universe ought to be (that is, a priori philosophical principles), Galilei and Kepler went and looked to see what was there. (21–23) (Note that an additional scientist was added).

There is a widespread myth that science has been constantly at war with religion (e. g., Galileo). Many secular philosophers were opposed to Galileo because of his criticism of Aristotle and many religious intellectuals supported him (at least initially). Also, one should consider the politics of Catholics versus Protestants. The Catholic Church was Aristotelian. (25)

The real conflict is not between science and religion but between two diametrically opposed worldviews: naturalism and theism. (28–30)

Naturalism asserts the cosmos is all there is or ever shall be. It is a closed system of cause and effect. Materialists are naturalists but some naturalists hold that mind and consciousness are to be distinguished from matter (that is, they are emergent properties). (29–30)

Case Study 7.2: Foundations of Personal Finance

The Christian worldview related to personal finance is principle driven and not data driven. There are investments that would fail to bring glory to God and there are investments that seek to bring glory to God and leads to human flourishing. Figure 7.3 illustrates a house build on a rock—it simply endures the battering through time. Figure 7.4 illustrates a house build on sand—one disruption such as a global pandemic will send it crashing down.

Figure 7.3. Illustration of House Built on a Rock[147]

---

[147]Photo by Philipp Mandler on Unsplash. Accessed October 22, 2024.

Figure 7.4. Illustration of House Built on Sand[148]

Biblically-based financial management can easily withstand the shifting sands of time.

Summary

We addressed two dominant worldviews, naturalism and Christianity. The Christian worldview was found to be the most compatible with science. Further, personal finance aligns better with observable reality.

---

[148]Photo by Emmanuel Acua on Unsplash. Accessed October 22, 2024.

Case Study 1: Sensate Versus Ideation: Budgeting

Family budgeting is a useful exercise when seeking to understand assets, liabilities, revenues, and expenses. A sensate-focused family will wrestle over who gets to consume scarce assets and revenues whereas an ideation-focused family will center on advancing family ideals. Consider a family of four, husband, wife, and two teenaged children. What key differences would you expect to emerge from an evening discussion around budgeting issues from a sensate-focused family and a Christ-centered family?

Case Study 2: Car Payments and the Christian Worldview

Suppose Bill drives an old Toyota Corolla (fifteen years old, 200,000 miles, two-door small car) and recently started his first full time well-paying job. Bill currently has limited savings. Although there is great freedom within the Christian worldview, what are the core issues on these two choices?

1. Continuing to drive the old car for another two year and then pays cash for every future car Bill may buy over his lifetime.
2. Purchase a new car on payments and then makes car payments for every future car Bill may buy over his lifetime.

Case Study 3: Charity: Naturalism Versus Christianity

Obviously, people from a variety of worldviews can be extremely charitable. Contrast the rational basis for charity in general from a naturalist worldview and a Christian worldview.

References

Lennox, John C., *God's Undertaker: Has Science Buried God?* (Oxford: Lion, 2009).

Moreland, J. P. and William Lane Craig, *Philosophical Foundations for a Christian Worldview* (Downers Grove, IL: InterVarsity Press, 2003).

Alvin Plantinga, *Where the Conflict Really Lies: Science, Religion, & Naturalism,* (New York: Oxford University Press, 2011).

Ruse, Michael, *Darwinism defended: A guide to the evolution controversies.* (Reading, MA: Addison-Wesley, 1982).

Chapter 8. Problem of Evil

Learning Objectives

- Contrast pain, suffering, and evil.
- Compare atheistic-based solutions to the problem of evil with theistic-based solutions.
- Explore biblical insights related to the problem of evil.
- Review selected Christian's experiences with evil, including the apostles and Horacio Spafford.

Opening Quotes

"Ideas have consequences, but ideas also have antecedents." (Source lost.)

"That feeling of over-due bills, of bills coming due, of accounts overdrawn, of tradesmen unpaid, of general money cares, is very dreadful at first; but it is astonishing how soon men get used to it. A load which would crush a man at first becomes, by habit, not only endurable, but easy and comfortable to the bearer. The habitual debtor goes along jaunty and with elastic step, almost enjoying the excitement of his embarrassments. ... But then, at last, the time comes when the excitement is over, and when nothing but misery is left. ... If a man could only think of that, as

he puts his name to the first little bill, as to which he is so good-naturedly assured that it can easily be renewed!"[149]

Overview

On any given day, various news outlets will report evil acts of humans from murder to thefts to racism. From these types of reports, it is implicitly assumed as fact that evil exists. Many worldviews, however, deny the existence of evil. Hence, we have a natural discord between many worldviews and the clear and indisputable fact that humans commit evil acts. In this chapter, the Christian's response to the presence of evil is explored in detail.

Pain, Suffering, and Evil

Our focus is on evil. First, it is important to distinguish between pain, suffering, and evil. Pain is the "physical suffering or discomfort caused by illness or injury."[150] To my knowledge, every worldview admits the existence of pain. Pain is very useful as it deters us from many activities, such as placing my hand on a hot stove. From the poorest to the richest among us, everyone experiences pain. For some who suffer, pain can be temporarily alleviated with having access to drugs. Unfortunately, often these very pain medicines cause future pain in terms of addictions and/or side effects. There may be pain in painkillers!

Suffering is "the state of undergoing pain, distress, or hardship."[151] Our human existence to some degree, long-term or instantaneous, entails inherent suffering. If you have not suffered greatly yourself, then you know someone who has.

---

[149]Anthony Trollope, *Framley Parsonage* (New York: Dodd, Mead & Company, 1911), 1:182-183.
[150]*New Oxford American Dictionary*, provided on Mac computer.
[151]*New Oxford American Dictionary*, provided on Mac computer.

Suffering takes many forms, including both physical and mental. Enduring the pain of cancer is a common challenge for many. Even worse for some is the mental anguish of divorce or discord between people. Time often heals physical suffering, but for many, time does nothing for mental suffering. Again, to my knowledge, every worldview admits the existence of suffering.

Evil is distinctly different from pain and suffering and is often denied by various worldviews. Evil is "profound immorality, wickedness, and depravity, especially when regarded as a supernatural force."[152] As previously discussed, one immediately is confronted with the problem of the criterion. If a particular worldview asserts that a particular action is evil, then immediately we are confronted with some opposite action being good. Hence, there must be a criterion to decide, and we are off and running with the problem of the criterion.

Atheism and the Problem of Evil

Atheistic-based worldviews, such as naturalism, must deny the existence of evil even though it is all around us. The problem of evil causes significant discord for an atheistic-based worldview. The atheistic-based worldviews declare life's imperative as vacuous, completely without meaning. Therefore, you cannot measure progress if you have no idea where you are going. You may very well be regressing as opposed to progressing.

The logic progresses in the following way:[153]

Premise 1) If evil exists, then good exists lest you not know the difference.
Premise 2) Evil exists.
Premise 3) Good exists.
Premise 4) Premises 2 and 3 imply measurability.
Premise 5) Measurability implies an objective basis for moral

---

[152] *New Oxford American Dictionary*, provided on Mac computer.
[153] See Session 3 for an introduction.

law.
Premise 6) Moral law implies a moral lawgiver.
Conclusion) Therefore, that evil exists implies God exists.

Interestingly, many atheists have found their worldviews unlivable, particularly in their sunset years. The problem of evil is, however, also a challenge for theistic-based worldviews.

Theism and the Problem of Evil

A genuine concern for seekers and even Christ-followers is that if God is all-powerful and all-good, then why is there evil? Moreover, if God is all powerful, omnipotent, able to do anything, why does evil persist? If God is all powerful, then God can do anything, including removing evil. David Hume notes that Epicurus's ancient questions remain unanswered: "Is he [God] willing to prevent evil, but not able? then is he impotent. Is he able, but not willing? then is he malevolent. Is he both able and willing? whence then is evil?"[154]

One solution to the problem of evil is to introduce another attribute of God—God is all-knowing. If God is all-knowing, and we are not, then surely God has a very good reason for not removing evil currently. From three attributes, we could move on to a fourth—God is all-wise. If God is all-wise, then from His deep wisdom, evil serves a valuable purpose perhaps in displaying God's beauty. Moving from four attributes to five attributes—God is perfect in justice. The process could continue with all the known attributes of God.

From a Christian worldview, we learn that God is the very standard for His own actions and in no way owes us an explanation. As we do have the precious gift of the Bible, there are many insights to be gained regarding the problem of evil from examining what has been revealed.

---

[154]David Hume, Part 10 in *Dialogues Concerning Natural Religion* (Project Gutenberg, 2009), https://www.gutenberg.org/files/4583/4583-h/4583-h.htm.

Biblical Insights on the Problem of Evil

Based on the first book in the Bible, we learn that God's creation was very good. Yet in God's sovereignty, He allowed a tempter to approach humans. Clearly humans were given the freedom to choose to obey God's simple law, not to eat of a particular tree or to disobey in rebellion.

Genesis 1:31, 3:1, and 3:12

[31]And God saw everything that he had made, and behold, it was very good. And there was evening and there was morning, the sixth day. ... 3 [1]Now the serpent was more crafty than any other beast of the field that the Lord God had made. He said to the woman, "Did God actually say, 'You shall not eat of any tree in the garden'?" ... [12]The man said, "The woman whom you gave to be with me, she gave me fruit of the tree, and I ate."

Throughout the Bible, we learn that God behaves in ways that offend the values held by some people. For example, in Exodus we find God schooling Moses, and in the Psalms, we find the psalmist acknowledging that God does as He pleases rather than what the psalmist in his humanness might devise.

Exodus 33:18–19

[18]Moses said, "Please show me your glory." [19]And he said, "I will make all my goodness pass before you and will proclaim before you my name 'The LORD.' And I will be gracious to whom I will be gracious, and will show mercy on whom I will show mercy."

Psalm 115:1–3

[1]Not to us, O Lord, not to us, but to your name give glory, for the sake of your steadfast love and your faithfulness! [2]Why should the nations say, "Where is their God?" [3]Our God is in the heavens; he does all that he pleases.

When we demand that God give an account of himself, it usually goes unanswered. Job, a very righteous man who suffered greatly made such a demand, and God chose to respond in an unexpected way.

Job 23:1–7

> ¹Then Job answered and said: ²"Today also my complaint is bitter; my hand is heavy on account of my groaning. ³Oh, that I knew where I might find him, that I might come even to his seat! ⁴I would lay my case before him and fill my mouth with arguments. ⁵I would know what he would answer me and understand what he would say to me. ⁶Would he contend with me in the greatness of his power? No; he would pay attention to me. ⁷There an upright man could argue with him, and I would be acquitted forever by my judge."
> See also Job 31:35–40.

Job 38:1–5

> ¹Then the Lord answered Job out of the whirlwind and said: ²"Who is this that darkens counsel by words without knowledge? ³Dress for action like a man; I will question you, and you make it known to me. ⁴"Where were you when I laid the foundation of the earth? Tell me, if you have understanding. ⁵Who determined its measurements — surely you know! Or who stretched the line upon it?"

Job eventually understands that God is holy and is accountable to no one. Further, God's holiness leads Job to repent.

Job 42:1–6

> ¹Then Job answered the Lord and said: ²"I know that you can do all things, and that no purpose of yours can be thwarted. ³'Who is this that hides counsel without knowledge?' Therefore I have uttered what I did not understand, things too wonderful for me, which I did not know. ⁴'Hear, and I will speak; I will question you, and you make it known to me.' ⁵I had heard of you by the

hearing of the ear, but now my eye sees you; ⁶therefore I despise myself, and repent in dust and ashes."

From a Christian worldview, several conclusions can be drawn.
- We have no right to complain against God.
- God does not have to give us intellectually satisfying answers to the problems of evil.
- God's sovereignty is not to be questioned related to the problem of evil, rather to be underscored.
- God's Word and His truth is altogether reliable.
- God is holy, just, and good.

Christian Experience

In a world of deep pain, suffering, and obvious evil, how does the Christian worldview stand up? John Stott summarizes the choice before us.

> *I could never myself believe in God, if it were not for the cross. The only God I believe in is the One Nietzsche ridiculed as 'God on the cross.' In the real world of pain, how could one worship a God who was immune to it? I have entered many Buddhist temples in different Asian countries and stood respectfully before the statue of the Buddha, his legs crossed, arms folded, eyes closed, the ghost of a smile playing round his mouth, a remote look on his face, detached from the agonies of the world. But each time after a while I have had to turn away. And in imagination I have turned instead to that lonely, twisted, tortured figure on the cross, nails through hands and feet, back lacerated, limbs wrenched, brow bleeding from thorn-pricks, mouth dry and intolerably thirsty, plunged in Godforsaken darkness. That is the God for me! He laid aside his immunity to pain. He entered our world of flesh and blood, tears and death. He suffered for us. Our sufferings become more manageable in the light of his. There is still a question mark against human suffering, but over it we boldly stamp another mark, the cross that symbolizes divine suffering. "The cross of Christ ... is God's only self-justification*

in such a world as ours ...." "The other gods were strong; but thou wast weak; they rode, but thou didst stumble to a throne; But to our wounds only God's wounds can speak, And not a god has wounds, but thou alone."[155]

As the problem of evil is often a key stumbling, in the next section several followers of Jesus are identified who either suffered greatly and endured significant evils.

Fate of the Apostles

In the early foundational years of Christianity, the original twelve apostles suffered significantly for proclaiming Jesus as the resurrected savior. Although the historical accounts are sketchy at times, the following is a brief account of fourteen people, the original twelve apostles, Matthias appointed after Judas's betrayal and death, and Paul.

- Judas Iscariot – hung himself after betraying Jesus.
- Simon Peter – crucified upside down by Nero in Rome around AD 64.
- Andrew – crucified by Patras around AD 60.
- James – killed with sword by Herod in AD 44 (Acts 12:1–2).
- John – banished to the island of Patmos, died of old age.
- Philip – not sure, perhaps beheaded, stoned, or crucified upside down around AD 80.
- Bartholomew – martyred, not sure how, and perhaps in India.
- Thomas – killed by spear in Mylapore, India on July 3, AD 72.
- Matthew – killed by being burned, stoned, stabbed, or beheaded perhaps in Africa, AD 60.
- James, son of Alphaeus – beaten with a fuller's club and stoned in Ostrakine, Egypt.
- Jude – killed with an ax in Syria.
- Simon the Zealot – likely a martyr by crucifixion or by saw, location unclear.
- Matthias – likely stoned or beheaded, location unclear.

---

[155] See John R. W. Stott, http://www.goodreads.com/quotes/416309-i-could-never-myself-believe-in-god-if-it-were. Original in *The Cross of Christ*.

- Paul – not one of the original twelve, but considered an apostle, beheaded by Nero, AD 68.

Clearly, following Jesus had great cost. Would you endure this level of persecution if you knew Jesus was a liar or lunatic? I do not believe either of these to be a reasonable explanation for paying so great a cost. A few others are identified in Christian history who endured suffering and evil.

Case Study 8.1: Horatio G. Spafford

Horatio G. Spafford wrote the lyrics of the well-known Christian hymn, "It Is Well With My Soul," in 1873. Before turning to the hymn, a brief biography is provided.[156] Spafford was born in Troy, New York in 1828 and died in Jerusalem, Israel in 1888. He was a successful lawyer in Chicago and had invested heavily in Chicago real estate. He also served as a Presbyterian church elder and from all appearances was a follower of Jesus Christ.

The great fire of Chicago in 1871 destroyed most of his real estate investments. Two years later, law duties kept him from joining his wife and four daughters on a ship to England. On November 22, 1873, the ship was struck by another ship and sank in twelve minutes killing 226 people, including his four daughters. Anna Spafford telegrammed her husband simply, "Saved alone."

Horatio then traveled to meet his wife shortly after receiving news from Anna. He wrote most of the following lyrics as his ship passed near where his daughters had died:

It Is Well With My Soul
Horacio G. Spafford, 1873

When peace, like a river, attendeth my way,
When sorrows like sea billows roll;

---

[156]See https://en.wikipedia.org/wiki/Horatio_Spafford and references therein.

Whatever my lot, Thou has taught me to know,
It is well, it is well, with my soul.

Refrain:
It is well, (it is well)
With my soul, (with my soul)
It is well, it is well, with my soul.

Though Satan should buffet, though trials should come,
Let this blest assurance control,
That Christ has regarded my helpless estate,
And hath shed His own blood for my soul.

My sin, oh, the bliss of this glorious thought!
My sin, not in part but the whole,
Is nailed to the cross, and I bear it no more,
Praise the Lord, praise the Lord, O my soul!

For me, be it Christ, be it Christ hence to live:
If Jordan above me shall roll,
No pang shall be mine, for in death as in life
Thou wilt whisper Thy peace to my soul.

But, Lord, 'tis for Thee, for Thy coming we wait,
The sky, not the grave, is our goal;
Oh, trump of the angel! Oh, voice of the Lord!
Blessed hope, blessed rest of my soul!

And Lord, haste the day when my faith shall be sight,
The clouds be rolled back as a scroll;
The trump shall resound, and the Lord shall descend,
Even so, it is well with my soul.

Figure 8.1 is a copy of the original document. During a June 7, 2020, sermon, Pastor Alister Begg noted that in the third line in the original lyrics, Spafford uses the word "know" and not "say" (as is common today). The power of a personal relationship with Jesus Christ is more than just a coherent

Exploring the Philosophical Roots that Influence Financial Fruit

worldview that corresponds with reality. It is a growing, life-transforming, tactile experience where you "know" your Savior. The Apostle Paul expresses this same deep level of knowledge.

1 Timothy 1:12b

12bBut I am not ashamed, for I know whom I have believed, and I am convinced that he is able to guard until that day what has been entrusted to me.

Figure 8.1. Original Handwritten Draft of "It Is Well With My Soul"[157]

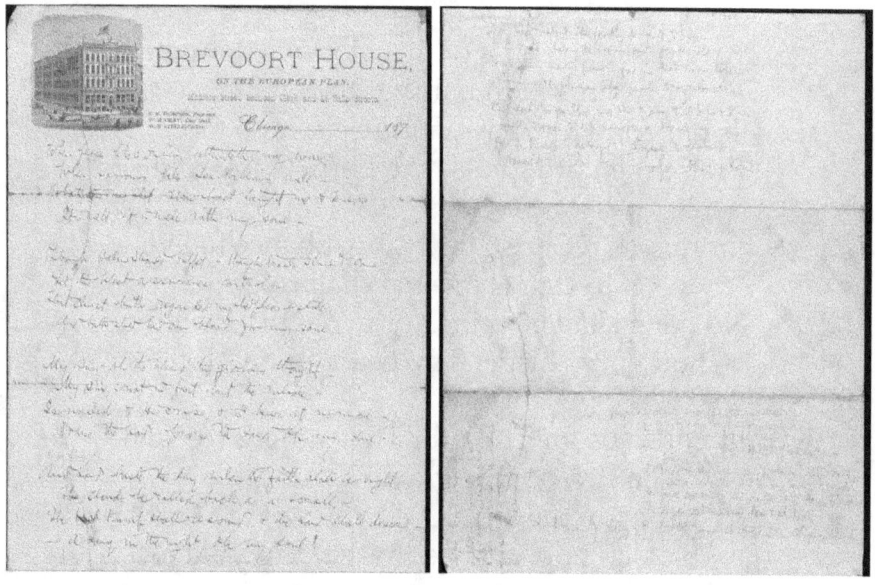

After traveling to England, the Spaffords had three more children where his only son died of scarlet fever at age four. Finally, they moved to Jerusalem to serve the poor. Clearly, Horatio experienced significant business loss as well as significant emotional pain. He did not live an easy life and suffered greatly.

---

[157]See https://www.loc.gov/item/mamcol.016/.

Enduring Financial Loss

Is it possible to invest in risky financial instruments or other financial opportunities and never suffer loss? Well, it depends. If your numeraire is currency units such as U. S. dollars, then the answer is no. Like boxing, you will suffer punishing losses if you choose to step into the ring.

If your numeraire is enduring eternal wealth, then the answer is yes indeed! For example, investing in a business startup will statistically most likely fail. If, however, the business startup is founded on biblical principles and centered on glorifying God and human flourishing, then during the season that the business existed, the business was generating enduring returns.

Many Christian businesses are deeply involved in making disciples of Jesus Christ. If the business was instrumental in the Christian maturation process, then clearly even after the business fails, the disciple is continuing the process of making other disciples.

Jesus promised that those who follow him will suffer.

Mark 8:34

34And calling the crowd to him with his disciples, he said to them, "If anyone would come after me, let him deny himself and take up his cross and follow me."

Thus, if the business foundation is based on solid biblical principles, then financial failure is not to be feared. Further, the future of the venture is ultimately in God's sovereign hand, so we do not need to be anxious. Rather we can focus solely on serving a faithful manager of God's resources and leave the results to Him.

Case Study 8.2: The Artist, His Faithful Father, and the Drunk[158]

Sam, married father of two middle school boys, unfortunately met Betty, a highly intoxicated driver, on a narrow bridge. In the accident that resulted, Betty escaped injury and Sam was left completely paralyzed apart from his left arm and right eyebrow. He further sustained significant brain damage limiting his ability to communicate.

Sam's wife abandoned him marrying Sam's best friend. Sam's father, Terry, took on the guardian role and cared for Sam over the next twenty-five years of his shortened life. Terry, a Christian, was asked by the judge overseeing the criminal case against Betty to speak to the court on Sam's behalf before sentencing. Although numerous potential responses are possible from a Christian and naturalistic worldview, what are potential responses?

How is justice ever provided for evil of this nature?

Summary

After defining pain, suffering, and evil, atheistic-based solutions to the problem of evil were compared with theistic-based solutions. Next, biblical insights related to the problem of evil were provided. Selected Christians' experiences with evil were provided, including the apostles and Horacio Spafford. Finally, in the context of evil, financial loss was examined.

---

[158] Although the names and facts are changed, the author knew Sam before this tragedy and watched his faithful father care for him until his death.

Case Study 1: Serving Those Who Steal from You[159]

"If a man steals your farm, teach him how to farm." Craig Deall's story is instructive for understanding Christian approaches to evil. Craig is a third generation white Zimbabwean. He grew up on his family's 3,000-acre farm. From a beer drinking harasser of Christians, whom he viewed as weak, he eventually became a follower of Jesus Christ. He was leading a highly successful farm, but now realizes that he loved the land and ruled the farm hands rather than loving the farm hands (upwards of 1,000 including dependents) and managing the land. During this season, Craig describes himself as a Christian streaker — having only the helmet of salvation on.

A political change resulted in Craig's family farm being stolen and his family migrating to a city. How does one respond to an evil act of this nature? As the referenced podcast reveals, Craig decided to love his enemies and teach them how to farm. To this day, Craig and his family have not been compensated for harm done, but Craig has been able to serve many African nations in resolving their food scarcity problem based on the Christian worldview.

Case Study 2: Jesus's Approach to Evil

Christianity is unique in that the Son of God suffered egregious evil at the crucifixion. Although impossible to completely plumb the depths of this topic, clearly Jesus trusted in God's providential care. The doctrine of God's sovereignty is immensely helpful when enduring significant evil.

---

[159] Based on several encounters with Craig Deall. See, for example, https://www.faithdrivenentrepreneur.org/podcast-inventory/2019/10/29/episode-80-serving-those-who-steal-from-you-craig-deall.

Case Study 3: An Unjust Death

Although the United States court system seeks to merit out justice, often it simply is not possible. For example, when someone is injured or dies due to someone else's negligence, it is impossible to adequately compensate for the loss of human functions or loss of human life. How does someone address this harm from different worldviews?

References

Hume, David, Part 10 in *Dialogues Concerning Natural Religion* (Project Gutenberg, 2009), https://www.gutenberg.org/files/4583/4583-h/4583-h.htm.

Stott, John R. W., http://www.goodreads.com/quotes/416309-i-could-never-myself-believe-in-god-if-it-were. Original in *The Cross of Christ*.

Trollope, Anthony, *Framley Parsonage* (New York: Dodd, Mead & Company, 1911).

Part 3. Fertilizing Financial Fruit

Recall the core premise for this book is that financial fruit grows on philosophical roots. In Part 1, the biblically-based philosophical roots were explored. Further, the rational basis for the Christian worldview was established. In Part 2, the various theological soils were introduced with the conclusion that the Christian worldview was most compelling.

Part 3 covers the remainder of the book, Chapters 9–13, focused on fertilizing financial fruit. Recall that to acquire enduring financial fruit, our philosophical roots need the best theological soil. Here the approach to nurturing the Christian worldview is sought, particularly within the context of personal finance.

In Chapters 9 and 10, the Bible is explored in detail. Chapter 9 addresses the charges that the Bible is at best hearsay or even worse heresy. The vast quantity of manuscript evidence is introduced related to biblical integrity.

In Chapter 10, the amazing, well-documented history contained in the Bible is explored as it speaks to its authenticity and reliability. Ultimately, the Christian worldview is based on news, and the Bible is an accurate portrayal of that news.

In Chapter 11, miracles are defined carefully, and the seven significant miracles recorded in the Gospel According to John are explored in detail. The chapter concludes with some statistical analysis of the likelihood of fulfilled prophesy.

In Chapter 12, the grand miracle of the resurrection of Jesus Christ is examined in detail. An application of Bayes's Theorem is provided to determine the likelihood that the early apostles all died for a lie. Following Bayes's Theorem application, Pascal's wager is considered and conclude the rational evidence for the bodily resurrection of Jesus Christ is conclusive. Subsequently, the implication for personal financial management is briefly explored.

In Chapter 13, the Christian duty to love our neighbor is carefully examined. From this perspective, the merits of biblically-based financial management are clearly established.

The book concludes in Chapter 14 with an examination of the nature of the harvest. A contrast is given from competing worldviews taken from recent opinion editorials addressing investment management processes drawn from either evolutionary theory or the Christian worldview. One will focus on either products (naturalist view) or people (imago Dei).

Chapter 9. The Bible as Hearsay or Heresy

Learning Objectives

- Refute the charge that the Bible is just hearsay.
- Refute the charge that the Bible is just heresy.
- Provide empirical evidence of the uniqueness of the Bible.

Opening Quote

2 Peter 1:16
16For we did not follow cleverly devised myths when we made known to you the power and coming of our Lord Jesus Christ, but we were eyewitnesses of his majesty.

Overview

In this chapter, the question of whether the Bible is just hearsay or actually heresy is considered carefully. These two charges are somewhat interrelated, and evidence to refute one can be used to refute the other. In the next chapter, the question of whether the Bible is reliable history is examined. The hearsay argument is addressed by examining the Bible itself. Was the Bible, particularly the New Testament, just written in response to a cultural movement? Alternatively, was the Bible just a nasty heresy written in an attempt to manipulate a cultural movement? These two questions are examined carefully here.

Hearsay, Heresy, or History

We start this analysis with three formal definitions:
- Hearsay – "information received from other people that one cannot adequately substantiate; rumor."[160]
- Heresy – "belief or opinion contrary to orthodox religious (especially Christian) doctrine."[161]
- History – "the study of past events, particularly in human affairs."[162]

From these three definitions, three hypotheses (H1, H2, and H3) are formally introduced:

- **H1:** The Bible is just hearsay. The Bible was written in response to a cultural movement.
- **H2:** The Bible is heresy. The Bible was written by a group in the 300s AD to manipulate a cultural movement.
- **H3:** The Bible is history. The Bible was written by the claimed authors and is authentic history. A cultural movement developed while the Bible was being written.

When evaluating documents, Aristotle notes that "the benefit of the doubt is to be given to the document itself, not arrogated by the critic to himself."[163] The first two hypotheses are carefully examined here and the third is examined in the next chapter.

---

[160] *New Oxford American Dictionary*, provided on Mac computer.
[161] *New Oxford American Dictionary*, provided on Mac computer.
[162] *New Oxford American Dictionary*, provided on Mac computer.
[163] Josh McDowell and Sean McDowell, *Evidence That Demands a Verdict: Life-Changing Truth for a Skeptical* World (Nashville, TN: Thomas Nelson, 2017), 68.

Is the Bible Just Hearsay?

Recall that hearsay is based on unsubstantiated information. Luke, a physician, wrote very concretely providing an enormous amount of specific information. Interestingly, much of this information has been attacked as false only to be later substantiated as historically plausible. The level of vicious attack speaks to the specificity given in the Bible. Consider the following passages, and note how Luke is not addressing philosophy, but rather seeks to "write an orderly account."

Luke 1:1–4

[1] Inasmuch as many have undertaken to compile a narrative of the things that have been accomplished among us, [2] just as those who from the beginning were eyewitnesses and ministers of the word have delivered them to us, [3] it seemed good to me also, having followed all things closely for some time past, to write an orderly account for you, most excellent Theophilus, [4] that you may have certainty concerning the things you have been taught.

Luke 3:1–2

[1] In the fifteenth year of the reign of Tiberius Caesar, Pontius Pilate being governor of Judea, and Herod being tetrarch of Galilee, and his brother Philip tetrarch of the region of Ituraea and Trachonitis, and Lysanias tetrarch of Abilene, [2] during the high priesthood of Annas and Caiaphas, the word of God came to John the son of Zechariah in the wilderness.

Now if the whole Bible is merely hearsay, why does it give such explicit detail? There have been countless cases where "higher critics" have argued that something is wrong in accounts like the one above. It is well-known that these objections have been fully resolved over the past 100 years or so. Thus, I conclude that a current unresolved problem may not be an error, just a lack of information. Luke continues in Acts to appeal to well-known events.

Acts 2:22

²²"Men of Israel, hear these words: Jesus of Nazareth, a man attested to you by God with mighty works and wonders and signs that God did through him in your midst, as you yourselves know – "

Acts 26:24-26

²⁴And as he was saying these things in his defense, Festus said with a loud voice, "Paul, you are out of your mind; your great learning is driving you out of your mind." ²⁵But Paul said, "I am not out of my mind, most excellent Festus, but I am speaking true and rational words. ²⁶For the king knows about these things, and to him I speak boldly. For I am persuaded that none of these things has escaped his notice, for this has not been done in a corner."

When writing hearsay, you would not accuse one of your key leaders (Paul) as being out of his mind. Generally, you would write about what a great person he is. In other passages, the authors appeal to eyewitness testimony, not hearsay.

John 19:35

³⁵He who saw it has borne witness – his testimony is true, and he knows that he is telling the truth – that you also may believe.

1 John 1:3

³that which we have seen and heard we proclaim also to you, so that you too may have fellowship with us; and indeed our fellowship is with the Father and with his Son Jesus Christ.

As seen in this Chapter's opening quote, Peter asserts firsthand knowledge as an eyewitness. Remember, Jesus prophesied that Peter would die by crucifixion. Further, he abandoned Jesus the night before his crucifixion. Years later Peter defends Jesus Christ as Lord. Something radical clearly happened to Peter.

Thus, Peter explicitly rejects the hearsay argument here. There are numerous other insights. For example, Luke and Acts were written sequentially. All extant evidence points to Paul being beheaded in Rome. Why wasn't that fact included at the end of Acts? Consider perhaps that Acts was written before Paul's death. This puts the record of Luke nearly at Jesus' lifetime. Many scholars hold that Matthew was written before Luke.

The Bible clearly points to eyewitnesses thus rejecting the hearsay argument. Also, given that the New Testament contains numerous embarrassing accounts of Jesus's followers. For example, the Corinthian church was deep in sexual sin, Peter fights with Paul, and so forth. One must conclude that it is not a carefully devised fable. Given the explicit historical details and given that have only recently been verified, one can reasonably conclude the New Testament is a historical document not just hearsay.

Case Study 9.1: Bible as Hearsay and Personal Finance

Even ardent atheists are reluctant to suggest the Bible is simply hearsay—a compilation of rumors. If the Bible is simply hearsay, then there is no compelling reason to consider its teaching related to personal finance. We may apply a few proverbs to our leadership approach, but that is about all.

Without a biblical foundation, we simply must take the position of ownership as opposed to stewardship. We would have to look elsewhere for guidance.

We turn now to consider whether the Bible, particularly the New Testament, is just a cleverly devised heresy.

Is the Bible Promoting a Heresy?

Recall a heresy is a belief that is contrary to some religious doctrine. Is the Christian worldview simply a heresy designed to attract folks away from Judaism to Christianity? From the outset, early Christian writers documented that Jesus Christ was born within a Jewish family and sought to fulfill the law.

Matthew 5:17

17"Do not think that I have come to abolish the Law or the Prophets; I have not come to abolish them but to fulfill them."

Without the context of the Old Testament, much of the content of the New Testament is incoherent. Consider the following proclamation of John the Baptist.

John 1:29

29The next day he saw Jesus coming toward him, and said, "Behold, the Lamb of God, who takes away the sin of the world!"

Within Old Testament doctrine, the sacrifice of lambs was to cover sin, not take it away. Thus, John the Baptist's assertion is heretical and deeply incoherent, unless Jesus is the Son of God—a perfect sacrifice for our sins. Jesus himself often asserted claims that would be deemed heretical and were often interpreted as such by those around him.

John 10:30-31

30"I and the Father are one." 31The Jews picked up stones again to stone him.

Jesus routinely asserts claims that seem mythical at best and heretical at worst. C. S. Lewis, an English literature scholar and a person with deep knowledge of mythology, makes the following observation regarding Christianity and myth:

Now as myth transcends thought, Incarnation transcends myth. The heart of Christianity is a myth which is also a fact. The old myth of the Dying God, without ceasing to be myth, comes down from the heaven of legend and imagination to the earth of history. It happens — at a particular date, in a particular place, followed by definable historical consequences. We pass from a Balder or an Osiris, dying nobody knows when or where, to a historical person crucified (it is all in order) under Pontius Pilate. By becoming fact it does not cease to be myth: that is the miracle. I suspect that men have sometimes derived more spiritual sustenance from myths they did not believe than from the religion they professed. To be truly Christian we must both assent to the historical fact and also receive the myth (fact though it has become) with the same imaginative embrace which we accord to all myths. The one is hardly more necessary than the other.[164]

Also, if heretical, why do Luke and Acts contain medical terms typical of physicians? Luke was in fact a physician. Why would you need a physician if crafting a heresy?[165]

Before leaving the charge of hearsay or heresy, a few observations are made regarding manuscript evidence related to the New Testament.

Direct Manuscript Evidence

The New Testament (NT) is one of the best attested historical documents in existence. Here are a few observations:
- John Rylands Library (AD 130) – portions of John. This fragment destroyed a carefully developed theory by Baur that John was not written until about 160 AD.
- Bodmer Papyrus II (AD 150-200) – contains most of John. Sir Frederic G. Kenyon concludes based on this

---

[164] C. S. Lewis, "Myth Became Fact," in *God in the Dock* (Grand Rapids, MI: William B. Eerdmans Publishing Company, 1970), 66–67.

[165] It is beyond our scope to dive deeply into the medical terminology used by Luke. There has been much written on this subject. See, for example, R. J. Knowling, "The Medical Language of St. Luke," *The Biblical World* 20, no. 4 (October 1902): 260–271, https://www.jstor.org/stable/3137396 as well as numerous citations therein.

document and others, "No other ancient book has anything like such early and plentiful testimony to its text, and no unbiased scholar would deny that the text that has come down to us is substantially sound."

- Codex Vaticanus (AD 325-350) – contains nearly all of the Bible.
- Interestingly, there are more than 15,000 existing copies of various ancient versions of the NT. Historically, ancient literature was rarely translated into different languages. The NT has shown up in Syriac, Greek, and Latin. (The desire to share this good news compelled Christians to translate.)
- Syriac Versions – believed to have been produced around 150-200 AD. There are now more than 350 extant manuscripts today from the 400's in the ancient Syriac language.
- Latin Versions – "E. A. Lowe shows paleographical marks of it having been copied from a second century papyrus" (Codex Babbiensis which is in old Latin). Jerome produced the Latin Vulgate between AD 366-384.

Indirect Manuscript Evidence from Early Church Leaders

An interesting source of information is quotes from early church leaders. These writings, according to J. Harold Greenlee, " ... are so extensive that the NT could virtually be reconstructed without the use of NT MS."[166] Sir David Dalrymple claims to have found all but eleven verses referenced.[167]

There were many early church leaders, including Clement of Rome (AD 95) (appointed by Peter), Tertullian (AD 160–220), and Irenaeus (AD 130–202). Irenaeus claims he "... had the preaching of the Apostles still echoing in his ears and their doctrine in front of his eyes." Irenaeus quotes from Matthew,

---

[166] See Josh McDowell, *Evidence That Demands a Verdict*, Revised Edition, Volume 1, (San Bernardino, CA: Here's Life Publishers, Inc., 1986), 50.
[167] Ibid.

Mark, Luke, Acts, 1 Corinthians, 1 Peter, Hebrews, and Titus. Tertullian quotes the NT more than 7,000 times, where 3,800 of which are from the Gospels.

Ignatius (AD 70-11) quotes from Matthew, John, Acts, Romans and eleven other NT books. Others who quote from the NT include Polycarp (AD 70-156) (a disciple of John), Barnabas (AD 70), Hermas (AD 95), Tatian (AD 170), Clement of Alexandria (AD 150-212) (2,400 of his quotes are from all but three books of NT), Hippolytus (AD 170-235) (1,300 references to NT), Justin Martyr (AD 133), Origen (AD 185-254) (compiled more than 6,000 works, quotes NT more than 18,000 times), and Cyprian (died AD 258) (quotes approximately 740 OT and 1,030 NT).

According to Geisler and Nix, "... a brief inventory ... will reveal that there were some 32,000 citations of the NT prior to the time of the Council of Nicea (325 AD) (the time the "higher critics" claimed a heresy developed) ...."[168]

F. E. Peters states that "... the works that made up the Christians' NT were the most frequently copied and widely circulated books of antiquity."[169]

Manuscript evidence includes over 5,300 Greek, over 10,000 Latin Vulgates, over 9,300 other early versions in a variety of languages, and there are over 24,000 total manuscripts of at least portions of the NT which still exist today. *The Iliad* by Homer has only 643 manuscripts, the first complete text dating from the thirteenth century.[170] Further, *The Iliad* is set near the end of the Trojan War but written around 400 years later. This pales in comparison to the New Testament writings.

---

[168] Ibid, 52.
[169] Ibid, 39.
[170] Ibid.

Case Study 9.2: Bible as Heresy and Personal Finance

Heresy implies an explicit effort to conceal the truth. As the resurrection is the central event of all of Christianity, its falsehood would negate the Christology found throughout the entire Bible. The lack of eternality would render Bible-based personal finance pointless.

Fortunately, the abundance of historical documents provides us warrant to reject the heresy argument. The historicity of the Bible gives us confidence in the integrity of its financial teachings.

Summary

In this chapter, the arguments that the Bible is just hearsay or heresy was examined. The hearsay argument is addressed in the Bible itself and rejected. Rather than the New Testament being written in response to a cultural movement, the New Testament was found to be documenting empirically verifiable historical events. Further, the Bible was not just a nasty heresy written to manipulate a cultural movement.

Case Study 1: Problem of Currently Unknown Explanation

Within the vast flow of financial information that travels around each day, there is an unceasing desire for explanation. We have all heard reports like the following: "The stock market was down today 100 points due to comments made by Fed chair." Clearly, the words uttered by the Fed chair did not directly cause stock prices to fall. Rather, a vast number of folks likely processes these comments as well as many other unreported events and concluded that they wanted to sell specific shares of stock. This selling pressure results in the decline in price so buyers can be found to clear the trades.

How can investors develop the capacity to make financial decisions when they know that they do not know all the available market information? One possible solution is to focus more on the investable funds purpose (needs-driven) rather than potential future price movements (view-driven).

Case Study 2: Biblical Integrity and Personal Debt

"Running into debt isn't so bad. It's running into creditors that hurts."[171] There are numerous Bible passages that address personal debt. If the Bible is as it claims to be, God's Word, then heeding its admonitions would be wise. Consider Proverbs 22:7. What is the main insight from this assertion?

Proverbs 22:7
The rich rules over the poor, and the borrower is the slave of the lender.

Case Study 3: Biblical Integrity, Borrowing, and Generosity

"Who was the world's greatest humorist? The person who named future credit card bills, 'easy payments.'"[172] Again, there are numerous Bible passages that address personal debt. Consider Psalm 37:21. What are the main insight from the behavior of the wicked and the righteous? What are the

---

[171]Source lost.
[172]Source lost.

implications for keeping your yearning below your earning related to giving?

Psalm 37:21
The wicked borrows but does not pay back, but the righteous is generous and gives;

References

Primary sources for this material include

Habermas, Gary R., *The Verdict of History*, (Monarch Books, 1990).

Lewis, C. S., *God in the Dock: Essays of Theology and Ethics*, (Grand Rapids, MI: William B. Eerdmans Publishing Company, 1970).

McDowell, Josh, *A Ready Defense: The Best of Josh McDowell*, (Nashville, TN: Thomas Nelson Publishers, 2021).

McDowell, Josh, *Evidence That Demands a Verdict*, Revised Edition, Volumes 1 and 2, (San Bernardino, CA: Here's Life Publishers, Inc., 1986).

McDowell, Josh, *The New Evidence That Demands a Verdict*, (Nashville, TN: Thomas Nelson Publishers, 1999).

Chapter 10. The Bible as History

Learning Objectives

- Explore five key aspects of the Bible: best, inspired, believable, logical, and eternal.
- Review several unique attributes of the Bible within a historical context.

Opening Quote

"The Bible stands like a rock undaunted, through the raging storms of time. Its pages burn with the truth eternal, and they glow with the light sublime." Haldor Lillenas, 1917.

Overview

We briefly explore several unique attributes of the Bible within a historical context. Based on the evidence, the Bible is not hearsay or heresy, rather it is clear and reliable history.

The Bible Is Simply the Best Book

Here are a few interesting facts related to the Bible.

1. The Bible was written over a 1,500 year span and by over forty authors. These authors include Moses, a political leader professionally trained in Egypt, Peter, a fisherman, Amos, a herdsman, Joshua, a military general, Nehemiah, a cupbearer, Daniel, a prime minister, Luke, a doctor, Solomon, a king, Matthew, a tax collector, Paul, a rabbi, and so on.
2. The Bible was written in different places: Moses in the wilderness, Jeremiah in a dungeon, Daniel on a hillside and in a palace, Paul inside prison, Luke while traveling, John on the isle of Patmos, and so on.
3. The Bible was written at different times: David in times of war, Solomon in times of peace. It was written in different moods: some at the height of joy, others in the depths of despair.
4. The Bible was written on three different continents: Asia, Africa, and Europe.
5. The Bible was written in three different languages: Hebrew, Aramaic, and Greek.
6. The Bible covers literally hundreds of controversial subjects. These subjects are addressed in harmony and continuity from Genesis to Revelation.
7. The Bible has one singular theme: God's redemption of man.
8. The Bible is deeply coherent. According to F.F. Bruce, "Any part of the human body can only be properly explained in reference to the whole body. And any part of the Bible can only be properly explained in reference to the whole Bible."[173]
9. The Bible corresponds with empirical observations today. Karl Barth notes, "Take your Bible and take your newspaper, and read both. But interpret newspapers from your Bible."[174]
10. The Bible is the number one best seller of all time. According to Guinness World Records, "Although it is impossible to obtain exact figures, there is little doubt that the Bible is the world's best-selling and most widely distributed book. A survey by the Bible Society concluded that around 2.5 billion copies were printed between 1815 and 1975, but more recent

---

[173] Josh McDowell, *Evidence That Demands a Verdict*, Vol. 1, 17.
[174] See *Time Magazine*, May 1, 1966. Quoted by Pastor Geoff T. Sinibaldo at https://sinibaldo.wordpress.com/2015/03/05/on-barth-the-bible-and-the-newspaper/.

estimates put the number at more than 5 billion."[175] No other book comes anywhere close.

Here's a challenge: take ten authors, all from one walk of life, one generation, one mood, one continent, one language, and read them concerning one controversial topic. Would all these authors agree? What would you have if you did this? You would not get the deep coherence found within the Bible.

Personally, the deep wisdom and insights given in the Bible related to personal finance are astounding. The biblical perspective of wealth management has been personally helpful and has benefited many that have taken Bible-based personal finance classes.[176]

The Bible Is Infallible, Inerrant, and Inspired

Many within the Christian community believe that the Bible was infallible and inerrant in its original draft. Further, many also believe the Bible to be inspired by God. Infallible indicates that it is absolutely trustworthy. Inerrancy indicates that it is absolutely without error.

Case Study 10.1: Logic Applied to Inspiration

Consider the following logic:

Premise> God cannot err and is trustworthy.
Observation> Bible is God's Word.
Conclusion> Bible cannot err and is trustworthy.

Assuming the premise is true, then if one concludes the observation is true, then the conclusion logically follows.

---

[175]See https://www.guinnessworldrecords.com/world-records/best-selling-book-of-non-fiction.
[176]For the detailed curriculum, see http://www.robertebrooks.org/project/personal-finance/.

Admittedly, asserting the Bible is God's Word is a very strong observation; there are no other candidate documents that come anywhere close to it. Since the Bible is inspired by God, what inferences can be made regarding its personal finance claims?

The Bible itself asserts to be inspired or God-breathed.

2 Timothy 3:16

16 All Scripture is breathed out by God and profitable for teaching, for reproof, for correction, and for training in righteousness...

The Apostle Paul states he spoke in words taught by the Spirit.

1 Corinthians 2:13

13 And we impart this in words not taught by human wisdom but taught by the Spirit, interpreting spiritual truths to those who are spiritual.

Frequently, Biblical authors quoted scripture with authority. For example, eighty different times the Bible uses the phrase, "It is written." A few selected verses are given below. For example, when wise men came to Jerusalem from the east, they asked King Herod where the King of the Jews would be born. The religious leaders knew immediately, and their answer is recorded in Matthew 2:5-6.

Matthew 2:5–6

5 They told him, "In Bethlehem of Judea, for so it is written by the prophet: 6 "'And you, O Bethlehem, in the land of Judah, are by no means least among the rulers of Judah; for from you shall come a ruler who will shepherd my people Israel.'"

The religious leaders in Jerusalem who quoted Micah 5:2 understood it to refer to the coming Messiah. Note that Micah was likely written during the last third of the eighth century BC.

Micah 5:2

²But you, O Bethlehem Ephrathah, who are too little to be among the clans of Judah, from you shall come forth for me one who is to be ruler in Israel, whose coming forth is from of old, from ancient days.

We will examine prophesy in more detail in the next chapter. For now, just note that Jesus could not control where he would be born. Jesus quoted the Old Testament as authoritative and historically reliable.

Matthew 4:4

⁴But he answered, "It is written, "'Man shall not live by bread alone, but by every word that comes from the mouth of God.'"

Luke 24:46

⁴⁶and said to them, "Thus it is written, that the Christ should suffer and on the third day rise from the dead..."

Paul also quotes from the Old Testament numerous times as if it were authentic and reliable.

Romans 1:17

¹⁷For in it the righteousness of God is revealed from faith for faith, as it is written, "The righteous shall live by faith."

Jesus said the Old Testament spoke of him.

Luke 24:27

²⁷And beginning with Moses and all the Prophets, he interpreted to them in all the Scriptures the things concerning himself.

Luke 24:44

⁴⁴Then he said to them, "These are my words that I spoke to you while I was still with you, that everything written about me in the Law of Moses and the Prophets and the Psalms must be fulfilled."

John 5:39

³⁹You search the Scriptures because you think that in them you have eternal life; and it is they that bear witness about me,

Hebrews 10:7

⁷"Then I said, 'Behold, I have come to do your will, O God, as it is written of me in the scroll of the book.'"

Jesus said that not even the smallest part of a Hebrew letter could be broken.

Matthew 5:18

¹⁸For truly, I say to you, until heaven and earth pass away, not an iota, not a dot, will pass from the Law until all is accomplished.

The New Testament refers to the written record as the "oracles of God."

Romans 3:2

²Much in every way. To begin with, the Jews were entrusted with the oracles of God.

Hebrews 5:12

¹²For though by this time you ought to be teachers, you need someone to teach you again the basic principles of the oracles of God. You need milk, not solid food...

Writers are warned not to alter words.

Jeremiah 26:2

²"Thus says the LORD: Stand in the court of the LORD's house, and speak to all the cities of Judah that come to worship in the house of the LORD all the words that I command you to speak to them; do not hold back a word."

Revelation 22:18–19

¹⁸I warn everyone who hears the words of the prophecy of this book: if anyone adds to them, God will add to him the plagues described in this book, ¹⁹and if anyone takes away from the words of the book of this prophecy, God will take away his share in the tree of life and in the holy city, which are described in this book.

The Bible Is Believable

The Bible stands as a unique document in several ways. The Bible is unique in its survival through time. The Bible, compared with other ancient writings, has more manuscript evidence than any ten pieces of classical literature combined.

The Bible has withstood vicious attacks of its enemies as no other book. Many have tried to burn it, ban it, discredit it, outlaw it, disprove it, yet the Bible stands. Voltaire, who died in 1778, said that in one hundred years from his time Christianity would be swept from existence and passed into history. What actually happened? Voltaire was swept into history, while the circulation of the Bible continues to grow. Interestingly, only fifty years after Voltaire's death, Voltaire's printing press and his house were used by the Geneva Bible Society to produce Bibles!

The Bible has withstood scholastic attacks like no other document. The "assured results of higher criticism" continue to fall by the wayside, and the Bible stands. For example, the critics use to claim that Moses could not have written the Pentateuch (the first five books of the Bible) because, obviously and clearly, writing was not in existence at the time of Moses. The discovery of the "black stele," which contained the detailed laws of Hammurabi, demonstrated conclusively that writing existed before Moses. Dating methods indicate that the "black stele" was written three centuries before Moses's time. The critics also claimed there were never any Hittites. The results of archaeology have produced hundreds of references overlapping 1,200 years of Hittite civilization.

The Bible is the very foundation of the Christian worldview. As C. S. Lewis notes, "If you see through everything, then everything is transparent. But a wholly transparent world is an invisible world. To 'see through' all things is the same as not to see."[177] The clarity through which the Bible can explain current events and challenges is outstanding.

The Bible Is Very Logical

The following passages indicate that searching, reasoning, and considering the empirical evidence is encouraged.

Ecclesiastes 7:25

> *25I turned my heart to know and to search out and to seek wisdom and the scheme of things, and to know the wickedness of folly and the foolishness that is madness.*

Isaiah 1:18

> *18"Come now, let us reason together, says the LORD: though your sins are like scarlet, they shall be as white as snow; though they are red like crimson, they shall become like wool."*

---

[177]Lewis, *The Abolition of Man*, 91.

Acts 1:3

³He presented himself alive to them after his suffering by many proofs, appearing to them during forty days and speaking about the kingdom of God.

The Greek word for "proofs" in Acts 1:3 is tekmerion meaning signs, indubitable tokens, or clear proofs. There is no other event in ancient history so well documented as the resurrection of Jesus Christ. The resurrection is examined in detail in Chapter 12.

Within personal finance, the Bible is deeply logical. For example, numerous cautions are given related to debt and diversifying is encouraged.

Deuteronomy 28:43–45

⁴³The sojourner who is among you shall rise higher and higher above you, and you shall come down lower and lower. ⁴⁴He shall lend to you, and you shall not lend to him. He shall be the head, and you shall be the tail. ⁴⁵"All these curses shall come upon you and pursue you and overtake you till you are destroyed, because you did not obey the voice of the LORD your God, to keep his commandments and his statutes that he commanded you."

Proverbs 22:7

⁷The rich rules over the poor, and the borrower is the slave of the lender.

Ecclesiastes 11:1–5

¹Cast your bread upon the waters, for you will find it after many days. ²Give a portion to seven, or even to eight, for you know not what disaster may happen on earth. ³If the clouds are full of rain, they empty themselves on the earth, and if a tree falls to the south or to the north, in the place where the tree falls, there it will lie. ⁴He who observes the wind will not sow, and he who regards the clouds will not reap. ⁵As you do not know the way the spirit comes to the bones in the womb of a woman with child, so you do not know the work of God who makes everything.

The Bible Is Eternal

The Bible asserts itself to be an everlasting document.

2 Peter 3:10
¹⁰But the day of the Lord will come like a thief, and then the heavens will pass away with a roar, and the heavenly bodies will be burned up and dissolved, and the earth and the works that are done on it will be exposed.

Psalm 119:89
⁸⁹Forever, O LORD, your word is firmly fixed in the heavens.

Luke 21:33
³³"Heaven and earth will pass away, but my words will not pass away."
See also Matthew 24:35 and Mark 13:31.

Bible as History and Personal Finance

The key financial insight here is that the true worldview implemented leads to human flourishing. We cannot live on hearsay or heresy, but a true and living history is a completely different matter. After forty years of wandering and being attended to by God, the Israelites knew the importance of God's word.

Deuteronomy 8:3
³And he humbled you and let you hunger and fed you with manna, which you did not know, nor did your fathers know, that he might make you know that man does not live by bread alone,

but man lives by every word that comes from the mouth of the LORD.

Jesus picks up on this during His first temptation in the wilderness.

Matthew 4:1–4

¹Then Jesus was led up by the Spirit into the wilderness to be tempted by the devil. ²And after fasting forty days and forty nights, he was hungry. ³And the tempter came and said to him, "If you are the Son of God, command these stones to become loaves of bread." ⁴But he answered, "It is written, "'Man shall not live by bread alone, but by every word that comes from the mouth of God.'"
See also Luke 4:1–4.

After feeding the 5,000 and walking on water, Jesus declares clearly that God's living word is nourishment enough for life's challenges including financial struggles.

John 6:35

³⁵Jesus said to them, "I am the bread of life; whoever comes to me shall not hunger, and whoever believes in me shall never thirst."

Real human flourishing comes from working within reality wherein we are placed. Figure 10.1 illustrates a fish in water. Clearly, if the fish sought to survive on land, it would die even though an abundance of food is all around. Rejecting the God-infused reality of life around us will eventually cause significant damage.

Figure 10.1 Illustration of Fish Working within Its Environment[178]

As followers of Jesus, we were meant to do more than just survive in the living water and with the bread of life. We were meant to soar as illustrated in Figure 10.2. As eagles catch the thermal drafts to soar so we too should entrust our lives to the living God by believing in Jesus and feasting on His precious Word.

Figure 10.2 Illustration of Soaring within Its Environment[179]

---

[178]Photo by Will Turner on Unsplash. Accessed October 23, 2024.
[179]Photo by Mathew Schwartz on Unsplash. Accessed October 23, 2024.

Case Study 10.2: "The Bible Stands"

In 1917, Haldor Lillenas wrote the lyrics to a simple, yet clear, song related to the Bible as history. The last five sections form an acrostic of BIBLE.

The Bible Stands
Haldor Lillenas, 1917
The Bible stands like a rock undaunted,
through the raging storms of time.
Its pages burn with the truth eternal,
and they glow with the light sublime.

The Bible stands every test we give it,
for its author is divine.
By faith alone I accept to live it,
and to know it and make it mine.

The Bible stands though the rocks may tumble,
it will firmly stand though the earth may crumble.
I will plant my feet on its firm foundation,
for the Bible stands.

As previously mentioned, one cannot live based on hearsay or heresy. The historicity of the Bible lends support for planting our family squarely on it through faith in Jesus Christ.

Summary

Several unique attributes of the Bible were explored within a historical context. Based on the valid data, significant evidence was shown that the Bible is not hearsay or heresy, rather it is clear and reliable history. What remains is whether you plant your feet on the Bible's firm foundation or not. The choice is yours.

Case Study 1: Founding Documents

Consider the following statements from Declaration of Independence (July 4, 1776 version) in the United States of America and the Preamble to the Constitution of the People's Republic of China (March 14, 2004 version).

Declaration of Independence Quote

> We hold these truths to be self-evident, that all men are created equal, that they are endowed by their Creator with certain unalienable Rights, that among these are Life, Liberty and the pursuit of Happiness.[180]

Preamble to the Constitution of the People's Republic of China Quote

> After waging protracted and arduous struggles, armed and otherwise, along a zigzag course, the Chinese people of all nationalities led by the Communist Party of China with Chairman Mao Zedong as its leader ultimately, in 1949, overthrew the rule of imperialism, feudalism and bureaucrat-capitalism, won a great victory .... Since then the Chinese people have taken control of state power and become masters of the country.
>
> After the founding of the People's Republic, China gradually achieved its transition from a New-Democratic to a socialist society. The socialist transformation of the private ownership of the means of production has been completed, the system of exploitation of man by man abolished and the socialist system established.[181]

Compare and contrast these two foundations regarding their theological roots and philosophical foundations.

---

[180]Declaration of Independence, July 4, 1776.
[181]Preamble to the Constitution of the People's Republic of China (March 14, 2004 version) available at http://www.npc.gov.cn/zgrdw/englishnpc/Constitution/2007-11/15/content_1372962.htm.

Case Study 2: Jefferson County, Alabama Sewage Problem

To settle lawsuits over raw sewage dumped into the Black Warrior and Cahaba rivers, Jefferson County in 1996 entered a consent decree whereby the county agreed to begin a twelve-year, $1.5 billion upgrade of its wastewater system.

1. If you were the advisor to Jefferson County, how would you determine the optimal amount of debt?
    a. $0
    b. $0.5 billion
    c. $1.0 billion
    d. $1.5 billion
    e. Other

Appraise the county's decision to borrow $1.5 billion. "An interest-rate swap gives the county the flexibility to time the market by hopping in and out of the variable rate liability as short-term interest rates rise and fall," according to the Jefferson County Finance Director.

2. Appraise this perspective related to forecasting rates considering James 4:13–17.

James 4:13–17

[13]Come now, you who say, "Today or tomorrow we will go into such and such a town and spend a year there and trade and make a profit" — [14]yet you do not know what tomorrow will bring. What is your life? For you are a mist that appears for a little time and then vanishes. [15]Instead you ought to say, "If the Lord wills, we will live and do this or that." [16]As it is, you boast in your arrogance. All such boasting is evil. [17]So whoever knows the right thing to do and fails to do it, for him it is sin.

Case Study 3: Borrowing Under the Old Testament Law

According to Moses in Deuteronomy, is Shakespeare's admonition, "Neither a borrower nor lender be" correct?

Deuteronomy 15:6

> [6]For the LORD your God will bless you, as he promised you, and you shall lend to many nations, but you shall not borrow, and you shall rule over many nations, but they shall not rule over you.

Deuteronomy 28:12

> [12] The LORD will open to you his good treasury, the heavens, to give the rain to your land in its season and to bless all the work of your hands. And you shall lend to many nations, but you shall not borrow.

References

Primary sources for this material include:

Gary R. Habermas, *The Verdict of History*, (Monarch Books, 1990).

Josh McDowell, *Evidence That Demands a Verdict*, Revised Edition, Volumes 1, (San Bernardino, CA: Here's Life Publishers, Inc., 1986).

Chapter 11. Miracles

Learning Objectives

- Define and explain miracles.
- Illustrate the deep coherence of recorded miracles.
- Explore prophesy as supporting the Christian worldview.

Opening Quote

Luke 18:27
[27]*But he said, "What is impossible with man is possible with God."*

Overview

Miracles are a source of much consternation by Biblical critics. The sheer force used to nitpick details is indicative of a worldview on the ropes. In this chapter, miracles are carefully defined focusing on the Biblical definition. The motivation of the documented miracles in the Gospel According to John are shown to demonstrate how miracles primarily serve as a sign. Further, a deep dive into one of Daniel's prophesies is explored and the chapter concludes by listing several prophesies related to Jesus Christ.

Miracles Defined

Miracles are often defined as violations of natural law. Natural laws are typically scientific generalizations based on numerous empirical observations. The Bible makes no such definition.

Miracles in the Bible are defined simply as mighty acts. What distinguishes miracles from natural law is purely a man-made distinction. Consider the following logical approaches to miracles depending on one's worldview.

Atheist Claim

Assume an atheist here is simply a non-theist, someone who does not have a belief in deities.
Premise: Miracles occur only if it can be conclusively demonstrated that the event was not caused by any presently known or unknown natural law.
Observation: We do not know all presently unknown natural laws.
Conclusion: Miracles cannot be proven to occur.

Weak Theist Claim

Premise: Miracles occur only if it can be conclusively demonstrated that the event was not caused by any presently known natural law.
Observation: We observe an apparent violation of known natural laws.
Conclusion: Miracles are proven to occur.

Strong Theist Claim

Premise: Miracles are certainly possible.
Observation: The Bible presents reliable, eyewitness accounts, clear prophecies, extra-Biblical evidence supports the existence of miracles, and I have personally experienced miracles.

Conclusion: Therefore, miracles occur, and my belief that they occur is perfectly rational.

Note that defining miracles as mighty acts of God allows for God's intervention without necessarily violating current human conceptions of natural laws. In no way does this definition explain away all miracles. By any account, the very first verse in the Bible is miraculous.

Genesis 1:1

1In the beginning, God created the heavens and the earth.

Any rational human would realize that if the first verse turns out to be true, then every other recorded miracle would be rather trivial to the universe's creator. From Isaiah, God actively created all things on the earth and continues that creative activity to this day.

Isaiah 42:5

5Thus says God, the Lord, who created the heavens and stretched them out, who spread out the earth and what comes from it, who gives breath to the people on it and spirit to those who walk in it...

The heart of the Bible is the gospel of Jesus Christ. Paul records it this way.

1 Corinthians 15:1–6

1Now I would remind you, brothers, of the gospel I preached to you, which you received, in which you stand, 2and by which you are being saved, if you hold fast to the word I preached to you — unless you believed in vain. 3For I delivered to you as of first importance what I also received: that Christ died for our sins in accordance with the Scriptures, 4that he was buried, that he was raised on the third day in accordance with the Scriptures, 5and that he appeared to Cephas, then to the twelve. 6Then he appeared to more than five hundred brothers at one time, most of whom are still alive, though some have fallen asleep.

Note the appeal to empirical evidence when writing to the Corinthian church. This is not some contrived philosophy, rather tactile and evidentiary. Seven miracles recorded in the Gospel According to John are examined. It is important to note that there is only one gospel; however, there are four accounts of it given in the first four books of the New Testament (Matthew, Mark, Luke, and John). Ezekiel, when describing the glory of the Lord, writes about four living creatures each with four faces.

Ezekiel 1:10

[10]As for the likeness of their faces, each had a human face. The four had the face of a lion on the right side, the four had the face of an ox on the left side, and the four had the face of an eagle.

One view of the four accounts of the gospel is related to Ezekiel's vision. Matthew depicts Jesus as the King of the Jews (lion), Mark depicts Jesus as a suffering servant (ox), Luke depicts Jesus as human, and John depicts Jesus as a heavenly King (eagle). Whether intentional or not, it is a useful aid in understanding the four accounts of the gospel. The seven miracles in the Gospel According to John are now presented.

Miracles Recorded in the Gospel According to John

Jesus did many things that were interpreted at the time as miraculous. John only records seven major miracles or signs. Why? Although it may never know for sure, here one explanation is presented. John explains to us why these signs were recorded.

John 20:30–31

30Now Jesus did many other signs in the presence of the disciples, which are not written in this book; 31but these are written so that you may believe that Jesus is the Christ, the Son of God, and that by believing you may have life in his name.

It is important to note the role of a sign. Figure 11.1 provides a humorous example. Now upon seeing this road sign, it is understandable to pull over, take pictures, and have a chuckle or two. Clearly, that is not the purpose of this sign; however, this sign is pointing to something of significance. Apparently, at this location, cows do sometimes slip off the cliffs above and may fall on cars. In the Gospel According to John, these signs were recorded so that you may entrust your life to Jesus Christ and conjoin into a deeply fulfilling relationship with God.

Figure 11.1 Illustration of Sign's Role[182]

---

[182]See https://www.roadtrafficsigns.com/caution-falling-cows-funny-road-sign/sku-k-9916. Accessed October 23, 2024.

In the same way, it is important not to fixate on miracles only to completely miss the sign's intention. Table 11.1 presents the seven signs aligned with the seven declarations Jesus made regarding himself. For example, in John 2:1–11 the first recorded sign is Jesus turning water into wine. We could fixate on the exact physical mechanism Jesus used to produce this miracle, contrive some sort of explanation of his trickery, or even explain why some writer made up this story. Alternatively, we could seek to understand what the sign was pointing toward. Later in John, Jesus declared that he was the true vine, and that genuine life was found in him. (See John 15:1ff.) Pastor Adrian Rogers further aligns these seven signs with God's potential purposes, such as providing joy for your disappointments.

Table 11.1 Seven Signs in the Gospel According to John

Jesus Christ is God's ...:[183]	Physical Miracle	Jesus Christ's "I am ..."
Joy for your disappointments	Water to wine, 2:1–11	True vine, 15:1
Assurance for your doubts	Nobleman's son healed, 4:46–54	Way, truth, and life, 14:6
Strength for your disabilities	Invalid at the pool, 5:1–16	Good shepherd, 10:11
Satisfaction for your desire	Feeding of 5,000, 6:1–13	Bread of life, 6:35
Peace for your despair	Storm at sea, 6:15–21	The door, 10:7
Light for your darkness	Blind man sees, 9:1–7	Light of the world, 8:12
Life for your death	Dead man lives, 11:1–46	Resurrection and life, 11:25

If you take the time to work through these seven signs, you will see a deep coherence within the Bible that is very

---

[183]Column one based on Adrian Rogers, *Believe in Miracles but Trust in Jesus* (Wheaton, IL: Crossway, 1997). All references in this table are to verses in the Gospel According to John, New Testament, Bible.

difficult to simply explain away. Let us turn to prophesy and consider whether it is simply coincidence or a mighty act of God.

Prophecy

Throughout history there have been various claims of prophetic utterances allegedly supporting some person or cause. Prophecy in this context is simply a prediction, whereas prophesy says that a specific thing will happen.

As seen above, there are numerous prophesies that actually were fulfilled by Jesus Christ. Jesus explains that these prophesies were related to him when speaking to the two disciples on the road to Emmaus.

Luke 24:27

> [27]*And beginning with Moses and all the Prophets, he interpreted to them in all the Scriptures the things concerning himself.*

Peter in his sermon to the Gentiles expresses the same idea.

Acts 10:42–43

> [42]*"And he commanded us to preach to the people and to testify that he is the one appointed by God to be judge of the living and the dead.* [43]*To him all the prophets bear witness that everyone who believes in him receives forgiveness of sins through his name."*

Often Jesus spoke in parables that lacked concreteness, frustrating some of his followers. Jesus indicates that it is intentional.

Matthew 13:10–12

> [10] Then the disciples came and said to him, "Why do you speak to them in parables?" [11] And he answered them, "To you it has been given to know the secrets of the kingdom of heaven, but to them it has not been given. [12] For to the one who has, more will be given, and he will have an abundance, but from the one who has not, even what he has will be taken away.

If prophesies like parables are not clear, then perhaps prophesy fulfillment is simply random chance. Let us examine this claim carefully.

Case Study 11.1: Prophesy Fulfillment as Random Chance

Suppose prophecy follows a binomial distribution (fulfilled, not fulfilled) with a probability, p, of fulfillment. Most biblical scholars have identified at least 25 prophecies fulfilled regarding the betrayal, trial, death, and burial of Jesus Christ all of which were fulfilled in one 24-hour period. There are 109 fulfilled prophecies concerning the first coming of Jesus Christ. If we assume the probability of fulfillment is 50% ($p = 1/2$), is it possible that these fulfillments were just by chance?

If $p = 1/2$, then $(1/2)^{25} = 2.98 \times 10^{-8}$ or 1-in-33,554,432.

If $p = 1/2$, then $(1/2)^{109} = 1.54 \times 10^{-33}$ 1-in-649,037,107,316,853,453,566,312,041,152,512.

The odds of this set of events happening by chance is the same chance of picking a particular flea at random from one of 87 billion fleas on each of 87 billion dogs owned by each of 87 billion people (population of 20 earths). Rationally there must be a better explanation. One obvious explanation is that the Bible is simply a God-directed love letter that includes prophecies that empirically validate its authenticity.

We now turn to a single prophecy.

What Day Would the Messiah Be Executed?

Although this prophecy has numerous interpretations, regardless one ends up very near the day of Jesus Christ's death.

Daniel 9:25–26

>25*Know therefore and understand that from the going out of the word to restore and build Jerusalem to the coming of an anointed one, a prince, there shall be seven weeks. Then for sixty-two weeks it shall be built again with squares and moat, but in a troubled time.* 26*And after the sixty-two weeks, an anointed one shall be cut off and shall have nothing. And the people of the prince who is to come shall destroy the city and the sanctuary. Its end shall come with a flood, and to the end there shall be war. Desolations are decreed.*

The Hebrew word for week is (Strong's # 7620) shabuwa` (shaw-boo'-ah) literally, sevened, i.e., a week (specifically, of years): KJV— seven, week.[184] In context, this same word indicates years.

Genesis 29:27–28

>27*"Complete the week of this one, and we will give you the other also in return for serving me another seven years."* 28*Jacob did so, and completed her week. Then Laban gave him his daughter Rachel to be his wife.*

The prediction in Daniel 9:1 was given in 539–538 BC. Daniel 9:25 states the initiating event was the order to restore and rebuild Jerusalem. This order is given in Nehemiah 2 dated as March 14, 445 BC. Let's do some math:

- 69 "weeks" = 69 x 7 = 483 years after the initiating event.

---

[184]There is a numbering system for every word in the Bible. Hence, Strong's number 7620 is helpful to find other uses of this exact same word.

- A prophetic year is 360 days. (See Daniel 7:25, 12:7, Revelation 12:14; 11:2, 13:5; 11:3, 12:6.)
- 483 years x 360 days/year = 173,880 days.
- Gregorian calendar days (365 days/year + leap-years).
- March 14, 445 BC to March 13, AD 32 = (445 years + 32 years − 1 year) x 365 = 173,740 days (ignoring leap-years).
- March 14, AD 32 to April 6, AD 32 = 24 days.
- Leap-year rule: Year/4 = yes, year/100 = no, and year/400 = yes.
- 445 BC to AD 32 implies 119 possible leap years.
- Years 300 BC, 200 BC, and 100 BC are not leap-years, but year 400 BC is.
- Total days between March 14, 445 to April 6, AD 32 = 173,740 + 24 + 119 − 3 = 173,880.

There are several concerns with this calculation that have been given over the years. These concerns miss the main point. Regardless of how this prediction is interpreted, Jesus Christ is the only representative that came anywhere close to fulfilling this prediction. There is no other.

We present an alternative explanation. Can we confirm the start date for the prophecy which calculates the date on which Jesus presented himself as Messiah in Daniel 9:25? In the fifth century B.C. a Hebrew named Nehemiah, then cup bearer to the Medo-Persian king Artaxerxes, wrote of the command to restore and rebuild Jerusalem.

Nehemiah 2:1–2

¹In the month of Nisan, in the twentieth year of King Artaxerxes, when wine was before him, I took up the wine and gave it to the king. Now I had not been sad in his presence. ²And the king said to me, "Why is your face sad, seeing you are not sick? This is nothing but sadness of the heart." Then I was very much afraid.

Nehemiah went on to explain that he was sad because he had heard reports that the city of his people, Jerusalem, was still desolate. Nehemiah requested that he be allowed to go back to

Jerusalem and rebuild the city. King Artaxerxes granted his wish on the spot and gave him official documents for easy passage. This occurred, we are told in the month of Nisan, in the twentieth year of Artaxerxes Longimanus's reign.

Artaxerxes Longimanus ascended to the throne of the Medo-Persian empire in July 465 BC.[185] The twentieth year of his reign would have begun in July 446 BC. The decree occurred approximately nine months later in the month of Nisan (March/April on our calendar). By Hebrew tradition when the day of the month is not specifically stated (as in Artaxerxes decree), it is given to be the first day of that month. Consequently, the very day of Artaxerxes' decree was the first day of the Hebrew month Nisan in 445 BC. The first day of Nisan in 445 BC corresponds to the fourteenth day of March. These dates were confirmed through astronomical calculations at the British Royal Observatory and reported by Sir Robert Anderson.[186]

The prophecy states that 69 weeks of years (173,880 days using the 360 day prophetic year) after the command goes forth to restore and rebuild the city of Jerusalem the Messiah will come. If we count forward 173,880 days from March 14, 445 BC, we arrive at April 6, AD 32.

How could Daniel, writing in 537 BC, have known this in advance? How could anyone contrive to have this prediction documented over five centuries in advance?

There is in fact, another way to check the accuracy of this date. In the Gospel According to Luke, chapter three, it states that in the fifteenth year of the reign of Caesar Tiberius, Jesus was baptized by John the Baptist and began his ministry. It is well established that the reign of Caesar Tiberius began with his coronation on August 19th in the year AD 14.[187] Most scholars believe Jesus was baptized in the fall season. It therefore follows that the ministry of Jesus started with his baptism in the Fall of AD 28, the fifteenth year of reign of Caesar Tiberius. The day that a Roman ruler ascends the throne begins his first year. The

---

[185] Encyclopedia Britannica, 1990 ed.
[186] Robert Anderson, *The Coming Prince* (Grand Rapids, MI: Kregel, 1984).
[187] The Encyclopedia Britannica, 1990. Micropedia.

ministry of Jesus spanned four Passovers or about three and one half years.

The first Passover of Jesus' ministry would have been in the spring of AD 29. The fourth Passover of His ministry was the day of his crucifixion and would have fallen in the year AD 32. The Passover in that year fell on April 10. The Passover holiday always occurs on the fourteenth day of Nisan in the Hebrew calendar. This corresponds to the first full moon after the spring equinox. Remarkably, according to Robert Anderson and the British Royal Observatory, the Sunday before that Passover was April 6, the very day that Jesus presents himself as King and exactly 173,880 days after the decree of Artaxerxes.

According to the principles of biblical higher criticism, this prophecy proves that the book of Daniel was written after the Gospel According to Luke. This is, of course, absurd because Daniel was translated into Greek (the Septuagint) nearly three centuries before Jesus was even born.

This prophecy is one of the most astonishing proofs that God transcends time and can see the end from the beginning with incredible precision. Here are numerous other prophecies regarding Jesus Christ given in the Bible. Like in a court of law, it is easy to nitpick with details of each prophecy. Given the sheer volume of prophecies, nitpicking really starts to look as if one does not want to be persuaded by evidence.[188]

List of Prophesies

Prophecy Given	Prophecy Fulfilled	Comments
Daniel 9:25-26	Luke 23:54	Day of Messiah's Death
Genesis 3:15	Luke 23:33	Messiah's foot will be injured, seed of a woman
Isaiah 53	Luke 23	Numerous references to Messiah's abuse and death
Isaiah 50:6	Matthew 26:67	Messiah is beaten
Micah 5:1	Luke 22:63	Messiah is slapped in face

---

[188]Within the finance academic disciple, there is a pressing concern of selection bias. In this case, one may argue that the Bible as we know it today was selected in response to various books having fulfilled prophesies. The historical record simply does not permit selection bias as being a reasonable explanation.

Exploring the Philosophical Roots that Influence Financial Fruit

Psalm 22:16	Luke 23:33	Messiah's hands pierced
Zechariah 12:10	Luke 23:48-49	People mourn Messiah's death
Psalm 34:20	John 19:33	No bones are broken
Psalm 22:14	John 19:33-34	Poured out like water, bones out of joint
Genesis 12:1-3	Matthew 1:1, Galatians 3:8,16	Messiah lineage of Abraham
Genesis 17:19, 21:2	Luke 3:23,34, Romans 4:18ff	Messiah lineage of Isaac
Numbers 24:17	Matthew 1:2	Messiah lineage of Jacob
Genesis 49:10	Luke 3:33, Matthew 25:31-2	Messiah lineage of Judah
Ezekiel 21:27	Various	Israel will have no king until Jesus
Genesis 49:10	Luke 2:14, Romans 5:1	Shiloh = peace, Messiah shall bring peace
Isaiah 11:1, 10	Luke 3:23,32	Messiah lineage of Jesse
Jeremiah 23:5, 2 Samuel 7:12-16, Psalm 132:11	Luke 3:23, 31, Matthew 1:1, 9:27, Revelation 22:16	Messiah lineage of David
Micah 5:2	Luke 2:4	Messiah born in Bethlehem
Psalm 69:21	Matthew 27:34,48, John 19:28ff	Gall and vinegar
Isaiah 9:7	Luke 1:32,33	Heir to throne of David
Isaiah 7:14	Luke 1:26,27, 30, 31	Born of a virgin
Jeremiah 31:15	Matthew 2:16-18	Slaughter of children
Hosea 11:1	Matthew 2:14-15	Flight to Egypt
Isaiah 40:3-5	Luke 3:3-6	The way shall be prepared
Malachi 3:1	Luke 7:24, 27	Preceded by a forerunner
Malachi 4:5-6	Matthew 11:13-14	Preceded by Elijah
Psalm 2:7	Matthew 3:17	Declared the Son of God
Isaiah 9:1	Matthew 4:13-16	Galilean ministry
Psalm 78:2-4	Matthew 13:34, 35	Speak in parables
Deuteronomy 18:15	Acts 31:20,22	A prophet
Isaiah 61:1	Luke 4:18-19	Bind up the brokenhearted
Isaiah 53:3	John 1:11, Luke 23:18	Rejected by the Jews
Psalm 110:4	Hebrews 5:5, 6	Priest after the order of Melchizedek
Zechariah 9:9	Mark 11:7-11	Triumphal entry
Psalm 8:2	Matthew 21:15, 16	Adored by infants
Isaiah 53:1	John 12:37,38	Not believed
Psalm 41:9	Luke 22:47,48	Betrayed by a close friend
Zechariah 11:12	Matthew 26:14,15	Betrayed for thirty pieces of silver
Psalm 35:11	Mark 14:57,58	Accused by false witnesses
Psalm 35:19	John 15:24,25	Hated without reason
Isaiah 53:12	Mark 15:27,28	Crucified with malefactors
Psalm 22:7,8	Luke 23:35	Sneered and mocked
Psalm 69:9	Romans 15:3	Was reproached
Psalm 109:4	Luke 23:34	Prayer for His enemies
Psalm 22:17	Matthew 27:35,36	Soldiers gambled for His clothing
Psalm 22:1	Matthew 27:46	Forsaken by God
Isaiah 53:9	Matthew 27:57-60	Buried with the rich
Psalm 16:10, 49:15	Mark 16:6-7	To be resurrected
Psalm 68:18	Mark 16:19, 1 Corinthians 15:4	His ascension to God's right hand

Case Study 11.2: Miracles and Personal Finance

Recall that miracles in the Bible are defined simply as mighty acts. Thus, we should not be surprised at all that God works mightily in the affairs of His ambassadors. As we seek first His kingdom and engage in God's disciple-making business, it is not shocking to observe direct, tangible, God-given provisions.

The challenge is simple: Go find a disciple-making follower of Jesus and simply ask them if they believe God has ever provided for them in a miraculous way. In my experience, they will immediately point to several unique God-given provisions.

Interestingly, often the miraculous activity is financial in nature. God provides just in time as indicated in Philippians 4:19.

Philippians 4:19

> [19]*And my God will supply every need of yours according to his riches in glory in Christ Jesus.*

Summary

In this chapter, miracles are defined simply as a mighty act of God. Clearly, if God created the universe, then everything else is rather elementary. The potential motivation for the documented miracles in the Gospel According to John was shown to demonstrate how miracles primarily serve as a sign. A deep dive was taken into one of Daniel's prophesies and concluded by listing several prophesies related to Jesus Christ.

Case Study 1: Bible as a Best Seller

"According to Guinness World Records as of 1995, the Bible is the best-selling book of all time with an estimated 5 billion copies sold and distributed. Sales estimates for other printed religious texts include at least 800 million copies for the Qur'an and 190 million copies for the Book of Mormon. Also, a single publisher has produced more than 140 million copies of the Bhagavad Gita. The total number could be much higher. Among non-religious texts, the Quotations from Chairman Mao Tse-tung, also known as the Little Red Book, has produced a wide array of sales and distribution figures—with estimates ranging from 800 million to over 6.5 billion printed volumes."[189]

1) Why has the Bible been removed from bestselling lists?
2) What does the sheer quantities of sold Bibles suggest about human nature?

Case Study 2: When to Take Social Security[190]

The decision of when to take social security is personal and unique for everyone. Every year you defer after age sixty-two increases your benefit by about 7%. A 7% risk-free return is a good one, but it also involves life expectancy. Based strictly on the present value of expected benefit, age sixty-two is best if you live up to age eighty-three. From age eighty-three to eighty-six, one is better off having started at sixty-six. If you live past eighty-six, one is better off having started at seventy.

1. What are the most critical issues when making this decision?

---

[189] See https://en.wikipedia.org/wiki/List_of_best-selling_books.
[190] See https://www.ssa.gov/oact/cola/examplemax.html for more details.

Exploring the Philosophical Roots that Influence Financial Fruit

2. How does one's worldview impact the decision on when to take social security?

Worker with steady earnings at the maximum level since age 22

Retirement in Jan.	Retirement at age 62 [a]			Retirement at age 65 [b]			Retirement at age 66 [c]			Retirement at age 67 [d]			Retirement at age 70 [e]		
		Monthly benefits			Monthly benefits			Monthly benefits			Monthly benefits			Monthly benefits	
	AIME	Initial	In 2023	AIME	Initial	In 2023	AIME	Initial	In 2023	AIME	Initial	In 2023	AIME	Initial	In 2023
2021	11,098	2,324	2,675	10,074	2,841	3,270	9,979	3,113	3,583	9,704	3,306	3,806	9,150	3,895	4,484
2022	11,430	2,364	2,569	10,437	2,993	3,253	10,141	3,240	3,522	10,049	3,568	3,879	9,446	4,194	4,559
2023	12,427	2,572	2,572	10,824	3,279	3,279	10,503	3,506	3,506	10,217	3,808	3,808	9,628	4,555	4,555

Biblically, this and many other financial decisions should not be based on what is best for me; rather, it should be based on what is best for my family and those who may have to care for me during the sunset years.

Case Study 3: Debt and Personal Financial Decision-Making

Suppose a young family covenants to no longer take on new debts and seeks to pay off all existing debts over time. What do you suppose are the common consequences? Having witnessed decisions such as this one over many decades, a few common threads have appeared. Here are some selected observations:

1) It will be extremely hard, especially in the early years.
2) The family's materialistic desires will moderate, and personal financial decisions will increase in prudence as well as wisdom.
3) The family will increase in their generosity as the ever-present materialism attraction abates.
4) The family is better able to focus on the Great Commission and their particular God-called role.

References

Anderson, Robert, *The Coming Prince* (Grand Rapids, MI: Kregel, 1984).

Access Jesus, *List of Miracles Recorded in the Old Testament Bible*, (August 14, 2016), online. Downloaded on September 23, 2018, source apparently no longer available. Numerous lists are widely available online, however.

Creation Studies Institute, *Miracles of the Bible*, Creation Studies Institute, Accessed September 23, 2018 (apparently no longer available, see https://creationstudies.org/). Taken from Henry M. Morris, *The Biblical Basis for Modern Science*, (Grand Rapids, MI: Baker Book House, 1984).

Rogers, Adrian, *Believe in Miracles but Trust in Jesus* (Wheaton, IL: Crossway, 1997).

Chapter 12. Resurrection of Jesus Christ

Learning Objectives

- Explore Jesus's claims regarding his own resurrection.
- Ponder twelve compelling reasons favoring the resurrection of Jesus Christ.
- Introduce Bayes's Theorem and apply it to selected evidence related to the resurrection of Jesus Christ.
- Review Pascal's Wager as a decision framework for appraising probabilities assigned to the resurrection of Jesus Christ.

Opening Quote

Matthew 28:6
⁶"He is not here, for he has risen, as he said. Come, see the place where he lay."

Overview

In this chapter, details of the physical bodily resurrection of Jesus Christ is examined. First, exactly what did Jesus Christ claimed he would do. Second, twelve compelling reasons are identified to believe that Jesus Christ did rise bodily from the grave. Third, just for fun a mathematical dive into Bayes's Theorem is presented (yes, rather technical) and explore applying it to the resurrection of Jesus Christ. Finally, Pascal's Wager is presented as a decision framework for appraising the resulting probabilities from applying Bayes's Theorem.

Jesus's Claim

Before taking into consideration the empirical evidence favoring the physical bodily resurrection of Jesus Christ, it is essential to understand clearly what Jesus Christ said about himself and his mission. Let us start with a very unusual assertion by John the Baptist.

John 1:29–34

29The next day he [John the Baptist] saw Jesus coming toward him, and said, "Behold, the Lamb of God, who takes away the sin of the world! 30This is he of whom I said, 'After me comes a man who ranks before me, because he was before me.' 31I myself did not know him, but for this purpose I came baptizing with water, that he might be revealed to Israel." 32And John bore witness: "I saw the Spirit descend from heaven like a dove, and it remained on him. 33I myself did not know him, but he who sent me to baptize with water said to me, 'He on whom you see the Spirit descend and remain, this is he who baptizes with the Holy Spirit.' 34And I have seen and have borne witness that this is the Son of God."

In John 1:29 above, a clear statement is given that John the Baptist believed Jesus to be the "Lamb of God." In Hebrew culture, it was understood that lambs are sacrificed to cover sins. John indicates that this lamb would be different. He "takes away the sin of the world!" Now consider the outrageous assertion by Jesus Christ found in John 10:30.

John 10:30

30"I and the Father are one."

Here, Jesus clearly identifies himself as God. Amazingly, some people try to reinterpret this verse giving it a false understanding. The people who heard Jesus make this declaration clearly understood, for they sought to kill him for blasphemy.

Jesus clearly predicted that he would suffer and be killed as illustrated below in Mark 8:31. He also clearly stated that he would be resurrected.

Mark 8:31

31And he began to teach them that the Son of Man must suffer many things and be rejected by the elders and the chief priests and the scribes and be killed, and after three days rise again.

In Matthew 27:63 below, the leaders in Jerusalem understood what Jesus asserted concerning his own resurrection.

Matthew 27:62–66

62The next day, that is, after the day of Preparation, the chief priests and the Pharisees gathered before Pilate 63and said, "Sir, we remember how that impostor said, while he was still alive, 'After three days I will rise.' 64Therefore order the tomb to be made secure until the third day, lest his disciples go and steal him away and tell the people, 'He has risen from the dead,' and the last fraud will be worse than the first." 65Pilate said to them, "You have a guard of soldiers. Go, make it as secure as you can." 66So they went and made the tomb secure by sealing the stone and setting a guard.

After the physical bodily resurrection of Jesus Christ from the dead, Jesus went out of his way to demonstrate that he was physical—not just an empirically unverifiable spirit or a ghost as seen in Luke 24:39 below.

Luke 24:36–49

> ³⁶As they were talking about these things, Jesus himself stood among them, and said to them, "Peace to you!" ³⁷But they were startled and frightened and thought they saw a spirit. ³⁸And he said to them, "Why are you troubled, and why do doubts arise in your hearts? ³⁹See my hands and my feet, that it is I myself. Touch me, and see. For a spirit does not have flesh and bones as you see that I have." ⁴⁰And when he had said this, he showed them his hands and his feet. ⁴¹And while they still disbelieved for joy and were marveling, he said to them, "Have you anything here to eat?" ⁴²They gave him a piece of broiled fish, ⁴³and he took it and ate before them.
>
> ⁴⁴Then he said to them, "These are my words that I spoke to you while I was still with you, that everything written about me in the Law of Moses and the Prophets and the Psalms must be fulfilled." ⁴⁵Then he opened their minds to understand the Scriptures, ⁴⁶and said to them, "Thus it is written, that the Christ should suffer and on the third day rise from the dead, ⁴⁷and that repentance for the forgiveness of sins should be proclaimed in his name to all nations, beginning from Jerusalem. ⁴⁸You are witnesses of these things. ⁴⁹And behold, I am sending the promise of my Father upon you. But stay in the city until you are clothed with power from on high."

The early church leaders understood that the physical bodily resurrection of Jesus Christ from the dead was the centerpiece of Christianity as evidenced in the early creeds. See, for example, the Apostle's Creed (AD 750~) below.

> *I believe in God, the Father almighty, creator of heaven and earth. I believe in Jesus Christ, his only Son, our Lord. He was conceived by the power of the Holy Spirit and born of the Virgin Mary. He suffered under Pontius Pilate, was crucified, died, and was buried. He descended to the dead. On the third day he rose again. He ascended into heaven and is seated at the right hand of the Father. He will come again to judge the*

living and the dead. I believe in the Holy Spirit, the holy catholic Church, the communion of saints, the forgiveness of sins, the resurrection of the body, and the life everlasting. Amen.

We now examine twelve selected reasons for believing Jesus Christ rose bodily from the dead.

Evidence for Jesus's Bodily Resurrection

We briefly identify twelve selected reasons favoring the conclusion that Jesus Christ rose bodily from the dead.

1. Eyewitness Accounts and Experiences

As previously mentioned, many disciples saw, felt, touched, and testified to Jesus's bodily resurrection. Remember that most of these same disciples suffered and died alone.

2. Early, Preserved Accounts of the Gospel

The centerpiece of Christianity is the gospel, not the prosperity gospel but the biblical gospel. As Paul articulates the biblical gospel in Corinthians.

1 Corinthians 15:1–4

[1]Now I would remind you, brothers, of the gospel I preached to you, which you received, in which you stand, [2]and by which you are being saved, if you hold fast to the word I preached to you — unless you believed in vain. [3]For I delivered to you as of first importance what I also received: that Christ died for our sins in accordance with the Scriptures, [4]that he was buried, that he was raised on the third day in accordance with the Scriptures...

Remember that Paul follows up this good news with numerous eyewitness accounts. The New Testament is filled with early, preserved accounts of the gospel. The New

Testament book of Acts contains numerous early sermons and testimonies related to Jesus' life, death, and resurrection.

3. Transformed from Fear to Martyrdom

The sheer number of people whose lives were transformed from cowering in fear to boldly proclaiming the gospel is an amazing historical fact. Given our inherent desire to avoid pain and suffering, people typically do not willingly die for what they know is a lie.

4. Empty Tomb

In the days after the secured tomb was found empty all the leaders in Jerusalem had to do was produce Jesus's body. They never did.

5. Resurrection Was Declared in Jerusalem

Again, in the days right after killing Jesus, the fearful disciples of Jesus were found boldly declaring to each other as well as to anyone who would listen that Jesus had risen bodily from the grave. These declarations were occurring right where it happened.

6. No Contrary Evidence

In recorded history, there is no evidence of a body or any other contrary evidence. There was a false rumor that some of the disciples stole the body. Since the tomb was empty, this rumor is not convincing, given that the tomb was secured and protected by guards. Further, if the body was stolen by the disciples, then they would not have endured such brutal suffering and martyrdom.

7. Some Jews Changed the Day of Worship

The Sabbath was a sacred and holy day on the Jewish calendar. What would possess Jews who believed Jesus was the prophesied Messiah, to change this day from Saturday to

Sunday? Given the physical, bodily resurrection of Jesus Christ occurred on Sunday, the celebration for what Jesus accomplished is the most reasonable explanation for this transition.

8. Conversion of Saul of Tarsus

What would possess a Jewish religious leader, Saul of Tarsus renamed Paul, to abandon his prestigious position in favor of following a dead Rabbi whose ministry was over due to the charge of blasphemy and execution? One rational explanation is that he encountered the resurrected Jesus. The fact that the Apostle Paul wrote a large portion of the New Testament suggests that he did not go insane. Clearly, insane people do not write such world-changing materials.

9. Key Initial Evidence Given to Women

In the Jewish culture at the time of the resurrection, women were marginalized members of society. If you were going to create a myth surrounding a blatant lie, you would not have made women lead characters in the myth.

10. Physical Resurrection—the Cornerstone

The emerging religious cult, as some believe, could have easily made Jesus's resurrection a spiritual one. That is, just say that he rose spiritually from the grave. Given that it would be unverifiable, you could just proceed with your new religious cult. By asserting a physical, bodily resurrection, you introduce the messiness of physicality and all the associated required empirical evidence.

11. Fulfilled Prophesy

From Genesis through Malachi, the Old Testament provides numerous clear and precise predictions of a coming Messiah who would suffer and die for transgressions. From the Messiah's birthplace to the date of his crucifixion, it was all clearly predicted.

12. Clarity of Biblical Teaching Related to Finance

If Christianity was merely a cruel myth fabricated by cunning people, then you would not expect to find deep and abiding wisdom related to personal and corporate wealth management. The Bible presents clear and coherent truth claims related to financial management starting in Genesis and ending in Revelation. Myths and frauds do not present coherent finance-related claims that deeply correspond to the empirical observations of our day. Given the empirical evidence of the resurrection of Jesus Christ, it is reasonable to consider deeply Jesus's teaching on finance.

We could continue with many more reasons supporting the physical bodily resurrection of Jesus Christ from the dead; I suspect by this point you get the general idea that the empirical and rational evidence is overwhelming. The next section is rather technical and can easily be skipped, but for fun some technical mathematics are given for the purpose of appraising the rationality of believing that Jesus Christ rose bodily from the dead.

Bayes's Theorem and the Resurrection[191]

Thomas Bayes (1701-1761) introduced a mathematical framework that bears his name for assessing the likelihood of undecided claims. Around the same period, David Hume (1711-1776) argued that miracles are extremely unlikely and therefore claims of Jesus's resurrection are likely false. Using Bayes' theorem, one can easily demonstrate that although one claim favoring the resurrection may not be compelling, multiple claims when rationally considered results in persuasive evidence.

Before introducing Bayes's theorem, an illustration is

---

[191] Based initially on materials produced by Professor Lionel Martellini.

given for how probabilities are updated based on new data. Our illustration is based on known objective probabilities something rare in philosophy or finance. The illustration's objective is useful in understanding the basic mechanics of how evidence influences one's acceptance of the various historical claims. The key insight is not so much the influence of one piece of evidence related to a particular truth claim, rather, it is understanding the weight of numerous pieces of evidence related to a particular truth claim. The approach taken here is widely used to solve numerous mathematical problems and has proven deeply fruitful in many financial applications.

Suppose there are have ten marbles, where four are blue and six are red. One of the blue marbles is striped, and three are solid. Four of the red marbles are striped, and two are solid.[192] Figure 12.1 illustrates the assumed population of marbles.

Figure 12.1. Illustration of Probability Updating
(Ten marbles: one striped blue, three solid blue, four striped red, two solid red)

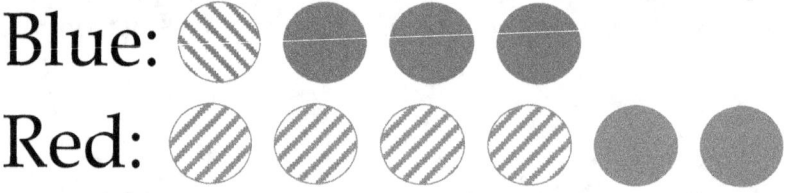

The probability of randomly picking a blue marble is four out of ten or $\Pr(Blue) = 40\%$, whereas the probability of picking a striped marble is five out of ten or $\Pr(Striped) = 50\%$. Note, however, if all you know is that the randomly drawn marble is striped, then the probability that it is red is four out of five or $\Pr(Red \mid Striped) = 80\%$ (Read: the probability of observing a red marble given that the marble is striped.)

---

[192]Ok, for the technically inclined reader, the white stripes would require naming the colors say reddish and bluish.

Technical Details of Bayes's Theorem

This section is solely for those interest in wrestling with the technical details. It can easily be skipped.

We now generalize the analysis. Let A denote red marbles and B denote striped marbles. Thus, symbolically the probability of A given B can be expressed as

$$\Pr(A|B) = \frac{\Pr(A \text{ and } B)}{\Pr(B)} = \frac{\Pr(A \cup B)}{\Pr(B)}, \qquad (12.1)$$

where the symbol ∪ denotes union or "and." From the example above,

$$\Pr(Red | Striped) = \frac{\Pr(Red \text{ and } Striped)}{\Pr(Striped)} = \frac{0.4}{0.5} = 0.8 \text{ or } 80\%.$$

Suppose there are two truth claims, A and B, where A is a particular proposition and B is a particular piece of evidence. You assign probabilities to these two truth claims, Pr(A) and Pr(B). The prior belief or prior probability of a particular proposition being true is defined as Pr(A). The Pr(A | B) is the posterior belief or posterior probability of a particular proposition being true. That is, the new information provided by evidence B results in adjusting the probability of proposition A being true.

Note by symmetry, if the truth claim serving as the proposition and the truth claim serving as the evidence is switched,

$$\Pr(B|A) = \frac{\Pr(B \text{ and } A)}{\Pr(A)} = \frac{\Pr(B \cup A)}{\Pr(A)}. \qquad (12.2)$$

In our marble example,

$$\Pr(Striped | Red) = \frac{\Pr(Striped \text{ and } Red)}{\Pr(Red)} = \frac{0.4}{0.6} = 0.67 \text{ or } 67\%.$$

Rearranging Equations (12.1) and (12.2), note

$$\Pr(A \cup B) = \Pr(B)\Pr(A|B) \text{ and} \qquad (12.3)$$

$$\Pr(B \cup A) = \Pr(A)\Pr(B|A). \qquad (12.4)$$

Again, in our example,

$$\Pr(Red \text{ and } Striped) = \Pr(Striped)\Pr(Red \mid Striped) = 0.5(0.8) = 0.4 \text{ and}$$

$$\Pr(Striped \text{ and } Red) = \Pr(Red)\Pr(Striped \mid Red) = 0.6(0.67) = 0.4.$$

Note if the right-hand side of Equations (12.3) and (12.4) are equated,

$$\Pr(B)\Pr(A \mid B) = \Pr(A)\Pr(B \mid A). \tag{12.5}$$

Rearranging Equation (12.5), Bayes's theorem is given.

Bayes's Theorem

Assuming two events, truth claims, or propositions, denoted A and B, and the probability of B is positive, then

$$\Pr(A \mid B) = \Pr(A)\frac{\Pr(B \mid A)}{\Pr(B)}. \tag{12.6}$$

Considering again our marble example,

$$\Pr(Striped \mid Red) = \Pr(Striped)\frac{\Pr(Red \mid Striped)}{\Pr(Red)} = 0.5\left(\frac{0.8}{0.6}\right) = 0.67 \text{ and}$$

$$\Pr(Red \mid Striped) = \Pr(Red)\frac{\Pr(Striped \mid Red)}{\Pr(Striped)} = 0.6\left(\frac{0.67}{0.5}\right) = 0.8.$$

When evaluating historical claims, it is helpful to provide an alternative measure for the marginal probability of B. Let the symbol $\neg$ denote "not." Thus, $\neg A$ is read "not A" and hence $\Pr(\neg A)$ is the probability not A is true, or A is false. Thus, in our marble case, not Red is equivalent to Blue. One helpful representation for $\Pr(B)$ is

$$\Pr(B) = \Pr(B \mid A)\Pr(A) + \Pr(B \mid \neg A)\Pr(\neg A). \tag{12.7}$$

In the marble example,

$$\Pr(Red) = \Pr(Red \mid Striped)\Pr(Striped) + \Pr(Red \mid \neg Striped)\Pr(\neg Striped)$$

$$= 0.8(0.5) + 0.4(0.5) = 0.6$$

Thus, an alternative version of Bayes's theorem can be expressed as

$$\Pr(A \mid B) = \Pr(A)\frac{\Pr(B \mid A)}{\Pr(B \mid A)\Pr(A) + \Pr(B \mid \neg A)\Pr(\neg A)}. \tag{12.8}$$

After this effort, Bayes's theorem is applied to historical truth claims.

Bayes's Theorem and the Resurrection of Jesus Christ

Suppose you are a skeptic considering the specific core claim of Christianity, that is, whether Jesus Christ rose bodily from the dead. Within the Bayes's Theorem framework, consider the following definitions:

A - truth claim or proposition (e.g., A - "Jesus Christ rose bodily from the dead") and

$\neg A$ - truth claim or proposition (e.g., $\neg A$ - "Jesus Christ *did not* rise bodily from the dead").

Further, being a skeptic and following Hume, you assign the likelihood of Jesus rising as very remote say one percent of one percent (known as a basis point in the investing world) or

$Pr(A)$ - prior belief or prior probability
[e.g., $Pr(A) = 0.01\%$ or 0.0001].

Thus,

$Pr(\neg A)$ - prior belief or prior probability
[e.g., $Pr(\neg A) = 99.99\%$ or 0.9999].

You now conduct a detailed study of the evidence related to the historical person known as the Apostle Peter. He is an interesting character and portrayed as very human. You consider a second truth claim:

B - second truth claim or proposition (evidence) (e.g., B - "Apostle Peter's zeal in proclaiming that Jesus Christ rose bodily from the dead, especially after Peter's own prior denial the night before Jesus was crucified").

You know people do not typically suffer and die to promote what they know is a lie. You remain extremely skeptical but realize Peter was not the bravest of characters, hence you determine:

$Pr(B|A)$ - likelihood [e.g., $Pr(B|A) = 75\%$ or 0.75, because Peter was unlikely to suffer and die to promote a cultural movement when he knew the resurrection was a lie]. Read: "Apostle Peter's zeal in proclaiming Jesus Christ rose bodily from the dead, given his own denial assuming Jesus Christ actually rose bodily from the dead."

Further, you concoct nefarious reasons motivating Peter to promote a lie and determine:

$Pr(B|\neg A)$ – likelihood [e.g., $Pr(B|\neg A)$ = 10% or 0.1]. Read: "Apostle Peter's zeal in proclaiming Jesus Christ rose bodily from the dead, given his own denial assuming Jesus Christ *did not* actually rise bodily from the dead."

Based on Bayes's Theorem,

$$Pr(A|B) = Pr(A)\frac{Pr(B|A)}{Pr(B|A)Pr(A) + Pr(B|\neg A)Pr(\neg A)}$$

$$= 0.0001\frac{0.75}{0.75(0.0001) + 0.1(0.9999)} \quad (12.9)$$

$$= 0.0001\frac{0.75}{0.100065}$$

$$= 0.0007495 \text{ or approximately } 0.075\%$$

Based on this analysis, the skeptic's view of the likelihood that Jesus Christ rose bodily from the dead has increased by a factor of about 7.5 (initial probability of 0.01% and posterior probability of 0.075%. Although this increase in probability does not seem like much, remember that the life transformation of Peter is simply one of hundreds of factual evidence favoring the resurrection.

Case Study 1: Bayes's Theorem and the Twelve Apostles

As an example, assuming the same probability structure for each of the additional twelve apostles, the following set of outcomes are produced for the thirteen apostles who all suffered after the resurrection of Jesus Christ. Table 12.1 shows the resulting mathematical calculations. Based on repeated use of Bayes's Theorem, the likelihood of Jesus rising bodily from the dead is virtually 100%.

Exploring the Philosophical Roots that Influence Financial Fruit

Table 12.1. Bayesian Updating of the Likelihood of the Bodily Resurrection from the Dead

Bayes Theorem and the Resurrection

Event (1) Event (i)	Pr(A|B) Pr(Res|Peter) Pr(Res|i)	Pr(A) Pr(Res) Pr(Res|i-1)	Pr(B|A) Pr(Peter|Res) Pr(i-1|Res)	Pr(¬A) Pr(¬Res) Pr(¬Res|i-1)	Pr(B|¬A) Pr(Peter|¬Res) Pr(i-1|¬Res)	Apostle
0		0.01%	75%	99.99%	10%	
1	0.07495%	0.07%	75%	99.93%	10%	Peter
2	0.55941%	0.56%	75%	99.44%	10%	Andrew
3	4.04836%	4.05%	75%	95.95%	10%	James
4	24.03743%	24.04%	75%	75.96%	10%	John
5	70.35530%	70.36%	75%	29.64%	10%	Philip
6	94.68075%	94.68%	75%	5.32%	10%	Bartholomew
7	99.25649%	99.26%	75%	0.74%	10%	Thomas
8	99.90022%	99.90%	75%	0.10%	10%	Matthew
9	99.98668%	99.99%	75%	0.01%	10%	James, son of Alphaeus
10	99.99822%	100.00%	75%	0.00%	10%	Jude
11	99.99976%	100.00%	75%	0.00%	10%	Simon the Zealot
12	99.99997%	100.00%	75%	0.00%	10%	Matthias
13	100.00000%					Paul

What conclusions can you draw from this analysis? Even if some of the probability assumptions are modified, the same general conclusion follows: The best explanation is that Jesus Christ rose bodily from the grave.

We now turn to what has become known as Pascal's Wager. The goal is to explore a rational framework for establishing the threshold of probability that would transition a person from believing a particular truth claim as false to one who now believes a particular truth claim as true.

Pascal's Wager

According to Wikipedia,

> *Blaise Pascal (19 June 1623 – 19 August 1662) was a French mathematician, physicist, inventor, writer and Catholic theologian. He was a child prodigy who was educated by his father, a tax collector in Rouen. Pascal's earliest work was in the natural and applied sciences, where he made important contributions to the study of fluids, and clarified the concepts of*

pressure and vacuum by generalising the work of Evangelista Torricelli. Pascal also wrote in defence of the scientific method.

Regarding Pascal's Wager, Alan Hájek concludes, "Pascal's Wager is a watershed in the philosophy of religion. As we have seen, it is also a great deal more besides."[193] Before specifying the wager, the concept of utility is defined. Hájek notes the following:

> *In any decision problem, the way the world is, and what an agent does, together determine an outcome for the agent. We may assign utilities to such outcomes, numbers that represent the degree to which the agent values them. It is typical to present these numbers in a decision matrix, with the columns corresponding to the various relevant states of the world, and the rows corresponding to the various possible actions that the agent can perform.*

Alan Hájek summarizes Pascal's Wager in the following way:

1. Either God exists or God does not exist, and you can either wager for God or wager against God. The utilities of the relevant possible outcomes are as follows, where f_1, f_2, and f_3 are numbers whose values are not specified beyond the requirement that they be finite:

	God exists	*God does not exist*
Wager for God	∞	f_1
Wager against God	f_2	f_3

---

[193] See Alan Hájek, "Pascal's Wager", in *The Stanford Encyclopedia of Philosophy*, ed. Edward N. Zalta (Summer 2018), https://plato.stanford.edu/archives/sum2018/entries/pascal-wager/. Hájek is a widely cited professor of philosophy at Australian National University. All Hájek quotes that follow this come from the same source.

2. *Rationality requires the probability that you assign to God existing to be positive, and not infinitesimal.*
3. *Rationality requires you to perform the act of maximum expected utility (when there is one).*
4. *Conclusion 1. Rationality requires you to wager for God.*
5. *Conclusion 2. You should wager for God.*

The main insight is that a "Wager for God" results in a positive infinite expected utility regardless of the finitely assigned probability that "God does not exist." Assuming any positive probability assigned to "God exists" will result in a positive infinite expected utility.

There are many criticisms of Pascal's Wager, but it remains a powerful way to frame evaluation of various decisions. Alan Hájek concludes,

> *Pascal's Wager vies with Anselm's Ontological Argument for being the most famous argument in the philosophy of religion. Indeed, the Wager arguably has greater influence nowadays than any other such argument – not just in the service of Christian apologetics, but also in its impact on various lines of thought associated with infinity, decision theory, probability, epistemology, psychology, and even moral philosophy.*

In summary, based on Pascal's Wager, once you have established a positive probability favoring the bodily resurrection of Jesus Christ, then entrusting your life to Jesus Christ is the only rational response.

Case Study 2: Finance and Jesus's Resurrection

Because the physical bodily resurrection of Jesus Christ is not only historically plausible, but a biblical necessity, all of life changes materially. The world we find ourselves occupying is

God-infused and teeming with living water and the bread of life.

The simple charge to go and make disciples is impossible from a human perspective. Fortunately, God is at work all around us and we simply must join Him in what He is already doing. If you are a follower of Jesus, then plead with Him to open your eyes to the lost but seeking all around you. Ask God for one person to assist along the way.

I remember riding in a car in a large city within a country deeply hostile to Jesus Christ. The government official who was driving described the burden he felt for his entire nation as the vast majority of its citizens do not have a personal relationship with God through Jesus Christ. For you see, this person had recently met Jesus, and his life was radically transformed from meaningless secular pursuits to serving in a deeply meaningful divine commission as God's ambassador.

It is easy for us to feel the pressure in our soul for the despair of entire nations. It is much more challenging to invite our colleague at work to coffee to serve as God's ambassador and introduce them to Jesus Christ. My friend understood his need to identify just a few people through prayer to whom he could proclaim the good news of salvation.

Figure 12.2 illustrates the daunting challenge of serving as God's ambassador to the world, but it starts by one person loving another person enough to share the gospel of Jesus Christ. Ask God to give you one more person to disciple.

Figure 12.2. Illustration of the Disciple-Making Challenge[194]

Summary

In this chapter, the physical bodily resurrection of Jesus Christ was examined in detail. First, it was shown what Jesus Christ claimed he would do. Second, twelve compelling reasons to believe that Jesus Christ did, by empirical fact, rise bodily from the grave were identified. Third, a deep mathematical dive into Bayes's Theorem was conducted and explored applying it to the resurrection of Jesus Christ. Finally, Pascal's Wager was introduced as a decision framework for appraising the resulting probabilities from applying Bayes's Theorem.

Case Study 1: Coke Consolidated

"At Coca-Cola Consolidated, we strive to fulfill our Purpose — to honor God in all we do, to serve others, to pursue excellence, and to grow profitably. At the core of our culture is a focus on

---

[194] Photo by Pema G. Lama on Unsplash. Accessed October 23, 2024.

service. Our teammates have a passion for serving each other along with our consumers, our customers, and our communities."

Note: 20-Year holding period rate of returns:
- 16.1% COKE (Coke Consolidated, Not Woke)
- 10.0% SPY (Benchmark, SP 500 Index ETF)
- 7.5% KO (Coca Cola Company, Woke)

Thus, can God-honoring companies be profitable? How can a corporate chaplain aid in a company fulfilling its marketplace mission?

Case Study 2: Bayes's Theorem Redone

We repeat Table 12.1 but with much more "conservative" probabilities. Specifically, rather than use 0.01% probability of Jesus' resurrection, use 0.0000001% probability. Further, assume these disciples were highly averse to persecution and there was only a 60% chance they would follow Jesus, given that Jesus Christ rose. Again, these disciples being highly risk averse, are assumed to have only a 5% chance of following Jesus Christ given Jesus Christ did not actually rise. The table below shows the resulting mathematical calculations. Based on repeated use of Bayes's Theorem, the likelihood of Jesus rising bodily from the extremely likely.

Bayes Theorem and the Resurrection

Event (1) Event (i)	Apostle	Posterior Probability Pr(A|B) Pr(Res|Peter) Pr(Res|i)	Prior Probability Pr(A) Pr(Res) Pr(Res|i-1)	Likelihood Pr(B|A) Pr(Peter|Res) Pr(i-1|Res)	Prior Probability Pr(¬A) Pr(¬Res) Pr(¬Res|i-1)	Likelihood Pr(B|¬A) Pr(Peter|¬Res) Pr(i-1|¬Res)	Implied Prior Probability Pr(B)
0							
1	Peter	0.000001%	0.0000001%	30%	100.000000%	5%	5.0000000%
2	Andrew	0.00000%	0.0000006%	30%	99.9999994%	5%	5.0000002%
3	James	0.00002%	0.0000036%	30%	99.9999964%	5%	5.0000009%
4	John	0.00013%	0.0000216%	30%	99.9999784%	5%	5.0000054%
5	Philip	0.00078%	0.0001296%	30%	99.9998704%	5%	5.0000324%
6	Bartholomew	0.00467%	0.0008%	30%	100.00%	5%	5.00019%
7	Thomas	0.02799%	0.0047%	30%	100.00%	5%	5.00117%
8	Matthew	0.16768%	0.0280%	30%	99.97%	5%	5.00700%
9	James, son of Alphaeus	0.99771%	0.1677%	30%	99.83%	5%	5.04192%
10	Jude	5.70185%	0.9977%	30%	99.00%	5%	5.24943%
11	Simon the Zealot	26.62150%	5.7018%	30%	94.30%	5%	6.42546%
12	Matthias	68.52161%	26.6215%	30%	73.38%	5%	11.65538%
13	Paul	92.88798%	68.5216%	30%	31.48%	5%	22.13040%

Again, what conclusions can you draw from this application of Bayes's Theorem? The final results are robust even if some of the probability assumptions are modified. The best explanation is that Jesus Christ rose bodily from the grave.

Case Study 3: Bayes's Theorem with Pascal's Wager

Recall with any reasonable application of Bayes's Theorem to the behavior of the twelve disciples and Paul, the probability that Jesus Christ rose bodily from the grave is essentially 100%. Recall from Pascal's wager, regardless of the amounts given for the other three possibilities, once should wager for God. What is the rational implication for someone who examines this evidence and rejects Jesus Christ? Perhaps it has more to do with seeking to live autonomously from God and desiring not to submit to God's rule and reign.

References

Hájek, Alan, "Pascal's Wager", in *The Stanford Encyclopedia of Philosophy*, ed. Edward N. Zalta (Summer 2018), https://plato.stanford.edu/archives/sum2018/entries/pascal-wager/.

Chapter 13. Loving Your Neighbor

Learning Objectives

- Understand the link between loving your neighbor and Christian apologetics.
- Consider hospitality as the key to honing your worldview.
- Explore the link between the Christian worldview and leadership as well as finance.

Opening Quote

A life based on cost-benefit analysis "... believes in nothing, cares for nothing, enjoys nothing, loves nothing, hates nothing, finds purpose in nothing, lives for nothing and only remains alive because there is nothing for which to die." Dorothy Sayers

Overview

There is a link between loving your neighbor and Christian apologetics. Love is the overarching compelling argument favoring the truthfulness of the Christian worldview.

Hospitality is the key to honing your worldview. Learning to serve others, particularly the sojourners amongst us, entails the essence of working out one's relationship with Jesus Christ. Next, how the Christian worldview impacts both leadership and finance is explored.

Love as the Compelling Argument

With any philosophical worldview, we need to understand its entailments. It is important to think through the logical coherence and empirical correspondence of a worldview. The final piece is the implied lifestyle that results. Is life really "red in tooth and claw" and merely meaningless "survival of the fittest," or is life deeply meaningful, full of hope, and worthy of expending unconditional love? Jesus addresses this issue clearly. Consider the challenging question posed to Jesus by a lawyer.

Matthew 22:35–40

> *35 And one of them, a lawyer, asked him a question to test him. 36 "Teacher, which is the great commandment in the Law?" 37 And he said to him, "You shall love the Lord your God with all your heart and with all your soul and with all your mind. 38 This is the great and first commandment. 39 And a second is like it: You shall love your neighbor as yourself. 40 On these two commandments depend all the Law and the Prophets."*

Note that the lawyer was seeking to test Jesus with his question. Apparently, in that day there was a debate regarding which of the ten commandments was the greatest. Jesus basically answered all of them within his summary answer. The key insight is that a right relationship with God results in a loving relationship with other people.

As explained in John below, Jesus gives a new commandment to his disciples.

John 13:34–35

> ³⁴"A new commandment I give to you, that you love one another: just as I have loved you, you also are to love one another. ³⁵By this all people will know that you are my disciples, if you have love for one another."

Followers of Jesus Christ are to be marked with a genuine love for each other. The key hallmark of true followers of Jesus Christ is the love they have for each other as well as a passion to make disciples. Paul summarizes this keystone of the Christian worldview in 1 Corinthian 13.

1 Corinthians 13

> ¹If I speak in the tongues of men and of angels, but have not love, I am a noisy gong or a clanging cymbal. ²And if I have prophetic powers, and understand all mysteries and all knowledge, and if I have all faith, so as to remove mountains, but have not love, I am nothing. ³If I give away all I have, and if I deliver up my body to be burned, but have not love, I gain nothing. ⁴Love is patient and kind; love does not envy or boast; it is not arrogant ⁵or rude. It does not insist on its own way; it is not irritable or resentful; ⁶it does not rejoice at wrongdoing, but rejoices with the truth. ⁷Love bears all things, believes all things, hopes all things, endures all things. ⁸Love never ends. As for prophecies, they will pass away; as for tongues, they will cease; as for knowledge, it will pass away. ⁹For we know in part and we prophesy in part, ¹⁰but when the perfect comes, the partial will pass away. ¹¹When I was a child, I spoke like a child, I thought like a child, I reasoned like a child. When I became a man, I gave up childish ways. ¹²For now we see in a mirror dimly, but then face to face. Now I know in part; then I shall know fully, even as I have been fully known. ¹³So now faith, hope, and love abide, these three; but the greatest of these is love.

It is important to note that the word for love used in this passage is rather unique to Christianity. According to Wikipedia,

Agape has been expounded on by many Christian writers in a specifically Christian context. C. S. Lewis uses agape in The Four Loves *to describe what he believes is the highest level of love known to humanity: a selfless love that is passionately committed to the well-being of others.*

It is stunning to contrast followers of Jesus Christ who are committed to loving God and loving others with the reality on the ground in this modern era. Paul Vallely writes in 2014,

The Centre for the Study of Global Christianity in the United States estimates that 100,000 Christians now die every year, targeted because of their faith – that is 11 every hour. The Pew Research Center says that hostility to religion reached a new high in 2012, when Christians faced some form of discrimination in 139 countries, almost three-quarters of the world's nations.

All this seems counter-intuitive here in the West where the history of Christianity has been one of cultural dominance and control ever since the Emperor Constantine converted and made the Roman Empire Christian in the 4th century AD.

Yet the plain fact is that Christians are languishing in jail for blasphemy in Pakistan, and churches are burned, and worshippers regularly slaughtered in Nigeria and Egypt, which has recently seen its worst anti-Christian violence in seven centuries.[195]

The primary response for Christians is not retaliation, though often justice is sought. The mandated response is to love our enemy—an admittedly impossible task outside of a life transformed by redemption found in Jesus Christ. Consider the teaching of Jesus Christ recorded in the Gospel According to Matthew.

---

[195] See https://www.independent.co.uk/voices/comment/christians-the-worlds-most-persecuted-people-9630774.html.

Matthew 5:43–48

⁴³"You have heard that it was said, 'You shall love your neighbor and hate your enemy.' ⁴⁴But I say to you, Love your enemies and pray for those who persecute you, ⁴⁵so that you may be sons of your Father who is in heaven. For he makes his sun rise on the evil and on the good, and sends rain on the just and on the unjust. ⁴⁶For if you love those who love you, what reward do you have? Do not even the tax collectors do the same? ⁴⁷And if you greet only your brothers, what more are you doing than others? Do not even the Gentiles do the same? ⁴⁸You therefore must be perfect, as your heavenly Father is perfect.

Case Study 1: Foundations for Farming (FfF)[196]

The following excerpt comes from Foundations for Farming:

Through FfF, farmers learn the minimal requirements to become self-sufficient and generate surplus from their land. With our best practices farmers escape poverty, have healthy diets, improve the environment, and generate enough income to build a better future for themselves and their families. FfF's training is based on a holistic, biblical, character-based approach that relies on personal transformation to achieve lasting behavior modification and results. ...

FfF's mantra is: On Time, At standard, Without waste, and with joy. If you apply these principles to any business, invariably in the end you will make a profit. Profit is the fruit of faithfulness. ...

Our mentoring program helps small-scale farmers achieve an average yield of 8 T/Ha, which is significantly higher than the

---

[196] Based on several encounters with Craig Deall. See, for example, https://www.faithdrivenentrepreneur.org/podcast-inventory/2019/10/29/episode-80-serving-those-who-steal-from-you-craig-deall.

national average of 0.4 T/Ha in Zimbabwe.[197]

Isaiah 58:10–11

¹⁰if you pour yourself out for the hungry and satisfy the desire of the afflicted, then shall your light rise in the darkness and your gloom be as the noonday. ¹¹And the Lord will guide you continually and satisfy your desire in scorched places and make your bones strong; and you shall be like a watered garden, like a spring of water, whose waters do not fail.

How is FfF different from delivering food to the needy in poor countries?

So how do we love our neighbor, even if they hate us? Given the opportunity, let us consider hospitality.

Hospitality as the Gateway to the World[198]

Hospitality is the opposite of avoidance or at the extreme — cruelty. Opening your home and sharing a meal with your neighbors is the essence of serving and loving them. Your neighbors can be across the street or from across the globe. In our home, we have been blessed to have people literally from all over the world visit in our home. Since we live in a college town and the rest of the world sends their best and brightest to our colleges and universities, through various activities we often find people at our table from many different countries.

One customary activity for welcoming our guests is to play various games. This often helps to break the awkwardness when language is taxing. Further, when weather is conducive,

---

[197] http://foundationsforfarming.org/. "A hectare (symbol: ha) is a unit of area that is accepted in the International System of Units (SI). It is primarily used to measure land area. One hectare is equal to 10,000 square meters and is equivalent to approximately 2.471 acres." (https://www.unitconverters.net/area/hectare-to-acres.htm.)

[198] For an insightful book that addresses this topic, see Rosaria Butterfield, *The Gospel Comes with a House Key: Practicing Radically Ordinary Hospitality in Our Post-Christian World* (Wheaton, IL: Crossway, 2018).

we especially enjoy sharing time outdoors. We have a small green on our front yard and a tee box 65 yards away. Since many foreign scholars are more academic than athletic, a golf lesson is a fun distraction (and potentially dangerous for anyone standing around).

One Thanksgiving Day we had six guests, four from China, one from Saudi Arabia, and one from Israel. When picking up one of these guests as they often do not have cars, the guest asked whether the US holiday of Thanksgiving was a religious holiday. Due to the deep Christian roots to Thanksgiving, that sparked a great discussion.

During this same occasion we realized we had perhaps chosen the wrong gaming activity. That year our six children had taken an interest in airsoft target shooting. Airsoft involves plastic guns that take plastic pellets for ammunition. These guns look real apart from an orange tip. Rather than a turkey shoot, as for some a traditional Thanksgiving activity, we set up a balloon board for target shooting. Here we witnessed a Muslim passing an air rifle to a Jew. It was a bit cringeworthy for sure. It turned out, however, that these two scholars—mortal national enemies in their home countries—really enjoyed meeting each other, and the discussions that ensued that evening were ones for the ages. Given we homeschooled our children, it was a classic lesson in global affairs. Clearly, it was easy for us to help our children better understand global issues while having sojourners at our table who often had lived out these same issues.

At the time of this writing, we find ourselves often interacting with Persians, and we are learning much about the rich Persian history. It is important to note that listening is a fine art. As our house guests have many questions and our home is a safe place to ask these questions, it is crucial to listen. Behind every question is the questioner, and behind every questioner is not only a worldview but experiences that include pain and suffering. Some of our guests have personally observed the very present evil of oppression and injustice common in their countries. It is heartbreaking to realize the deep pain and suffering inflicted on people intentionally by other people.

Where do they turn for justice? How do they restore life's meaning and hope for the future?

A lawyer seeking to understand what it takes to inherit eternal life questioned Jesus. Jesus replied that the lawyer should love God and love his neighbor. Being a typical lawyer, he sought further clarification.

Luke 10:29–37

> [29]But he, desiring to justify himself, said to Jesus, "And who is my neighbor?" [30]Jesus replied, "A man was going down from Jerusalem to Jericho, and he fell among robbers, who stripped him and beat him and departed, leaving him half dead. [31]Now by chance a priest was going down that road, and when he saw him he passed by on the other side. [32]So likewise a Levite, when he came to the place and saw him, passed by on the other side. [33]But a Samaritan, as he journeyed, came to where he was, and when he saw him, he had compassion. [34]He went to him and bound up his wounds, pouring on oil and wine. Then he set him on his own animal and brought him to an inn and took care of him. [35]And the next day he took out two denarii and gave them to the innkeeper, saying, 'Take care of him, and whatever more you spend, I will repay you when I come back.' [36]Which of these three, do you think, proved to be a neighbor to the man who fell among the robbers?" [37]He said, "The one who showed him mercy." And Jesus said to him, "You go, and do likewise."

It is indisputable that the teaching of Jesus Christ has transformed life on this earth and His teaching that urges us toward hospitality. Jürgen Habermas notes that western culture has never been the same. He states:

> *Universalistic egalitarianism, from which sprang the ideals of freedom and a collective life in solidarity, the autonomous conduct of life and emancipation, the individual morality of conscience, human rights and democracy, is the direct legacy of the Judaic ethic of justice and the Christian ethic of love. This legacy, substantially unchanged, has been the object of continual critical appropriation and reinterpretation. To this day, there is*

no alternative to it. And in light of the current challenges of a postnational constellation, we continue to draw on the substance of this heritage. Everything else is just idle postmodern talk.[199]

Case Study 2: Tuscaloosa International Friends

"Incorporated as a community organization in 1972, Tuscaloosa International Friends (TIF) is a community organization dedicated to providing opportunities for international visitors to learn more about life in the United States and for local residents to learn more about other cultures. TIF sponsors picnics, dinners, parties, and a friendship family program."[200]

One rewarding opportunity to show hospitality is building friendships and meeting the needs of our international guests within our own communities. Many people do not realize that large numbers of international students train at universities near you. For the most part, these international students do not have the capacity reciprocate your generosity. Showing hospitality in this way is a great opportunity to compare various worldviews.

The link between the Christian worldview and one's vocation is explored. Given its pervasiveness throughout all vocations, leadership and finance are the focus.

---

[199] Jürgen Habermas, *Time of Transitions* (Malden, MA: Polity Press, 2006), 150–151. This is a translation of an interview from 1999. According to the Stanford Encyclopedia of Philosophy website, Jürgen Habermas currently ranks as one of the most influential philosophers in the world. See https://plato.stanford.edu/entries/habermas/. It is important to note that Habermas is not a Christian.

[200] See https://international.ua.edu/programs-activities/tuscaloosas-international-friends/. See, also, https://www.tuscaloosainternationalfriends.com/.

The Servant Leader[201]

Ken Blanchard, a prolific author focused on leadership, offers an interesting perspective:

> *Business and beliefs. Jesus and your job. Personal and professional. Servant and leader. Even seeing those words paired together makes many people uneasy. Our sophisticated culture encourages us to draw lines and keep our spiritual lives separate from our secular lives. Faith is for Sundays or family gatherings only. Right? (8)*

Blanchard's views on leadership changed after his eyes were opened "to the power of the Word" referencing the Bible. He concludes,

> *I realized that Christians have more in Jesus than just a great spiritual leader; we have a **practical and effective leadership model** for all organizations, for all people, for all situations. (9)* (bold is italics in original)

Blanchard has identified Jesus as a practical and effective leader. How can a simple tradesman from Nazareth have the key insights to so many different fields of study? Any conclusion other than Jesus is God's son, that He rose bodily from the grave, and the Bible contains his authentic teachings is logically difficult given the depths of biblical insights. Leadership and finance are just two of many.

We conclude with selected Bible-based financial management ideas.

---

[201] Quotes in this section taken from Ken Blanchard and Phil Hodges, *The Servant Leader Transforming Your Heart, Head, Hands & Habits* (Nashville, TN: Thomas Nelson, 2003).

Bible-Based Financial Management[202]

One of the interesting insights gained from an in-depth study of the Bible focusing on finance is the clear change of numeraire. The dictionary defines numeraire as "… an item or commodity acting as a measure of value or as a standard for currency exchange."[203] One interpretation is that there are at least two types of numeraires, currency (transitory) and metaphysical (enduring). We all know the transitory nature of money. There are numerous jokes along these lines. "Money talks! I heard it once. It said, 'goodbye.'" "Do you know why they call it cold cash? Because you do not get to hold it long enough for it to get warm!" As with much humor, there are truths embedded.

Enduring wealth is different as it never dissolves. Consider the following Bible verses.

Proverbs 15:16–17

> [16]Better is a little with the fear of the Lord than great treasure and trouble with it. [17]Better is a dinner of herbs where love is than a fattened ox and hatred with it.

Proverbs 8:10–11, 18

> [10]Take my instruction instead of silver, and knowledge rather than choice gold, [11]for wisdom is better than jewels, and all that you may desire cannot compare with her. … [18]With me are riches and honor, enduring wealth and prosperity.

Proverbs 13:11

> [11]Wealth gained hastily will dwindle, but whoever gathers little by little will increase it.

---

[202]For more insights on personal finance, see http://www.robertebrooks.org/project/personal-finance/.
[203]New Oxford American Dictionary on my Mac computer.

Proverbs 22:1

¹A good name is to be chosen rather than great riches, and favor is better than silver or gold.

Clearly, many of the challenges facing modern business practice and finance in particular would solve themselves if the primary motivation was love for others. If we genuinely love our co-workers, bosses, suppliers, clients, and other stakeholders, then so many challenges would vanish. The economic cost of monitoring is staggering. Small businesses that have sought to adopt various portions of the Christian worldview typically see the cost of monitoring decline. If your staff seeks to honor God and love others, it fosters a much more enjoyable work environment, and customers are attracted.

It is important to note that from a Christian worldview no one is perfect except Jesus Christ. Thus, every boss, supplier, client, or staff member will fail in some way. Interestingly, the mechanisms for forgiveness and restoration found in the Christian worldview is deeply helpful. The challenge is loving your neighbor, who may be next door or across the globe, enough to invest in them. It is not enough to just spend time together; we must proclaim God's precious word to the lost and dying all around us.

Summary

Love is the compelling argument for the Christian worldview. Loving our neighbors, even if they hate us, is the consequence of taking Jesus's yoke upon us.

Love can be shown in many ways. Just a few here are illustrated here from loving those who stole your family farm to loving our international guests residing in our hometown. Showing hospitality within our homes is a blessing, particularly to those who do not have the means to reciprocate.

Case Study 1: The Golden Rule

The well-known Golden Rule in Matthew 7:12 is followed by contrasting a narrow way versus a wide way.

Matthew 7:12–14

> *12"So whatever you wish that others would do to you, do also to them, for this is the Law and the Prophets. 13"Enter by the narrow gate. For the gate is wide and the way is easy that leads to destruction, and those who enter by it are many. 14For the gate is narrow and the way is hard that leads to life, and those who find it are few."*

1) Based on this passage, how are people of "the Way" to be different?
2) What does the contrast between the wide gate and the narrow gate suggest?

Case Study 2: Eternal Life and the Marketplace

Consider John 14:1–4.

John 14:1–4

> *1"Let not your hearts be troubled. Believe in God; believe also in me. 2In my Father's house are many rooms. If it were not so, would I have told you that I go to prepare a place for you? 3And if I go and prepare a place for you, I will come again and will take you to myself, that where I am you may be also. 4And you know the way to where I am going."*

1) Based on this passage, what is the natural state of our hearts?
2) How does our eternality influence our marketplace activities?

Case Study 3: Continental Realty Group

The Continental Reality Group notes the following:

> We partner with Apartment Life on each of our housing assets as creating and fostering healthy communities is central to our mission in housing investment and development. Through our partnership with Apartment Life, there are dedicated housing coordinators placed at each property where they live full time and spend dedicated hours each month welcoming new residents and creating community engagement. A healthy and connected community increases resident retention and reduces turnover costs. We care deeply about the residents in our communities and want to impact them in positive ways.[204]

- Apartment Life has served 1.3 million units since 2000
- Is ministering to apartment dwellers a way to fulfill the Great Commission? How is it financially justified?

References

Blanchard, Ken, and Phil Hodges, *The Servant Leader Transforming Your Heart, Head, Hands & Habits* (Nashville, TN: Thomas Nelson, 2003).

Bloom Jon, "'Invictus' Redeemed," Desiring God, August 22, 2014. Provides poems, William Ernest Henley, "Invictus," and Dorothy Day, "Conquered." See http://www.desiringgod.org/articles/invictus-redeemed.

Butterfield, Rosaria, *The Gospel Comes with a House Key: Practicing Radically Ordinary Hospitality in Our Post-Christian World* (Wheaton, IL: Crossway, 2018).

Habermas, Jürgen, *Time of Transitions* (Malden, MA: Polity Press, 2006).

Hatch, Nathan O., "Evangelical Colleges and the Challenge of Christian Thinking," in *Making Higher Education Christian:*

---

[204] https://www.continentalrealtygroup.com/asset-strategy.

The History and Mission of Evangelical Colleges in America, ed. Joel A. Carpenter and Kenneth W. Shipps (Grand Rapids, MI: Eerdmans, 1987).

Hove, Rick, and Heather Holleman, *A Grander Story: An Invitation to Christian Professors* (Orlando, FL: Cru Press, 2017).

Lennox, John C., *God's Undertaker: Has Science Buried God?* (Oxford: Lion, 2009).

Liddon, Henry Parry, *Liddon's Bampton Lectures 1866* (London: Rivingtons, 1869).

Liftin, Duane, *Conceiving the Christian College* (Grand Rapids, MI: Eerdmans, 2004).

Metaxas, Eric, *Bonhoeffer Pastor, Martyr, Prophet, Spy* (Nashville, TN: Thomas Nelson, 2011).

Muggeridge, Malcolm, *The End of Christendom* quoted in William A. Dembski, *Intelligent Design The Bridge Between Science and Theology* (London, England: IVP Academic, 2002).

Plantinga, Alvin, "On Christian Scholarship." Available at http://www.veritas-ucsb.org/library/plantinga/ocs.html/.

Solzhenitsyn, Aleksandr, The Gulag Archipelago 1918–1956. See, for example, https://www.goodreads.com/quotes/13750-if-only-it-were-all-so-simple-if-only-there.

Chapter 14. The Nature of the Harvest

Learning Objectives

- Explore the financial implications of applying evolutionary theory or the Christian worldview to finance.
- Provide a chapter-by-chapter summary of major financial implications of one's philosophical foundation.
- Review two poems and selected quotes summarizing this material.

Opening Quote

"Christian scholars view their work as larger than themselves, larger than itself. They look not only at what they're studying but also along it, so as to see its Christ-centered implications. This tethering of the temporal to the eternal provides meaning and significance and beauty to what they do and generates the highest motivation for excellence. Their study becomes virtually an act of worship. They work not merely to understand the created order, as worthwhile as that goal is within itself; they also study the created order to deepen their understanding and appreciation of, and ultimately their relationship with, the One

who fashioned it and who occupies its center, its Creative Orderer, the Lord Jesus Christ.[205]" Duane Liftin

Overview

This book wraps up by contrasting the application of evolutionary theory and the Christian worldview to financial decision-making. Selected insights gained from each chapter of the book are then highlighted. Finally, several applicable quotes are provided.

From Jesus to Wall Street[206]

This section contrasts financial decision based on two philosophical foundations, specifically Christian theism and evolutionary theory. Details of the evolutionary theory perspective is given in Drew Estes' *From Darwin to Wall Street: Harnessing Evolutionary Theory for Smarter Investments*. A concise rebuttal based on theism is given in the article *From Darwin to Wall Street: A Rebuttal*.[207] Here the focus is on Christianity rather than theism though it borrows heavily from the rebuttal article.

Estes asserts:

> "A product, whether a good or a service, is a firm's DNA, and products comprise many sub-units, or 'premes.' The preme is the gene of commerce; they are the 'units of heredity' differentiating product-lines. Accordingly, premes are the primary 'replicators'

---

[205] Duane Liftin, *Conceiving the Christian College* (Grand Rapids, MI: Eerdmans, 2004), 75. Quoted in Rick Hove and Heather Holleman, *A Grander Story: An Invitation to Christian Professors* (Orlando, FL: Cru Press, 2017), 46.
[206] This section is based in part on an opinion editorial (Op-Ed 24-O5) available at https://www.robertebrooks.org/project/opinion-editorials/.
[207] For the rebuttal to Estes' article, see *From Darwin to Wall Street: A Rebuttal*, available at https://blogs.cfainstitute.org/investor/ (05 November 2024).

of commerce, and firms, like organisms, are merely their 'survival machines.'" [208]

Conclusions drawn from Estes' work are eminently reasonable within the naturalist worldview. If existence somehow led to essence, then harnessing insights from evolutionary theory within investment management may prove useful. But what if, in fact, essence somehow led to existence?[209] The core problem within finance is its philosophical core; that is, the worldview upon which our analytical frameworks are based.

In his book *What I learned About Investing From Darwin*, Prasad defines evolutionary biology as

> *"the study of the causes and nature of the evolution of organisms since the beginning of life on Earth."*[210]

The core challenges of evolutionary biology, however, rests with explanations of how life began from non-life, how inorganic matter began from non-matter, and so forth. A more general definition of evolutionary biology is taken from Wikipedia,

> *"Evolutionary biology is the subfield of biology that studies the evolutionary processes (natural selection, common descent, speciation) that produced the diversity of life on Earth."*[211]

---

[208] See Drew Estes, *From Darwin to Wall Street: Harnessing Evolutionary Theory for Smarter Investments*, available at https://blogs.cfainstitute.org/investor/ (22 August 2024). See also https://destes.substack.com/p/commercial-evolution as well as a podcast, https://podcasts.apple.com/us/podcast/drew-estes-cfa-investing-through-an-evolutionary-lens/id268942353?i=1000669640061.

[209] When discussing the Thomist cosmological argument, Moreland and Craig note, "A thing's essence is an individual nature that serves to define what that thing is. Now if an **essence** is to exist, there must be conjoined with that essence an **act of being**." (Bold in original.) See J. P. Moreland and William Lane Craig, *Philosophical Foundations for a Christian Worldview*, 2nd edition, (Downers Grove, IL: InterVarsity Press, 2017), p. 477. For example, I am a soul (essence) and I have a body (existence).

[210] See Pulak Prasad, *What I Learned About Investing From Darwin*, (New York, NY: Columbia University Press, 2023), p. 1.

[211] See https://en.wikipedia.org/wiki/Evolutionary_biology, accessed on October 9, 2024.

Exploring the Philosophical Roots that Influence Financial Fruit

I share Estes' and Prasad's frustration with the lack of intellectual rigor found within the finance profession in general and within investments in particular. If the philosophical foundation is sand or even primordial goo of some sort, then no among of clever construction will produce a house that can withstand life's storms or an investment process that is beneficial.

As explored previously, naturalism, the philosophical foundation of evolutionary theory, is in direct conflict with the Christian worldview. Given this discord, it is reasonable to surmise that if you start from a different philosophical foundation most likely you will end with a substantially different financial management process. Thus, to summarize the key points in this book, a review is made between the finance implications of two different philosophical foundations, naturalism and Christianity.

The philosophical foundation is critical to the financial management process. Thus, as we argue in this book, it is important for clients of financial professionals to fully understand financial professional's philosophical foundations. An entity's culture emanates from the stated or even unstated philosophical foundations and culture drives all strategy.

Estes laments,

> "No other science is so thoroughly ignored by its practitioners. The reason is that economics went astray by borrowing ideas from physics. ... Economics should instead borrow ideas from evolutionary biology."

The finance professional's departure from science may more reasonably be the result of wholesale adoption of evolutionary theory. Alvin Plantinga clearly articulates the conflict between theistic worldviews and other worldviews, particularly within the sciences. This conflict is especially acute within the social sciences such as finance.

> "Scholarship and science are not neutral, but are deeply involved in the struggle between Christian theism, perennial naturalism

and creative anti-realism. And the unhappy fact is that at present (and in our part of the world) it is the latter two that are in the ascendancy. Christian theism has perhaps made some small steps back in recent years; but it is surely the minority opinion among our colleagues in Western universities."[212]

C. S. Lewis reformulated Alfred North Whitehead's explanation of why the scientific revolution emerged out of medieval Europe due to the belief in God's rationality.

"Men became scientific because they expected law in nature, and they expected law in nature because they believed in a lawgiver."[213]

There are good reasons to be concerned about building financial decision-making processes on evolutionary theory. Ludwig Wittgenstein notes that scientific description falls way short of explaining anything within the universe.

"The great delusion of modernity is that the laws of nature explain the universe for us. The laws of nature describe the universe, they describe the regularities. But they explain nothing."[214]

Finally, Malcolm Muggeridge scoffs at the religious adherence to evolution as an explanation of our universe.

"I myself am convinced that the theory of evolution, especially the extent to which it's been applied, will be one of the great jokes in the history books in the future. Posterity will marvel

---

[212]Alvin Plantinga, "On Christian Scholarship." Available at http://www.veritas-ucsb.org/library/plantinga/ocs.html/
[213]Attributed to C. S. Lewis, quoted in John C. Lennox, *God's Undertaker: Has Science Buried God?* (Oxford: England: Lion, 2009), p. 21.
[214]Attributed to Ludwig Wittgenstein.

that so very flimsy and dubious an hypothesis could be accepted with incredible credulity that it has."[215]

In full disclosure, I have spent decades teaching quantitative finance and recently co-authored a PhD-level book, *Financial Pricing of Financial Derivatives*,[216] but do not suffer from physics envy. In fact, my interactions with physicist suggest they perhaps envy quantitative finance. For quantitative finance is much more interesting as it has the curse of dimensionality, electrons with feelings, and often leads to human flourishing.[217]

In this book, we explored numerous rational and empirical justifications for building financial management processes on a Christian worldview. One of the most empirically justified observations is the biblical notion of sin. From a Christian perspective, sin is simply missing the mark. Jesus set an impossibly high standard in Matthew 5:48.

Matthew 5:48

"You therefore must be perfect, as your heavenly Father is perfect."

Thus, from this perspective as Roman 3:23 concludes,

Romans 3:23

"for all have sinned and fall short of the glory of God."

As explored previously, naturalism must deny the existence of sin or even evil for that matter due to its atheistic

---

[215] See Malcolm Muggeridge, *The End of Christendom* quoted in William A. Dembski, *Intelligent Design The Bridge Between Science and Theology* (London, England: IVP Academic, 2002).

[216] See Robert E. Brooks and Don M. Chance, *Foundations of the Pricing of Financial Derivatives: Theory and Analysis*, Wiley, 2024 (https://www.wiley.com/en-us/Foundations+of+the+Pricing+of+Financial+Derivatives%3A+Theory+and+Analysis-p-9781394179664).

[217] The curse of dimensionality can be illustrated with the S&P 500 index being a 500 dimensional challenge. Electrons with feelings can be illustrated with well-known performativity and counter-performativity related to various financial valuation challenges, such as option valuation. See Donald MacKenzie, *An Engine, Not a Camera*, Cambridge, MA: MIT Press, 2006.

foundation. Thus, the starting point for financial analysis would be material items, such as products as Estes asserts.

Again, here we enumerated rational justifications for building financial decision-making processes on a Christian worldview. Further, the emergence of numerous funds focused on Biblically Responsible Investing (BRI) would simply be unwarranted under the philosophical worldview of naturalism. Alternatively, if Christianity is true, then BRI-based funds are not only warranted but are much more likely to be internally coherent as well as correspond with reality. In the next section, we review these two worldviews—naturalism and Christianity—once again with a focus on the financial management process.

Naturalism, Christianity, and Finance[218]

To the surprise of many, Plantinga rigorously defends the assertion that

> *"there is superficial conflict but deep concord between science and theistic religion, but concord and deep conflict between science and naturalism."*[219]

If Plantinga is right, then we have good reason to be concerned that financial decisions built on components of naturalism, such as evolutionary biology, lacks internal coherence as well as lacking correspondence to reality.

Naturalism

In Chapter 7, we saw that naturalism is "the philosophical belief that everything arises from natural properties and causes, and supernatural or spiritual explanations are excluded or discounted."[220] Clearly, naturalism implies atheism, but atheism does not imply naturalism.

It is important to note that from a naturalist worldview, some

---

[218] For a thorough analysis of theism, naturalism, and science, see Alvin Plantinga, *Where the Conflict Really Lies: Science, Religion, & Naturalism*, 2011.
[219] Alvin Plantinga, *Where the Conflict Really Lies: Science, Religion, & Naturalism*, 2011, ix.
[220] See, for example, https://www.naturalnavigator.com/news/2012/07/meaning-of-the-word-naturalism/.

form of evolutionary theory is exactly what you would expect. If existence exists and that is all that exists, then some explanation of modern complexity is demanded.

Christianity

Again, from Chapter 7, Christianity can be defined as, "Human beings and the universe in which they reside are the creation of the God who has revealed himself in Scripture" or "rough intersection of the great Christian creeds ... the result would be something like the 'Mere Christianity' of which C. S. Lewis spoke."[221] At the core of Christianity is the gospel of Jesus Christ and at the core of the gospel is the physical bodily resurrection of Jesus Christ.

The resurrection of Jesus Christ validates his teaching, including numerous financial principles. Humans are more than simply sensate animals. Life is more than determining what makes us most happy and pursuing financial transactions that facilitate this happiness. We are higher than the animals in the wild. There are clearly moral absolutes and if another person is harmed or worse, there is morally-based consequences. Financial decisions are not reduced to simply advancing my own narcissistic goals regardless of who may be hurt. The Golden Rule has a rational foundation and is worthy to be pursued.

Ideation, the formation of ideas, is preeminent over simple sensate beings. We are more than simply sensate animals seeking our own self-interest. There exist immutable, metaphysical ideas that are foundational to all decision-making, especially finance-related decisions.

Recall from Chapter 1, we posed three tests for truth, four questions to be answered, and five subjects to be studied. In this book, we argued that the Christian worldview easily satisfied the three tests for truth as this worldview is logically consistent, empirically adequate, and experientially relevant. Further, the Christian worldview coherently addresses origins, meaning, morality, and destiny. Finally, we presented financial applications for the five subjects related to God, reality,

---

[221] Plantinga, p. 8.

knowledge, morality, and humankind.

Recall from Chapter 7, the key objective from a Christian worldview is to conform ourselves to the reality around us. The cosmos in which we reside is living and abundant—teaming with abundance created as well as sustained by a loving God. Further, we know that humans are deeply flawed. We were created within a moral universe with an ingrained sense of right and wrong. Unfortunately, we have a never ending pull towards what is wrong. Absent God's grace and mercy, we are destined to sin and destruction. There is an obvious conflict between what we observe and what we know ought to be.

Deep within our being is the desire to align what we observe empirically with what we with our minds infer ought to be. We naturally seek the normative reason why.

Science and Financial Decision-Making

Recall from Chapter 7 that most social science fields such as finance, it is often impossible to conduct repeatable events, a standard often asserted to be scientific. Every day is unique, and humans are constantly learning and changing. For example, in almost every decade, the overall U.S. stock market total returns are positive and often significantly positive. In each decade, however, there is usually at least one significant drop in value more than 30% or so. Thus, although some patterns appear, they remain unreliable.

We agreed with Lennox that science is a "method of inference to the best explanation."[222] Finance seeks the best inference regarding present financial decisions, based on historical data viewed through the lenses of the embraced philosophical worldview.

The key is having a correct perspective within finance is having a correct understanding what it means to be human. This understanding aids in creating flourishing cultures and effective strategies. For example, understanding the reality of peoples' total depravity, including our own, aids in developing appropriate financial guardrails.

---

[222] John C. Lennox, *God's Undertaker: Has Science Buried God?* (Oxford, England: Lion, 2009), p. 32.

Within this book, we argued that there are only two compelling economic frameworks.

Two Economic Frameworks

At the heart of the clash of worldviews is essence and existence. Either essence precedes existence or existence precedes essence. The Christian worldview has essence preceding existence:

Genesis 1:1

"In the beginning, God created the heavens and the earth."[223]

From the naturalist worldview, existence precedes essence. As quoted in Chapter 3, Solomon asserts,

"I am an infinitesimal speck of carbon-based dust born in a time and place not of my choosing here for an incredible brief amount of time before my atoms are scattered back into the cosmos."[224]

The transition within economics away from a normative approach (what ought to be) to a positive approach (what is) is generally attributed to Friedman's work in 1966, but it likely goes much further back.[225] Modern economic analysis is positivist in flavor and fits well within naturalism. Biblically-based economic analysis is normative in flavor and often in direct contradiction to naturalism.[226]

In 1982, Warren T. Brookes in *The Economy in Mind* provided important insights regarding this clash of worldviews.[227] He

---

[223] See Genesis 1:1, Bible, English Standard Version. Available at https://www.biblegateway.com/passage/?search=Genesis%201%3A1&version=ESV.

[224] Emma Pattee, "Covid-19 makes us think about our mortality. Our brains aren't designed for that." *The Washington Post*, October 7, 2020, accessed online. Pattee is quoting Sheldon Solomon.

[225] See Milton Friedman, "The Methodology of Positive Economics," in *Essays In Positive Economics* (Chicago: Univ. of Chicago Press, 1966. See also Robert Brooks, Op-Ed 24-O4 *Tigers and Ghosts: Distinguishing Between Financial Risk and Uncertainty* available at https://robertebrooks.org/project/opinion-editorials/.

[226] For example, modern economic theory is founded upon the doctrine of scarcity. The biblically-based approach is founded upon the doctrine of abundance coupled with a stewardship mandate.

[227] Warren T. Brookes, *The Economy in Mind* (NY: Universe Books, 1982).

notes,

> "While the real economy has been growing daily more metaphysical, our economists and our accounting systems, it seems, have grown steadily more materialistic in their perspective."[228]

Further, Brookes provides a historical perspective.

> "Since economic thought first became formalized over two centuries ago, there have been essentially two different views about wealth. One view, first defined by Adam Smith and Jean-Baptiste Say, is that wealth is primarily metaphysical, the result of ideas, imagination, innovation, and individual creativity, and is therefore, relatively speaking, unlimited, susceptible to great growth and development. The other, espoused by Thomas Malthus and Karl Marx, contends that wealth is essentially and primarily physical, and therefore ultimately finite. The modern presentation of this view argues that since usable energy is steadily diminishing into entropy, all wealth is really cost to be shared more equitably."[229]

Note modern economic theory is founded upon the doctrine of scarcity. The biblically-based approach is founded upon the doctrine of abundance coupled with a stewardship mandate.

Brookes links his metaphysical perspective to religion.

> "The central message of nearly all religious prophets throughout history has been to look beyond these limited presentations of the physical senses into the ultimate potential of the mind and spirit. The common denominator of faith was and is the willingness to recognize that our real wealth comes not from finite natural resources or uncertain material conditions, but from the triumph of the metaphysical over the physical, of attitudes over appearances. Or in St. Paul's words, 'Through faith we understand that the worlds were framed by the word of God, so

---

[228]Brookes, p. 14.
[229]Brookes, p. 12.

that things which are seen were not made of things which do appear.'"[230]

We now turn to summary implications of these two clashing worldviews.

Products or people

Recall naturalism has a physical focus. Thus, when applying evolutionary theory to commerce, it is expected that the center of analysis rests on physical items, such as products. For example, Estes asserts,

> "Products, in other words, are like DNA. They are complex structures of subunits called premes, and premes, like genes within DNA, battle for inclusion in products. A preme is any attribute impacting a product's value proposition. It can be as minor as employees saying, 'My pleasure,' at Chick-fil-A or as major as iOS for Apple products."[231]

Christianity has a metaphysical focus. Thus, when applying the Christian worldview to commerce, it is expected that the center of analysis rests on the metaphysical, primarily people and especially firm leaders. For example, Chick-fil-A's corporate purpose is as follows:

> "To glorify God by being a faithful steward of all that is entrusted to us. To have a positive influence on all who come in contact with Chick-fil-A."[232]

Similarly, from Apple's website we find the following:

> "Apple conducts business ethically, honestly, and in full compliance with the law. We believe that how we conduct ourselves is as critical to Apple's success as making the best products in the world."

---

[230] Brookes, p. 25.
[231] See Drew Estes, *From Darwin to Wall Street: Harnessing Evolutionary Theory for Smarter Investments*, previously cited.
[232] See https://www.chick-fil-a.com/about/company.

Tim Cook, Apple's CEO asserts,

> "We do the right thing, even when it's not easy."[233]

Thus, it appears that corporate executives from widely diverse worldviews share their focus on essence, not existence.

It is eminently more reasonable that people are at the heart of replicating products. Estes claims,

> "(Ideas float) about like pollen ready to fertilize a receptive entrepreneur's mind."[234]

Ideas are inherently metaphysical, and pollen is physical. The naturalist would struggle to admit the existence of "ideas" beyond some brain activity. Ideas are inherent in the Christian worldview and the reasonableness of a person's idea rests in the correspondence between what is taking place in the entrepreneur's mind and the surrounding reality.

The growth of biblically responsible investing (BRI) products suggests there exists a significant number of investors who are seeking alternative ways to deploy their capital. There are now at least 90 BRI-based financial instruments.[235] The Bible presents numerous instructions for living. As C. S. Lewis notes,

> "In reality, moral rules are directions for running the human machine. Every moral rule is there to prevent a breakdown, or a strain, or a friction, in the running of that machine."[236]

Thus, companies that lean in the direction of "Mere Christianity" will function well and serve the needs of its shareholders.

We briefly introduce two exchange-traded funds (ETFs) with a BRI focus. Inspire Investing's Inspire 500 ETF (ticker: PTL

---

[233]See https://www.apple.com/compliance/.
[234]See Estes, previously cited.
[235]For more information regarding these products, see https://www.faithdriveninvestor.org/mutual-funds.
[236]C. S. Lewis, *Mere Christianity*, Book III, Chapter 1, page 59.

denoting Praise The Lord) is a passively managed fund charging only 9 basis points that seeks to track the Inspire 500 Index. This index is the largest 500 cap weighted stocks with "positive biblical values alignment as determined by Inspire Impact Scores greater than or equal to zero."[237] For example, Apple, Inc. has a -100 score (lowest possible) and hence is not a stock held in PTL. Sovereign's Capital Flourish Fund ETF (ticker: SOVF) is an actively-managed fund "consisting of 80-100 publicly traded companies that are among the most spiritually integrated firms, determined by our proprietary ranking methodology." SOVF managers have compiled a "proprietary database of 330 faith-aligned CEOs."[238] Due to its active management mandate, SOVF has a 75 basis point expense ratio. The mere existence of 330 identifiable faith-aligned executives suggest naturalism has not been embraced entirely within the business community.

It remains an empirical question how BRI-based investments will perform if focused solely on temporal total return. The mere existence of at least 90 BRI-based funds suggests that there exists a significant number of investors who desire to invest in funds consistent with their metaphysical values and not simply the best monetarily performing firms or products.[239]

We conclude this section, we an interesting Charles Darwin quote,

> *"With me the horrid doubt always arises whether the convictions of man's mind, which has been developed from the mind of the lower animals, are of any value or at all trustworthy."*[240]

We now review selected ideas presented in this book.

---

[237] See https://www.inspireetf.com/ptl.
[238] SOVF fact sheet for 6/30/2024. See https://www.scetfs.com/sovf/factsheet (accessed on 10/2/2024).
[239] For more information and analysis of BRI-based funds, see www.BRIQNewsletter.com.
[240] Quote attributed to Charles Darwin. See Plantinga, (2011), p. 316.

The Harvest

Recall the core premise for this book is that financial fruit grows on philosophical roots. Hence, we explored deeply the alternative philosophical roots and concluded that the Christian worldview was the most coherent and corresponds best to reality that surrounds us.

Chapter 1 focused on Christian apologetics and sought to make the connection to financial decision-making. One key insight illustrated in Case Study 1.1 Home Purchase was that regardless of the home selected, we are simply God's managers of his possessions not the owners. If we were designed by God to be his managers, then taking on the role of owner will not be fruitful.

In Chapters 2 and 3, a quick tour through the field of philosophy was given. These philosophical concepts are applied to the often not-so-popular topic of budgeting. The reason budgeting often is dysfunctional is not due to lack of knowledge or understanding, rather a life founded on a false worldview.

Biblically, we know that the universe is intricately designed and has amazing orderliness. The world was created and sustained by a rational God in an orderly process and has not mysteriously evolved out of chaos. The primary and essential character of wealth is not physical. It is not our material possessions, rather wisdom and discernment. With this understanding, we are better able to make financial decisions that lead to human flourishing.

Chapter 4 provides a financial perspective on the nature of information. The key insight is that a mechanistic-related explanation does not in any way negate an agency-related explanation. For example, accounting information provides the formal mechanistic explanation for a particular firm's activities over say a year. The manager's explanation for why they conducted various business activities provides more clarity on motivation. Thus, information plays a vital role in finance.

In Chapter 5, we reviewed briefly the nature of the theism debate and conclude that God's existence is a properly basic belief. Due to the theological beauty found in the Bible, we surmise that there are immutable moral laws, life is deeply meaningful, and there is a satisfying hope. This foundation was found to be much more robust than alternative worldviews.

Chapter 6 offered a quick review of competing worldviews introduced with the problem of the criterion. Particularism was foundational and the Christian worldview provided robust justification. In Chapter 7, a deep dive is taken on contrasting Christianity with naturalism. Thus, we are vindicated in basing financial decisions from a biblical perspective. If Christianity is true, then our challenge is managing God's abundance, not fighting over dwindling scarcity.

One of the hardest challenges facing every worldview, is the problem of pain, suffering, and evil. Though a difficult challenge indeed, Chapter 8 sheds light on this problem from both a theist and an atheist perspective. Most likely, severe financial loss will be facing some of us in the future. The strength of your relationship with God through Jesus Christ will govern how this difficult challenge will be faced.

At the core of the Christian worldview is the Bible. In Chapters 9 and 10, a careful examination is given on the Bible as merely hearsay, a manifest heresy, or clear history. Ultimately, the Christian worldview is simply news. The news of incarnation, life, death, and bodily resurrection. It is good news, indeed.

Though difficult to countenance in today's cultural scientism worldview, miracles were carefully explored in Chapter 11. Biblically, we know that God has communicated divine truths through miracles. The only other leading alternative is divine silence. Miracles were found to be signs that point us to a loving God who has provided abundantly for us despite our waywardness.

The centerpiece of the Christian worldview is the resurrection of Jesus Christ. In Chapter 12, we examined the physical, bodily resurrection of Jesus Christ finding ample evidence to support it. As a financial quant, it was insightful to apply Bayes's Theorem to the resurrection. Combined with Pascal's famous wager, the logical conclusion is Jesus rose bodily from the grave and our belief in this evidence is eminently justified.

So where does this exploration into the philosophical roots lead us? Chapter 13 present love as the overarching and compelling conclusion. Hospitality is an incredible joy and provides a gateway to the world. By loving others and serving them, one's own worldview is clarified. Because God loved us enough to sacrifice Jesus Christ, we are compelled to love others, particularly those who seek our harm.

There is deep contentment to be found in entrusting your life to Jesus Christ and seeking to mature as God's child. Generosity is a natural consequence.

We turn now to a Case Study showcasing two poems that help encapsulate our journey together exploring the philosophical roots that influence the resulting financial fruit.

Case Study 14.1: Precedence: Existence or Essence[241]

Worldviews can be easily categorized as those that assume existence precedes essence (e.g., naturalism) and those that assume essence precedes existence (e.g., the Christian worldview).

Poetry often can clearly communicate truth claims. The following two poems encapsulate these perspectives.

---

[241] See http://www.desiringgod.org/articles/invictus-redeemed.

Existence Precedes Essence
"Invictus" (Latin: Unconquered)
William Ernest Henley, 1875
Out of the night that covers me,
  Black as the pit from pole to pole,
I thank whatever gods may be
  For my unconquerable soul.
In the fell clutch of circumstance
  I have not winced nor cried aloud.
Under the bludgeonings of chance
  My head is bloody, but unbowed.
Beyond this place of wrath and tears
  Looms but the Horror of the shade,
And yet the menace of the years
  Finds and shall find me unafraid.
It matters not how strait the gate,
  How charged with punishments the scroll,
I am the master of my fate,
  I am the captain of my soul.

Essence precedes existence
"Conquered"
Dorothy Day (1930s?)
Out of the light that dazzles me,
  Bright as the sun from pole to pole,
I thank the God I know to be,
  For Christ – the Conqueror of my soul.
Since His the sway of circumstance,
  I would not wince nor cry aloud.
Under the rule which men call chance,
  My head, with joy, is humbly bowed.
Beyond this place of sin and tears,
  That Life with Him and His the Aid,
That, spite the menace of the years,
  Keeps, and will keep me unafraid.
I have no fear though straight the gate:
  He cleared from punishment the scroll.
Christ is the Master of my fate!
  Christ is the Captain of my soul.

Case Study 14.2: Napoleon's Question[242]

Recall our core premise for this book was that financial fruit grows on philosophical roots. To acquire enduring financial fruit, our philosophical roots need the best theological soil. Note that everything hinges on the person and work of Jesus Christ. Napoleon wrestled with Jesus Christ's leadership style:

> *When conversing, as was his habit, about the great men of the ancient world, and comparing himself to them, he turned, it is said, to Count Montholon with the enquiry, "Can you tell me who Jesus Christ was?" The question was declined, and Napoleon proceeded, "Well then, I will tell you. Alexander, Caesar, Charlemagne and I myself have founded great empires; but upon what did these creations of our genius depend? Upon force. Jesus alone founded His empire upon love, and to this very day millions will die for Him. ... I think I understand something of human nature; and I tell you, all these were men, and I am a man: none else is like Him; Jesus Christ was more than a man. ... I have inspired multitudes with such an enthusiastic devotion that they have died for me, ... but to do this it was necessary that I should be visibly present with the electric influence of my looks, my words, my voice. When I saw men and spoke to them, I lighted up the flame of self devotion in their hearts. ... Christ alone has succeeded in so raising the mind of man to the unseen, that it becomes insensible to the barriers of time and space. Across a chasm of eighteen hundred years, Jesus Christ makes a demand which is beyond all others difficult to satisfy; he asks for that which a philosopher may often seek in vain at the hands of his friends, or a father of his children, or a bride of her spouse, or a man of his brother. He asks for the human heart; he will have it entirely to himself. He demands it unconditionally, and furthermore his demand is granted. Wonderful! In defiance of time and space, the soul of man, with all its powers and faculties, becomes an annexation to the empire of Christ. All who sincerely believe in him experience that remarkable supernatural love*

---

[242]Henry Parry Liddon, *Liddon's Bampton Lectures 1866* (London: Rivingtons, 1869).

toward Him. This phenomenon is unaccountable; it is altogether beyond the scope of man's creative powers. Time, the great destroyer, is powerless to extinguish this sacred flame; time can neither exhaust its strength nor put a limit to its range. This is it, which strikes me most; I have often thought of it. This it is which proves to me quite convincingly the divinity of Jesus Christ."

If we conclude, as Napoleon did, that Jesus Christ is the Son of God, then we will submit to his rule and reign in our hearts. Only from this perspective does it make sense that we adhere to the financial teachings within the Bible.

Thank you for your time investment in this book. I hope you have found it helpful and would welcome your feedback. A few quotes that embrace our objectives are now given.

Encapsulating Quotes

Bonhoeffer helps us see the stark contrast between essentially naturalism and Christianity.

Christianity preaches the infinite worth of that which is seemingly worthless and the infinite worthlessness of that which is seemingly so valued.[243]

Aleksandr Solzhenitsyn reminds us that evil is ever present, even within each one of us.

If only it were all so simple! If only there were evil people somewhere insidiously committing evil deeds, and it were necessary only to separate them from the rest of us and destroy them. But the line dividing good and evil cuts through the heart

---

[243]Dietrich Bonhoeffer, quoted in Eric Metaxas, *Bonhoeffer Pastor, Martyr, Prophet, Spy* (Nashville, TN: Thomas Nelson, 2011), 85.

of every human being. And who is willing to destroy a piece of his own heart?[244]

Isaac Newton, famous mathematician, realized the amazing depth of God's created order. We now know this universe is far more intricate and complex than any early scientist realized.

> *I seem to have been only like a boy playing on the seashore ...whilst the great ocean of truth lay all undiscovered before me.*[245]

Nathan Hatch argues for "first-order Christian scholarship" to preserve a place for Christian-based rational thought.

> *The battle for the mind cannot be waged by mobilizing in the streets or on Capitol Hill, nor by denouncing more furiously the secular humanists. If we are to help preserve even the possibility of Christian thinking for our children and grandchildren, we must begin to nurture first-order Christian scholarship.*[246]

Summary

This chapter is the culmination of our journey together. This book wraps up by contrasting the application of evolutionary

---

[244] Aleksandr Solzhenitsyn, The Gulag Archipelago 1918–1956. See, for example, https://www.goodreads.com/quotes/13750-if-only-it-were-all-so-simple-if-only-there.

[245] Attributed to Isaac Newton. See, for example, https://writersalmanac.publicradio.org/index.php%3Fdate=2005%252F12%252F25.html.

[246] Attributed to Nathan Hatch. See https://www.cru.org/faculty/2016/our-academic-pursuits-the-need-for-excellence/. Nathan O. Hatch, "Evangelical Colleges and the Challenge of Christian Thinking," in *Making Higher Education Christian: The History and Mission of Evangelical Colleges in America*, ed. Joel A. Carpenter and Kenneth W. Shipps (Grand Rapids, MI: Eerdmans, 1987), 158. Quoted in Rick Hove and Heather Holleman, *A Grander Story: An Invitation to Christian Professors* (Orlando, FL: Cru Press, 2017), 48.

theory and Christian theism to financial decision-making. Christian theism was found to be eminently more reasonable. Selected insights gained from each chapter of the book were then highlighted. Finally, a few applicable quotes are provided. Again, thank you for your patience with this material.

Case Study 1: Home Purchase Decision Revisited

Recall we started our exploration by considering the home purchase decision. Is the home purchase decision simply an analytical and rational choice, or is there more that typically goes into it? Assuming young couple with two children, what are the key issues to be addressed?

There are several issues involved, including functional utility, maintenance cost, structural soundness, and overall safety. The often unspoken but profound driving factor in home purchase decisions relates to how we will be perceived among peers. This is not a tangible, physical, or utilitarian issue, rather an issue of human pride. Based on your experience with this book, has your answer changed?

Case Study 2: Philosophical Roots

Appraise the following statement: "There is a separation between how we manage our financial resources and our worldview. We simply seek to maximize our "utility" or risk-adjusted return and then let our worldview inform us of how to dispose of the resultant wealth."

References

Brookes, Warren T., *The Economy in Mind* (New York, NY:

Universe Books, 1982).

Brooks, Robert E., "From Darwin to Wall Street: A Rebuttal," available at https://blog.cfainstitute.org/investor/ (05 November 2024).

Brooks, Robert E., "Tigers and Ghosts: Distinguishing Between Financial Risk and Uncertainty," available at https://robertebrooks.org/project/opinion-editorials/ (Op-Ed 24-O4).

Brooks, Robert E. and Don M. Chance, *Foundations of the Pricing of Financial Derivatives: Theory and Analysis* (Hoboken, NJ: John Wiley & Sons, Inc., 2024).

Dembski, William A., *Intelligent Design The Bridge Between Science and Theology* (London, England: IVP Academic, 2002).

Estes, Drew, "From Darwin to Wall Street: Harnessing Evolutionary Theory for Smarter Investments," available at https://blog.cfainstitute.org/investor/ (22 August 2024).

Friedman, Milton, "The Methodology of Positive Economics," in *Essays in Positive Economics* (Chicago, IL: University of Chicago Press, 1966).

Hove, Rick, and Heather Holleman, *A Grander Story: An Invitation to Christian Professors* (Orlando, FL: Cru Press, 2017).

Lennox, John C., *God's Undertaker: Has Science Buried God?* (Oxford: Lion, 2009).

Lewis, C. S., *Mere Christianity* (Harper Collins, 1952).

Liddon, Henry Parry, *Liddon's Bampton Lectures 1866* (London: Rivingtons, 1869).

MacKenzie, Donald, *An Engine, Not a Camera*, (Cambridge, MA: MIT Press, 2006).

Metaxas, Eric, *Bonhoeffer Pastor, Martyr, Prophet, Spy* (Nashville, TN: Thomas Nelson, 2011).

Moreland, J. P. and William Lane Craig, *Philosophical Foundations for a Christian Worldview*, 2nd Edition, (Downers Grove, IL: InterVarsity Press, 2017).

Pattee, Emma, "Covid-19 Makes Us Think About our Mortality. Our Brains Aren't Designed for That." *The Washington Post*, October 7, 2020.

Plantinga, Alvin, "On Christian Scholarship." Available at

http://www.veritas-ucsb.org/library/plantinga/ocs.html/.

Plantinga, Alvin, *Where the Conflict Really Lies: Science, Religion, & Naturalism*, (New York: Oxford University Press, 2011).

Prasad, Pulak, *What I Learned About Investing From Darwin*, (New York, NY: Columbia University Press, 2023).

Bibliography

Access Jesus, *List of Miracles Recorded in the Old Testament Bible*, (August 14, 2016), online. Downloaded on September 23, 2018, source apparently no longer available. Numerous lists are widely available online, however.

Anderson, Robert, *The Coming Prince* (Grand Rapids, MI: Kregel, 1984).

https://www.bethinking.org/apologetics: Managed by the Universities and Colleges Christian Fellowship (UCCF) whose goal is to "make disciples of Jesus Christ in the student world."

Baucham, Jr., Voddie, *Expository Apologetics: Answering Objections with the Power of the Word* (Wheaton, IL: Crossway, 2015).

Blanchard, Ken, and Phil Hodges, *The Servant Leader Transforming Your Heart, Head, Hands & Habits* (Nashville, TN: Thomas Nelson, 2003).

Bloom Jon, "'Invictus' Redeemed," Desiring God, August 22, 2014. Provides poems, William Ernest Henley, "Invictus," and Dorothy Day, "Conquered." See http://www.desiringgod.org/articles/invictus-redeemed.

Brookes, Warren T., *The Economy in Mind* (New York, NY: Universe Books, 1982).

Brooks, Robert E., "From Darwin to Wall Street: A Rebuttal," available at https://blog.cfainstitute.org/investor/ (05 November 2024).

Brooks, Robert E., "Tigers and Ghosts: Distinguishing Between Financial Risk and Uncertainty," available at https://robertebrooks.org/project/opinion-editorials/ (Op-Ed 24-O4).

Brooks, Robert E. and Don M. Chance, *Foundations of the Pricing of Financial Derivatives: Theory and Analysis* (Hoboken, NJ: John Wiley & Sons, Inc., 2024).

Butterfield, Rosaria, *The Gospel Comes with a House Key: Practicing Radically Ordinary Hospitality in Our Post-Christian World* (Wheaton, IL: Crossway, 2018).

https://carm.org: Christian Apologetics and Research Ministry—contains a wide array of useful materials.

Carpenter, Joel A. and Kenneth W. Shipps *Making Higher Education Christian: The History and Mission of Evangelical Colleges in America*, ed. (Grand Rapids, MI: Eerdmans, 1987).

Chesterton, G.K., *St. Thomas Aquinas* (Grand Rapids, MI: Christian Classics Ethereal Library), available at https://www.ccel.org/ccel/c/chesterton/aquinas/cache/aquinas.pdf.

Craig, William Lane, *Reasonable Faith Christian Truth and Apologetics*, 3rd ed (Wheaton, IL: Crossway, 2008).

Creation Studies Institute, *Miracles of the Bible*, Creation Studies Institute, Accessed September 23, 2018 (apparently no longer available, see https://creationstudies.org/). Taken from Morris, Henry M., *The Biblical Basis for Modern Science*, (Grand Rapids, MI: Baker Book House, 1984).

Dembski, William A., *Intelligent Design The Bridge Between Science and Theology* (London, England: IVP Academic, 2002).

Dembski, William A., *The Design Inference: Eliminating Chance Through Small Probabilities*, Cambridge University Press, 1998.

Dubofsky, David, and Lyle Sussman, *Your Total Wealth: The Heart and Soul of Financial Literacy*, HSF Publishing, LLC, 2021.

Estes, Drew, "From Darwin to Wall Street: Harnessing Evolutionary Theory for Smarter Investments," available at https://blog.cfainstitute.org/investor/ (22 August 2024).

Flew, Anthony, "Parable of the Invisible Gardener," https://en.wikipedia.org/wiki/Parable_of_the_Invisible_Gardener.

Frame, John M., "God and Biblical Language: Transcendence and Immanence," in *God's Inerrant Word*, ed. J. W. Montgomery (Minneapolis: Bethany Fellowship, 1974). Quoted at https://www.thegospelcoalition.org/blogs/justin-taylor/the-invisible-vs-the-constant-gardener-parables-for-and-against-atheism/.

Friedman, Milton, "The Methodology of Positive Economics," in *Essays in Positive Economics* (Chicago, IL: University of

Chicago Press, 1966).

Geisler, Norman L. and Paul D Feinberg, *Introduction to Philosophy A Christian Perspective* (Grand Rapids, MI: Baker Academic, 1980).

Habermas, Gary R., *The Verdict of History*, (Monarch Books, 1990).

Habermas, Jürgen, *Time of Transitions* (Malden, MA: Polity Press, 2006).

Hatch, Nathan O., "Evangelical Colleges and the Challenge of Christian Thinking," in Carpenter, Joel A. and Kenneth W. Shipps *Making Higher Education Christian: The History and Mission of Evangelical Colleges in America*, ed. (Grand Rapids, MI: Eerdmans, 1987).

Hájek, Alan, "Pascal's Wager", in *The Stanford Encyclopedia of Philosophy*, ed. Edward N. Zalta (Summer 2018), https://plato.stanford.edu/archives/sum2018/entries/pascal-wager/.

Hove, Rick, and Heather Holleman, *A Grander Story: An Invitation to Christian Professors* (Orlando, FL: Cru Press, 2017).

Hume, David, Part 10 in *Dialogues Concerning Natural Religion* (Project Gutenberg, 2009), https://www.gutenberg.org/files/4583/4583-h/4583-h.htm.

Keller, Tim, *The Reason for God: Belief in an Age of Skepticism* (Dutton, 2008).

Keynes, John Maynard, *Essays in Biography* (New York: Horizon Press, 1951). Referenced at https://www.indstate.edu/cas/econ/introduction-economics/jm-keynes-requirements-economist.

Kinnier, Richard, ed., *The Meaning of Life* (Palazzo Editions, 2007).

Kreeft, Peter, *C. S. Lewis for the Third Millennium: Six Essays on the Abolition of Man* (San Francisco: Ignatius, 2011).

Lennox, John C., *God's Undertaker: Has Science Buried God?* (Oxford: Lion, 2009).

Lewis, C. S., *God in the Dock: Essays of Theology and Ethics*, (Grand Rapids, MI: William B. Eerdmans Publishing Company, 1970).

Lewis, C. S., *The Abolition of Man* (New York: The Macmillan Company, 1973).

Lewis, C. S., *Mere Christianity* (Harper Collins, 1952).

Lewis, C. S., *Miracles* (Harper Collins, 1947).

Lewis, C. S., *The Problem of Pain* (Harper Collins, 1940).

Liddon, Henry Parry, *Liddon's Bampton Lectures 1866* (London: Rivingtons, 1869).

Liftin, Duane, *Conceiving the Christian College* (Grand Rapids, MI: Eerdmans, 2004).

MacKenzie, Donald, *An Engine, Not a Camera*, (Cambridge, MA: MIT Press, 2006).

McDowell, Josh, *A Ready Defense: The Best of Josh McDowell*, (Nashville, TN: Thomas Nelson Publishers, 2021).

McDowell, Josh, *Evidence That Demands a Verdict*, Revised Edition, Volumes 1 and 2, (San Bernardino, CA: Here's Life Publishers, Inc., 1986).

McDowell, Josh, *The New Evidence That Demands a Verdict*, (Nashville, TN: Thomas Nelson Publishers, 1999).

Metaxas, Eric, *Bonhoeffer Pastor, Martyr, Prophet, Spy* (Nashville, TN: Thomas Nelson, 2011).

Moreland, J. P., Revised and Updated *Love Your God with All Your Mind: The Role of Reason in the Life of the Soul* (Colorado Springs, CO: NavPress, 2012).

Moreland, J. P. and William Lane Craig, *Philosophical Foundations for a Christian Worldview* (Downers Grove, IL: InterVarsity Press, 2003).

Moreland, J. P. and William Lane Craig, *Philosophical Foundations for a Christian Worldview*, 2nd Edition, (Downers Grove, IL: InterVarsity Press, 2017).

Morris, Henry M., *The Biblical Basis for Modern Science*, (Grand Rapids, MI: Baker Book House, 1984).

Myers, Jeff and David Noble, *Understanding the Times*, (Colorado Springs, CO: David C Cook, 2015).

Nash, Ronald, *Faith and Reason* (Academie Books, 1988).

Pattee, Emma, "Covid-19 Makes Us Think About our Mortality. Our Brains Aren't Designed for That." *The Washington Post*, October 7, 2020.

Plantinga, Alvin, "On Christian Scholarship." Available at

http://www.veritas-ucsb.org/library/plantinga/ocs.html/.

Plantinga, Alvin, *Where the Conflict Really Lies: Science, Religion, & Naturalism*, (New York: Oxford University Press, 2011).

Portnoy, Brian, *The Geometry of Wealth: How to Shape a Life of Money and Meaning*, Harriman House, 2018.

Prasad, Pulak, *What I Learned About Investing From Darwin*, (New York, NY: Columbia University Press, 2023).

Rogers, Adrian, *Believe in Miracles but Trust in Jesus* (Wheaton, IL: Crossway, 1997).

Ruse, Michael, *Darwinism defended: A guide to the evolution controversies*. (Reading, MA: Addison-Wesley, 1982).

Solzhenitsyn, Aleksandr, The Gulag Archipelago 1918–1956. See, for example, https://www.goodreads.com/quotes/13750-if-only-it-were-all-so-simple-if-only-there.

Spitznagel, Mark, *The Dao of Capital Austrian Investing in a Distorted World*, Wiley, 2013.

Strobel, Lee, *The Case for a Creator* (Zondervan, 2004).

Strobel, Lee, *The Case for Faith* (Zondervan, 2000).

Strobel, Lee, *The Case for Christ* (Zondervan, 1998).

Taleb, Nassim, *Fooled by Randomness: The Hidden Role of Chance in the Markets and in Life* (New York: W. W. Norton, 2001).

Trollope, Anthony, *Framley Parsonage* (New York: Dodd, Mead & Company, 1911).

Willard, Dallas, "Language, Being, God, and the Three Stages of Theistic Evidence." Available at http://www.dwillard.org/articles/individual/language-being-god-and-the-three-stages-of-theistic-evidence.

Exploring the Philosophical Roots that Influence Financial Fruit

Major Bible References

OLD TESTAMENT

Genesis 1:1	129, 209, 268
Genesis 1:3, 6, 7, 9, 11, 14, 15, 20, 21, 24, 26	86
Genesis 1:26–27	93
Genesis 1:31, 3:1, and 3:12	166
Genesis 29:27–28	215
Exodus 33:18–19	166
Numbers 20:8	87
Deuteronomy 8:3	200
Deuteronomy 15:6	206
Deuteronomy 28:12	206
Deuteronomy 28:43–45	199
2 Samuel 6:14–16	119
1 Chronicles 12:32	124
Nehemiah 2:1–2	216
Job 23:1–7	167
Job 28:1-28	19
Job 38:1-5	167
Job 42:1-6	167
Psalms 1:1–6	129
Psalm 19:1–3	87
Psalm 19:7–11	113
Psalm 33:6	88, 110
Psalm 37:21	190
Psalm 115:1–3	166
Psalm 119:89	200
Psalm 139:13–14	114
Proverbs 8:10–11, 18	254
Proverbs 13:11	254
Proverbs 15:16–17	254
Proverbs 22:1	255
Proverbs 22:7	189, 199
Ecclesiastes 11:1–5	199
Ecclesiastes 12:11–14	22
Ecclesiastes 7:25	198
Isaiah 1:18	198
Isaiah 42:5	209
Isaiah 58:10–11	249
Jeremiah 26:2	197
Jeremiah 29:11	115
Ezekiel 1:10	210
Daniel 9:25–26	215
Micah 5:2	195

NEW TESTAMENT

Matthew 2:5–6	194
Matthew 4:1–4	201
Matthew 4:4	195
Matthew 5:17	184
Matthew 5:18	196
Matthew 5:43–48	248
Matthew 5:48	264
Matthew 7:12–14	256
Matthew 9:1–2	31
Matthew 9:6–7	87
Matthew 11:28–30	22
Matthew 13:10–12	214
Matthew 22:23–33	44
Matthew 22:35–40	245
Matthew 27:62–66	226
Mark 8:31	226
Mark 8:34	173
Luke 1:1–4	181
Luke 3:1–2	181
Luke 6:46–49	129
Luke 9:23–24	129
Luke 10:29–37	251
Luke 21:33	200
Luke 24:27	195, 213
Luke 24:36–49	227
Luke 24:44	196
Luke 24:46	195
John 1:1–3, 10	88, 110
John 1:2	62
John 1:29	184
John 1:29–34	225
John 5:39	196
John 6:35	201
John 10:10	150
John 10:30	226
John 10:30–31	184
John 13:34–35	246
John 14:1–4	256
John 14:6	150
John 15:9–11	129
John 18:33–38	150
John 18:4–6	87
John 19:35	182
John 20:24–29	31
John 20:30–31	211
Acts 1:3	199
Acts 2:22	182
Acts 10:42–43	213
Acts 17:17–21	16

Exploring the Philosophical Roots that Influence Financial Fruit

Reference	Page
Acts 17:28	62
Acts 22:1-2a	89
Acts 25:16	89
Acts 26:1–3	16
Acts 26:24-26	182
Romans 1:17	195
Romans 1:18–32	116
Romans 3:2	196
Romans 3:23	264
Romans 8:3–4	66
Romans 8:28	114
Romans 11:33	21
1 Corinthians 2:13	194
1 Corinthians 3:10–11	130
1 Corinthians 8:6	88, 110
1 Corinthians 13	246
1 Corinthians 15:1–4	228
1 Corinthians 15:1–5	147
1 Corinthians 15:1–6	209
1 Corinthians 15:12–19	45, 55
2 Corinthians 5:14–15	66
2 Corinthians 10:5	124
Ephesians 2:8–10	118
Philippians 1:15–18	89
Philippians 1:7, 16	17
Philippians 4:19	220
Colossians 1:16	114
Colossians 1:16–17	88, 110
Colossians 2:6–10	42
1 Timothy 1:12b	172
1 Timothy 6:17	115
2 Timothy 2:15	130
2 Timothy 3:16	194
2 Timothy 3:16–17	128
Hebrews 5:12	196
Hebrews 10:7	196
James 1:1–5	21
James 4:13–14a	90
James 4:13–17	205
1 Peter 2:9	114
1 Peter 3:13–17	88
1 Peter 3:15	14
2 Peter 3:10	200
1 John 1:3	182
Revelation 22:18–19	197
Revelation 4:11	62

www.ingramcontent.com/pod-product-compliance
Lightning Source LLC
Chambersburg PA
CBHW071018240526
45469CB00006BD/1971